Praise for *Called to Coach*

"We all know about Coach Bowden's accomplishments on the field and we probably won't see that again in college football in this day and age. What people might not know about Bobby Bowden is the man that he is, the person that he is, and the number of people he impacted, influenced, and inspired. He did it with such class and dignity in every way. As coaches, you wish maybe someday to be thought of as well as he is, not only in terms of what he accomplished but the way he did it."
—Nick Saban, head coach, University of Alabama

"I've had the privilege of knowing Bobby Bowden for more than thirty years. During my years of coaching at Nebraska, between 1980 and my last year of coaching in 1997, we played Florida State eight times. We won only twice and lost six times. Many of the games were very close and the winner would win the national championship. Through all of those years of competition, I always respected and admired Bobby Bowden greatly. He stands for the right things, is a man of principle, was always honest in recruiting, and exemplifies all that a Christian person should be. *Called to Coach* is a very interesting narrative of life in the coaching profession spanning nearly fifty years. I recommend the book highly."
—Tom Osborne, athletic director, University of Nebraska

"Coach Bowden transcends football. He is a man who leveraged his position as a winning football coach into a living example of the Christian values he believed in. Then he shared them with his players. He personifies the ultimate father in that he inspired us to be the best that we could be, helping us build our mind, body, and spirit through the game he loved. This book will deliver his message to others who will benefit—just like I have— from the life, the wisdom, and the grace that is Coach Bobby Bowden."
—Warrick Dunn, former NFL player, Tampa Bay Buccaneers and Atlanta Falcons

"Coach Bobby Bowden deserves a seat in the front row of the pantheon of the greatest football coaches. I love him as a man, as my big brother, and as my favorite preacher."
—Burt Reynolds, actor

"When I was a young coach, Bobby Bowden was a hero to me. As I got older, he became an example. For all of us, he has been a benchmark. He did things the right way and reached out to help so many of us through the years. He left anyone who was fortunate enough to be around him with a true understanding of what it means to be a coach."

—Mack Brown, head coach, University of Texas

"When Bobby speaks, I listen. When he writes, I read. You will be grateful you read this book. Then you will know why I, and millions of people, love and respect Bobby Bowden."

—Lou Holtz, former coach and college football analyst, ESPN

"We all know Bobby has been incredibly successful on the football field, but I believe his real success lies in how many lives he has touched as a mentor, teacher, and friend! I know he has touched my life and I am better for it."

—Kenny Chesney, country music artist

"Coach Bowden has had an enduring impact on an untold number of lives for such a long period of time. Aside from my father, Coach Bowden is the most influential man in my life. I'm certain there are countless others who could say the same thing. Any success I have in the coaching business I owe mostly to Coach Bowden."

—Mark Richt, head coach, University of Georgia

"Where would college football be without men like Bobby Bowden? I have long been a fan of his tireless dedication to athletic excellence, but it is his work off the field that makes me admire him even more. It is impossible to count the number of lives that have been influenced for the better by this great man. His leadership of young men made them champions both on and off the field."

—S. Truett Cathy, CEO, founder, Chick-fil-A, Inc.

CALLED TO COACH

Reflections on Life, Faith, and Football

BOBBY BOWDEN

with MARK SCHLABACH

FOREWORDS BY TONY DUNGY AND JOE PATERNO

HOWARD BOOKS
A DIVISION OF SIMON & SCHUSTER, INC.

New York · Nashville · London · Toronto · Sydney

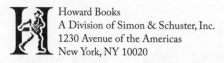 Howard Books
A Division of Simon & Schuster, Inc.
1230 Avenue of the Americas
New York, NY 10020

First Howard Books hardcover edition August 2010

HOWARD and colophon are trademarks of Simon & Schuster, Inc.

For information about special discounts for bulk purchases, please contact Simon & Schuster Special Sales at 1-866-506-1949 or business@simonandschuster.com.

The Simon & Schuster Speakers Bureau can bring authors to your live event. For more information or to book an event, contact the Simon & Schuster Speakers Bureau at 1-866-248-3049 or visit our website at www.simonspeakers.com.

Designed by Stephanie D. Walker

Manufactured in the United States of America

10 9 8 7 6 5 4 3 2 1

Library of Congress Cataloging-in-Publication Data

Bowden, Bobby.
  Called to coach / by Bobby Bowden with Mark Schlabach.
    p.   cm.
  1. Bowden, Bobby. 2. Football coaches—United States—Biography. 3. Florida State University—Football. I. Schlabach, Mark, 1972– II. Title.
  GV939.B66A3 2010
  796.332092—dc22   2010013196
  [B]

ISBN 978-1-4391-9597-0
ISBN 978-1-4391-9598-7 (ebook)

CONTENTS

Bobby Bowden:

For Ann—my beautiful bride of sixty-one years.

For all you have sacrificed to be my wife
and the matriarch of our family.

For always being my biggest fan and my unwavering defender.

For your strength and support that helped me
follow God's purpose for my life.

I may have been called to coach football, but more importantly,
I was called to be your husband.

———————————————

Mark Schlabach:

To Heather, Caroline, Jane, and Jack,
my championship team

FOREWORD

When I stepped down as head coach of the Indianapolis Colts after the 2008 football season I received a lot of notes congratulating me on my career. People were very kind in pointing out that in fifteen years as an assistant coach and thirteen years as a head coach, I had won my share of games and helped a good number of players. For twenty-eight years I'd gotten to do two things that I loved doing—coaching football and being around young men. I knew that God had blessed me tremendously and given me more than I could ever have hoped for when I began coaching in 1981.

I give you that background just to put into perspective what I think of when I'm asked about Bobby Bowden. Consider this—when Coach Bowden got his first head coaching job at Howard College in 1959 I was *four years old*. And one year after *I* retired, Bobby was still the head coach at Florida State University and I was sitting in his office because he was recruiting my son to play for the Seminoles.

God has truly given Coach Bowden what the Bible calls "good success." In fact, in forty-four seasons as a head coach, the last thirty-four at one institution, he enjoyed unprecedented success. Thirty-three straight winning seasons. Fourteen straight seasons with ten or more wins and finishing in the top five nationally. The numbers are incredible and I doubt that they'll be matched by anyone in the near future.

The greatness of Bobby Bowden, to me though, is not in the number of wins, the number of championships, or even the number of All-Americans he's coached. The wonderful thing to me is *how* he's done it.

Since 1996, when I became head coach of the Tampa Bay Buccaneers, I got to see firsthand how he did it at Florida State. As a first-time head coach living in Florida, I couldn't help but observe Coach Bowden. I was struck by how he won so consistently, but always did it with humility. And when there were losses they were handled with grace. It was a tremendous model for any young coach to follow.

I also noticed that Coach Bowden had an impact on his players off the field as well. I had the privilege of coaching quite a few of his former players over the years and most of them talked openly about the impression that he had made on them. From their very first week on campus— when he would take every one of his freshman players to church—they could be sure that he was concerned about them not just as athletes, but as men. He made sure they knew that he would always be there for them, long after their last game as a Seminole. I could personally attest to that as he would call me periodically to check on a player's progress. Not how they were playing, but how they were *doing*. He genuinely cared about them, and that caring was mutual. They had a feeling for him that you don't often see between a player and a coach. It was obvious that he had helped them grow not only as players but academically, socially, and spiritually as well.

Coach Bowden also did a great job of mentoring his staff and helping them grow. That was evident in the number of assistant coaches he had leave for head coaching positions and go on to run successful programs themselves. But it was not just the top assistant coaches that he mentored. Everyone in the office was important to him, and he always had their best interests at heart. Whether it was starting the workday a little later than is customary so the coaches could see their kids off to school or starting staff meetings with devotions that reminded what was really important in life, everyone benefited from the little things Coach

Bowden did. It didn't matter if you were the university president or the assistant custodian—when you came to the Florida State football office you were treated the same way, with warmth and dignity. That was the Bowden way.

How did that way develop? How did Coach Bowden learn the game of football so well and blend it with such a great outlook on life? Where did he get the ability to draw people together, inspire men to give more than they thought they could give, and do it in such a way that it would create such great loyalty among his staff and players? I believe when you read *Called to Coach* you'll see it all comes from his faith in Christ and how he was raised. Coach Bowden never left those roots and he was able to show that traits like honesty, loyalty, humility, and compassion never go out of style and don't create a generation gap.

The true measure of a coach, or anyone in a leadership role for that matter, is how they help those around them grow. And when you look at where many of the men that have been around Bobby Bowden are today, it's a great testimony to his ability to inspire greatness. Look beyond all the championships and the NFL All-Pros and you'll see a lot of very successful businessmen. You'll also see a great many successful husbands, fathers, and some of the best community servants we have in our country today. You'll even see some people like me, who never played or worked for him, but have learned and grown from watching him from afar. That, to me, is the true impact of the man. That's the Bobby Bowden legacy.

Tony Dungy

FOREWORD

When I think of Bobby Bowden, I think about what a great person he was for college football and the young people he coached. He was a tremendous coach, a greater man, and someone who cared deeply about his players and the sport of college football.

I have known Bobby Bowden for more than half a century. I first met Bobby when he visited Penn State's spring practice after he had just started coaching at Howard College in 1959. I coached against Bobby when he was the offensive coordinator and head coach at West Virginia. Penn State always seemed to have better players than he had, but our games were always very close. His teams were always well coached and disciplined.

Bobby was innovative from the start of his coaching career. I don't think people have ever given Bobby enough credit for some of the things he started in college football. At West Virginia during the 1960s and '70s, his teams were faking reverses and running reverses when no one else was doing it. He was open-minded and willing to try different things. I sent my coaches down to watch Florida State practice, and they came back and said, "Coach, they're so well organized and have so much enthusiasm."

Among the coaches I faced throughout my career, I don't know if anyone ever got more out of his teams than Bobby. The only coach I could compare Bobby to in those terms was Ara Parseghian, who coached at Miami (Ohio), Northwestern, and Notre Dame during the 1950s, '60s, and '70s. Bobby was at the top in the way he handled himself, his games-manship, his innovation, and his humbleness. He was never a guy who gloated after he beat you. You knew that if your team lost to one of Bobby's teams, you were licked by a good football team that played well. His teams always held on to the football, played great defense, and were disciplined.

I have deep respect for Bobby. He and his wife, Ann, became good friends of mine over the years. We spent a lot of time together while on Nike trips during the off-season. My wife, Sue, and I admired the way they handled their family and how loyal they were to them.

This book will be an inspiration to young coaches and college foot-ball fans everywhere. It will teach them about the ability to innovate, about being loyal to your coaching staff and being loyal to your school. I think it's a tremendous compliment to Bobby that very few of his assistant coaches ever left. A few of Bobby's assistants moved on to be-come head coaches, but most stayed because he was such a great person to work for.

I doubt if we'll ever see another team match what Florida State did during the 1990s. Bobby's teams won at least ten games and finished in the top five of the final Associated Press Top 25 poll for fourteen con-secutive seasons. It was absolutely amazing.

The press wrote that Bobby and I battled to finish with the most victories in the history of college football. I don't think either one of us was very concerned about the record. We had the same ideals and were just trying to win games the right way. It bothered me that the NCAA wanted to take victories away from Bobby near the end of his career. As far as I'm concerned, he still has those victories.

When it's all said and done, I hope we're not going to judge Bobby's career—or my career, for that matter—by a couple of victories. Bobby's contributions to college football go so much beyond wins and losses. I can only hope my legacy will be able to stand up to his in the sense of what we were able to do for our schools and the sport of college football.

Joe Paterno

CHAPTER 1

HOLDING
THE ROPE

The second day of January 2010 started like any other during the last half century as the head coach of a college football team. I awoke at four o'clock in the morning, started a fresh pot of coffee, and was joined at the breakfast table by Ann, my wife of sixty years. Together, we spent an hour reading Scripture. Our ritual has always been to start with Genesis, and when we finish Revelation, we go back and read the entire Bible again. When we finish reading each morning, we spend several minutes praying together.

God has answered so many of my prayers over the years that I'll never have enough time to thank Him for all my blessings. He blessed me with a wonderful family: my loving wife, six children and their spouses, twenty-one beautiful grandchildren, and five great-grandchildren. God also blessed me with the wonderful career He chose for me. I've always believed that God wanted me to be a football coach, that it was my calling. I believe God wants some people to be doctors, some to be lawyers, some to be teachers. I believe His purpose for me was to go into coaching and try to influence young men for Jesus Christ. He wanted me not only to teach them to be good people but also to surrender their lives to Him.

But though it seemed a day like any other, January 2, 2010, really was different. For the first time in forty-eight years, I didn't wake up as the head coach of a college football team. But I'm hardly ready for retirement. As far as I'm concerned, my work is not done. God still has a plan for me, and it is to spread His word to as many young people as possible. It is what I tried to do as the head football coach at South Georgia College, Howard College, West Virginia University, and Florida State University, and it's what I'll continue to do during the final years of my life.

It is no secret that I was not ready for my coaching career to end. I'd hoped to coach at Florida State for one more season. But after my team lost to the University of Florida, 37–10, in our final game of the 2009 regular season, I knew the end of my career might be near. We finished the 2009 regular season with a 6–6 record, and for the first time in my career as Florida State's coach, influential people were calling for me to retire. After we lost our final game to the Gators, I told the media I needed to go home and do some soul-searching. But when I awoke on November 29, I was determined to return to Florida State for one more season and turn the Seminoles around.

But I was not given the opportunity to do it. The day after we lost to the University of Florida, I received a call from an assistant athletic director at Florida State, who informed me that President Wetherell, one of my former players, wanted to meet with me the next morning. When T.K. and FSU athletic director Randy Spetman arrived at my office on Monday morning, I knew the news was not good. "Bobby, this isn't going to be pretty," T.K. told me.

After thirty-four seasons as Florida State's coach, in which my coaching staff and I led the Seminoles to 2 national championships and 316 victories, and 33 nonlosing seasons, I was asked to step down. Florida State's administration wanted to turn the program over to Jimbo Fisher, who had worked the previous three seasons as my offensive coordinator. Near the end of Jimbo's first season at Florida State in 2007, he was named head-coach-in-waiting, my eventual successor. The plan was for Jimbo to replace me as the Seminoles' coach at the end of the 2010 season.

President Wetherell gave me two options. The first option was to return to Florida State as an ambassador coach, in which I'd have no on-field duties during practices or games.

"Do you mean I'm the head coach, but can't go on the field?" I asked President Wetherell.

"Yes," he told me.

"Well, that option is out. What is the other option?"

President Wetherell answered, "The other option is that we won't renew your contract."

"Would you still want me to do the Seminole Booster Tour this spring?" I asked him.

"No, your contract would expire on January 4, 2010."

I went home and discussed the situation with Ann, and we both agreed that I had no choice. I couldn't stay at Florida State as an ambassador coach. I was going to be paid to sit behind a desk and do nothing. I felt like I would be stealing their money. I didn't think it would be a good situation for anyone.

I was not mad at the fans or Florida State. It was T.K. and the trustees that made the decision not to renew my contract after the Florida loss. I had gotten word earlier that they were all meeting at T.K.'s house to watch that game. After we lost, I thought to myself, "My goose is cooked." I know things don't always end the way you expect them to, but where was the loyalty you would think you'd get after thirty-four years of service? You can't imagine how many times those in charge told me over the last twenty years, "Bobby, you can coach as long as you'd like at FSU." But the termination ended my chances of winning four hundred games, as well as my chances to challenge my good friend Joe Paterno to be the winningest football coach in major college football history. With our entire offense from 2009 returning and a new defensive staff coming in, who knows?

I was disappointed because I thought I had one good fight left in me. I thought I was like Evander Holyfield, Muhammad Ali, or one of the other great heavyweight boxers, who kept climbing back into the ring for one more challenge. I remember when the legendary boxing writer Bert Sugar asked two-time heavyweight champion Floyd Patterson about being knocked down more than any other heavyweight fighter in history. "Yeah, but I got up more than any fighter in history," Patterson told him.

I wasn't ready for my fight to end. At the beginning of the twenty-first century, I watched my good friend Joe Paterno struggle as Penn State's coach. Joe had won more games than any other coach in major college football history, but Penn State wanted him to retire after his teams finished with losing records in four of the five seasons from 2000 to 2004, which enabled me to pass him. Joe would tell me about the Penn State president and athletic director coming to his house in an attempt to persuade him to retire. Joe told them, "Cool it. We're getting this thing straightened out; we're going to get better."

And Penn State did get better. The Nittany Lions went 11–1 in 2005 and beat my team by a 16–13 score in triple overtime in the 2006 Orange Bowl. I looked at the way Joe turned Penn State around, and I always thought I would do it at Florida State, too. But it never happened.

As I look back at my final season at Florida State in 2009, I can look at one play in each of our six losses and say, "If this hadn't happened or if that hadn't happened . . ." If we had won two more games, the possibility of a coaching change probably never would have come up. But that is the nature of the game. Al Groh, former coach of the NFL's New York Jets and the University of Virginia, told me one time, "Things seldom end the way you expect." He was so right.

I coached my last game at Florida State against West Virginia University in the Gator Bowl on New Year's Day 2010. It was bittersweet because West Virginia was the first school to offer me a major head coaching position, in 1970. My family and I spent ten years living in Morgantown, West Virginia, and I learned a lot about being a head coach during my time there. We have many good friends from West Virginia, and it is a place four of my children still call home. Bill Stewart, the Mountaineers' head coach, was a walk-on player on my first team at West Virginia.

The Gator Bowl and WVU were very gracious to Ann and me throughout the entire week. I really did not want to make a big deal about it being my last game as a head coach, but the Gator Bowl asked me to serve as marshal of its parade, and they honored me during pre-game ceremonies. More than three hundred of my former players were in attendance, and they stood in the cold rain to escort me from our team buses into the stadium. I was determined I was not going to let my emotions get the best of me, but it was pretty difficult seeing all of my boys again. I saw many players I hadn't seen in twenty-five years.

Before the game, they asked me to throw a flaming spear into the turf, which is a tradition at Florida State. I was concerned about all of the festivities surrounding me becoming a distraction for my team. I was nervous after the Mountaineers took a 14–3 lead late in the first quarter. Fortunately, my boys came back and we won the game, 33–21. It was a great way to end my coaching career.

I retired from coaching with 389 career victories—or 377, if you believe the NCAA record books. Really, my teams won 411 games, if you count the 22 wins we had at South Georgia College. But I have always been more concerned about the scoreboard He keeps up there. I believed my number one priority as a head coach was to make sure my players received an education and were taught to do things the right way. We won a lot of games at Florida State, but my greatest accomplishments were seeing my players become good husbands, fathers, and professionals.

A lot of times during my career, a mother would invariably write me a letter and tell me she was having problems raising her teenage son. "I'm worried he's headed down the wrong path," she would inform me. "Can you tell me what will help him become a success?"

I would always respond to the mothers with a handwritten letter, and I always gave each of them the same answer.

"Tell your son to get his priorities in order," I told them. "Tell him the number one priority in his life has to be God. That is the first priority. His second priority has to be his family, and his third priority has to be his education. Everything else comes after that. Tell the boy not to do anything that God would not want him to do. Tell him to ask God if he should do it. If he doesn't think God would want him to do it, he shouldn't do it."

That has always been the blueprint for my life. When I was a young man, I was so intent on doing well in football that I wasn't living my life the way God wanted me to live it. But I eventually realized football might not last a week if you tear your knee up. With one misstep, your career is over. I tell other football coaches the same thing. I tell them, "Don't let football become your god. If you do, you may become miserable."

Look at all the coaches who burn out quickly. They can't coach for very long because their priorities aren't in the right order. I've never put football ahead of God or my family. I believe it's the reason I lasted in the coaching profession for so long.

People ask me all the time what I want my legacy to be, and I've always said that when I retire, I hope people remember me for three things. I hope people believe I was one of the best who ever coached the game.

More important, I hope they say Bobby Bowden did it the right way.

The most important thing I hope people would say about me is that Bobby Bowden served God's purpose for his life. When I first became a college head coach, at South Georgia College in Douglas, Georgia, in 1955, I started a ritual of meeting with my team on the Friday night before a game. I started every one of my team meetings the same way—with a devotional. It was the night before the game, and I knew my players were nervous about the day ahead.

I would talk to them about how you become a Christian and how you become saved. Some may say I didn't have the right to do it, but I would much rather be spiritually correct than politically correct. Let's say a professor teaching a class mentions his religious beliefs. He has the right to do so. But you do not have to believe the professor if you do not want to. I wanted to give the message to every boy I coached, to give witness to him, and then I left it up to him to decide what to do with it.

Romans 10:9–10 teaches us that "if you confess with your mouth, 'Jesus is Lord,' and believe in your heart that God raised him from the dead, you will be saved. For it is with your heart that you believe and are justified, and it is with your mouth that you confess and are saved."

As Scripture teaches us, anyone who trusts in Him will never be put to shame. You have to believe, you have to have faith, and you must testify to it without shame. That's what I've tried to do throughout my life. I am not afraid to tell anybody about it. I told my boys to be the same way: never be ashamed of it.

I still remember receiving a late-night phone call when I was coaching at West Virginia during the 1970s. One of my players had been arrested for being drunk and getting into a fight. I picked the boy up from jail and told him to meet me in my office the next morning. When he arrived, I scolded him for his actions and told him I would not tolerate such behavior. I warned him I would kick him off the team if he did it again. "You know what you need?" I asked him as he was walking out the door. "You need God."

A week later, the young man showed up at my office again.

"I found Him," the player told me.

"Found who?" I asked.

"I found God," he said.

After returning to his dormitory room after our initial meeting, the player wandered into a Fellowship of Christian Athletes meeting and stayed long enough to listen. I never had a problem with the young man again.

Throughout my coaching career, I always felt like I was being led. I prayed about a lot of decisions that were made, and they usually turned out to be good choices. I always felt like some of the best things that happened to me came after God said no. I wanted to leave Florida State for the University of Alabama in 1987, but Alabama didn't offer me the job. It was very disappointing, but I felt like God was telling me Florida State was where I needed to be.

When Florida State told me it was time to retire, I felt like God must not have wanted me to stay. I still felt like they were wrong for turning me out, but I knew God was handling the situation, and He was in control. That's just how my faith goes.

I've always believed that every game we won at Florida State was won by our players, assistant coaches, support personnel, alumni, and fans. Teamwork is what helped the Seminoles win national championships in 1993 and 1999. They were special teams, and I tried to instill their work ethic and unity in every one of my teams thereafter. Before many of my seasons at Florida State, I talked to my players about holding the rope:

> *What did our 1993 national championship team and 1999 national championship team do that was in common? They held the rope!*
>
> *What does holding the rope mean? You are hanging from the edge of a cliff five hundred yards in the air. The only thing between you and falling to the ground is a piece of rope with the person of your choice on the other end.*
>
> *Who do you know that you can trust enough? Who do you know who has enough guts to withstand rope burn, watch blood drip from his hands, and still not let go?*
>
> *Look around and ask, "Who can I trust to hold the rope?" Who will let his hands bleed for me? If you can look at every member of your team and say they will hold the rope, then your team will win!*

My coaching career might be over, but I'm still holding the rope that really matters.

CHAPTER 2

I WILL
SERVE YOU

Even after a coaching career that spanned more than half a century, people ask me all the time why I became so interested in football. Football has always been a big part of my life. Almost from the day I was born, playing and coaching football were all I ever wanted to do. It just got into my blood.

Up until I was five, my family and I lived in the Woodlawn section of Birmingham, Alabama. Now, you have to understand: if you grew up in Alabama, you were a football fan. That's just the way it is in Alabama. In my case, the backyard of my family's home was adjacent to the east end zone of the Woodlawn High School football field. At the time, Woodlawn was a perennial state champion. They were *the* football team to beat in the city of Birmingham in the early 1940s. As a kid, I could step into our backyard and hear through the tall bushes growing across our fence the school band marching or the players practicing nearly every day. We had a garage that backed up to that fence, and I can remember my daddy getting a ladder so we could climb up on the roof of the garage and watch them practice. We would sit up there for hours every day. My father loved watching football, and I always loved watching it with him.

After I turned five, we moved three miles away, to a part of town called East Lake, into a small white-frame house that was half a block away from Berry Field, which was Howard College's football field. It was up on a hill, and I could see the Howard team practicing from my front lawn. During elementary school, I had to walk up that hill by the football field and the gymnasium, across campus, then two more blocks to get to school. I literally grew up on the Howard College campus.

Every autumn, I'd hear the sounds of boys playing football: kicking, tackling, grunting, things like that. Berry Field became my playground. I'd come home from school, load my pockets with unshelled peanuts and an apple, go meet my buddies, and we would play around with the tackling dummies or climb the fence. On Sundays, when Howard College wasn't practicing, the neighborhood kids would all go up there and play football. When I was about ten, my dad bought me my first football uniform. It was practically cardboard with thin shoulder pads and a little helmet. But the shirt had "Howard College Bulldogs" across the chest, so it was a very big deal to me.

My father, Bob Bowden, was born in Clayton, Alabama. His father died when my daddy was very young. My father had thirteen brothers and sisters, but not all of them survived. Back in those days, a lot of babies died at birth. After my grandfather died, my daddy had to help his mother support their family. When my father was only seven years old, he sold newspapers at the street corner outside Nick's Drug Store in Woodlawn. He worked the rest of his life, and I like to think I learned a strong work ethic and determination from him. My father eventually became a teller at the First National Bank in Birmingham, and he worked there for seventeen years. During the Great Depression, he managed to keep his job while others lost theirs. He eventually was promoted and handled loans for a home builder named W. E. Bishop. My father and Mr. Bishop became very close and decided to go into business together. They bought an office building in Woodlawn, named their company "Bowden and Bishop," and did quite well. I worked every summer for Mr. Bishop and did all the things nobody else wanted to do—carrying lumber, bricks, cement, even digging foundations. Looking back, that was some of the hardest work of my life.

My daddy was always a "Dadgumit!" man. He would say, "Dang it!" or "Dadgumit!" and would never take the Lord's name in vain. I heard "Dadgumit!" so much as a child, I guess it just grew on me. My father rarely used profanity, and my mother never swore at all.

My daddy was very active in our church, Ruhama Baptist, one of the oldest in Alabama, which we attended every Wednesday night and Sunday morning. We prayed together before every meal and before going to bed. My daddy sang in the choir all of his life, and both my parents taught Sunday school class. Daddy was in charge of the Sunday school class for the older high school students, which was attended by a lot of the football players from Woodlawn High School. A lot of those boys were my heroes when I was young. One of them was Jimmy Tarrant, who was an all-state back at Woodlawn High School and Howard College. Jimmy could have played at the University of Alabama, but he wasn't big enough. He later became one of Alabama's most famous high school football coaches.

My father was really a very good person. He had a happy personality and he was uninhibited, even boisterous. He was the kind of guy who was just always having a good time. He liked to tell us jokes, and I guess my sense of humor came from him. Any time I'm together with my sons—Terry, Tommy, Jeff, and Steve—we always ask one another, "Have you heard any good jokes?" Telling jokes and having a sense of humor has always been a Bowden thing, and I have my father to thank for that.

But my daddy also was a strict disciplinarian. If I did something bad, I would have to take off all my clothes, bend over a chair, and he would take off his belt and whack me on the rear end. Then I would get the same story every child is told: this hurts me more than it hurts you. When I was young, my mother had a nice chair with wooden armrests. For whatever reason, I sat in that chair one day and cut notches in it with my pocketknife. When my father got home from work that day, I had to take off all my clothes, and he whacked me with his belt. He was definitely from the old school when it came to punishment.

Another time, we were having initiation for the Boy Scouts. I had been initiated the previous year, and now it was my turn to initiate the new scouts. There were maybe five guys coming into our group, and when they got to the church, we made sure they all saw this jar of worms sitting on a table. Then we blindfolded the boys, told them to open their mouths, and then fed them spaghetti. Of course, they thought they were eating worms, so they spat them out, horrified.

But one boy had walked up to the front of the room and said, "I know what you're going to do!" Well, since he knew what was going to happen, I put a live worm in his mouth. My daddy was so mad, he had the other scouts form two lines and had them take off their belts. I had to run between the lines with every one of them whacking me on the rear end. Boy, they wore me out that day. Of course, my daddy took me home and wore me out again. It was not a good day.

My mother, Sunset Cleckler Bowden, was born and raised in Anniston, Alabama. She was very small when she was born, probably premature. When she was a baby, they said you could sit her in a coffeepot. She grew to be only five feet tall. My mother was a very sweet lady, and, of course, she loved her boy. You know how mothers are. In January 1943, I was thirteen years old and was walking home after playing basketball at the local YMCA. It was winter and my knees were aching terribly the entire way. When I got home, I took off my shoes, and my feet were swollen. My mother was terrified when she saw them, and she immediately called our family doctor. Back in those days, doctors still made house calls. The doctor rushed to our house to see me. He diagnosed me with rheumatic fever, which was considered a very serious illness at the time. It killed people. Later we were told that I had an enlarged heart. I remember my mother crying when the doctor left our house.

The doctors told my mother to put me in bed and told me not to get up for anything. They wouldn't even let me go to the restroom. My mother had to help me use a bedpan. I hated it. When the doctor came back to see me a second time, a few weeks later, I started getting out of bed, and he yelled at me, "No, don't get up! Don't get up! Lay back down!" It made me think I was dying. But that is how scared they were about rheumatic fever back then. My parents must have thought it was pretty serious, too, because over at Ruhama Baptist Church, every Sunday, the minister would say, "Pray for little Bobby Bowden."

Every Friday night during the fall of 1943, while I was still confined to my bed, I would listen to Woodlawn High School football games on the radio. Woodlawn won the Alabama state championship that season. Harry Gilmer, who grew up in my neighborhood, was the star tailback, and he led Woodlawn High to an undefeated record that season. I grew up idolizing Harry Gilmer. He went on to become an All-American at the University of Alabama, leading the Crimson Tide to a 1946 Rose Bowl win in Pasadena, California. He was one of the first players to throw a jump pass, and I would go out in the backyard and run, jump, and throw a pass just like Harry Gilmer did. My father bought me an electric football game while I was sick. It had the players who would slide across the field while the game board vibrated. My friends and I would pretend we were Doc Blanchard and Glenn Davis, who were "Mr. Inside" and "Mr. Outside," respectively, the great backs at the U.S. Military Academy.

While I was sick, I missed playing football more than anything else. The doctors told me I would not be active anymore and that I'd be in bed for the rest of my life. My legs ached so badly at times that I would cry myself to sleep some nights. After I had been sick for about six months, I remember my mother walking through the doorway to leave my bedroom. Before she left, she turned to me and asked, "Bobby, do you believe in prayer?"

I told her, "Of course, I do, Mother."

"Well, why don't you ask Him to heal you? He will," she said.

My mother would hold me in her arms, praying to God to heal me. I prayed all the time, too. It was kind of a pledge. I told Him, "If you heal me, I will serve You. If you let me play football again, I will try to serve You through sports."

And He did heal me.

Finally, after nearly a year in bed, I got clearance from the doctors to go back to school. But my orders were clear: no lifting weights, no running, no exercise of any kind, and absolutely no football. They told me I could go to school and come home and that was it. I was devastated. In 1944, I finally finished elementary school. I was always older than most of my classmates, and seemed even older after I fell behind in school because of my illness. I enrolled in Woodlawn High School in 1944. The doctors still would not let me exercise or play sports, so I joined the marching band. We would march at the football games and in parades. I played first trombone in the high school orchestra and even performed a solo at the University of Alabama summer band camp. For a while I also played in a jazz group called the Lee Jordan Band. I really loved music, but I still couldn't run or play sports, and I missed it dearly.

My mother knew how much I wanted to play football, so before my junior year she insisted on taking me to another specialist for a second opinion. It was there that I finally got the news I'd been praying for: the doctors pronounced me fit to play football again. I remember feeling like a heavy burden had just been lifted from me. I remember crying in that doctor's office, and my mother was crying, too. After waiting so long, I was finally getting the chance to do what I loved most. I went out for spring practice that year and was doing well. About two weeks before the first game in the fall of 1946, I went out for a pass in practice, fell down, and landed on my hand. When I got up, my thumb was bent backward. Kenny Morgan, my coach, looked at my thumb and started twisting it back into place, thinking it was only dislocated. He taped up my thumb and sent me back out to practice. My thumb was actually broken. It swelled up and hurt like mad, but I toughed it out. A few days later, I went to see the University of Alabama football team's doctor, who lived in Birmingham. He put my hand in a cast and told me my football season was over. After waiting so long to play again, I never even got into a game that first season at Woodlawn High. I was heartbroken again.

That year, I weighed only about 130 pounds—not too small for running backs at the time; most of the big backs weighed about 150 or 155 pounds. You just didn't have really big players back then. You might have one player who weighed more than 200 pounds, and if you weighed 215 pounds, they'd say you were too fat to play. My coach called me to his office one day after I broke my thumb.

"Bobby, would you be interested in dropping out of school?" he asked me. "If you drop out for one semester, I think I can get you another year of eligibility. You can get bigger and might be able to get a scholarship to college."

I talked to my parents about it, and we decided that was what we would do. For the next few months, I worked around the house and didn't do much of anything else. But I would still go up to the high school and play football on the weekends with my friends. The next fall, I went back out for football again, this time weighing about 140 pounds. I was a backup halfback and played in some of the games. In my senior year, the coaches moved me to right halfback, and I was senior cocaptain of the team, which was a big honor to me. During both of my football seasons at Woodlawn High School, we played all of our games at Legion Field in Birmingham. At times there were eighteen thousand fans in attendance. The high school games were always big in Birmingham because there were only five high school teams in the city. Nearly every season, Woodlawn High School and Ramsay High School would rank number one and number two in the city, but my team never won a city championship.

Despite everything, I would not have traded my childhood for anything. I believe my illness as a child brought me closer to my family and to God. I believe it made me a better person, a better father, and a better coach. Looking back now, it's easy to see the lesson I learned at such a young age: if something bad has happened to you and you have faith, then something good is bound to happen. I've always believed that. I came to believe that faith, prayer, and a willingness to serve God will get you through everything.

Growing up, especially after a game of touch football, my friends and I would just lie there on the grass, looking up at the sky. Before long, one of my friends would say, "That cloud looks like a goose flying through the air."

Someone else would say, "That cloud looks like a horse galloping through a pasture." It would go on and on, with each of us using our imagination as only children do.

But one day one of my friends asked, "I wonder if God is up there?"

We always think about God being "up there," you know? Even though we know He's everywhere, we always think of Him being "up there" in the clouds with the flying geese and galloping horses.

While we lay there in the grass pondering that question, someone else said, "I wish He would stick His head out so I could see Him."

Wouldn't that be nice? If we could see God, everyone would believe in Him. But because we can't see Him, not everyone believes.

But I've always believed in God.

I know Jesus made the invisible visible. I have never seen God. I've never seen the wind, either, but I know it's there. I've felt a chilling gust blow across my face in the dead of winter, and felt a cool breeze bring much-needed relief during the sweltering days of summer. I've felt the wind swirl through my hair. I've watched the wind push over trees and blow the leaves across my lawn.

That's kind of the way God is, too. Having read about Jesus in the Bible and learned about His life, how He walked on water, how He raised Lazarus from the dead, and how He raised Jairus's daughter from the dead, I know God is there. I know Jesus lived and I know how He died. I know He was buried for three days and came out of His tomb and lived for forty more days before He was lifted up into heaven.

And now that I have known Jesus, I know God.

My mother and father were both very devoted Christians. When I was really young, I thought I was required to join the church because my parents expected me to do it. But I kept putting it off and putting it off. Finally, one Sunday morning, when I was about ten or eleven years old, I said, "I'm going to join the church today."

As a Baptist, if you were ready to join the church, you walked down to the front after Sunday service and told the pastor you were ready to join the church and be saved. At least that was the way we did it at Ruhama Baptist. The reason you went down in front of everybody else is you were not supposed to be ashamed of it. It was almost like you were telling everyone around you, "Look at me, I want to be a Christian!"

So the day came when I thought it was time to accept Jesus Christ into my heart. Of course, being a young child, I thought that after I joined the church, I had only to be good and I would automatically go to heaven. If I was good on any given day, I thought I would get a plus from God. But if I was bad, I would get a minus. I thought God was grading me every day. I pictured God "up there" in a big, old chair with a big, long beard, watching over me and keeping score. That was what I imagined.

It wasn't until I was twenty-three years old that I found out that isn't the way it works. Not until I was a young father and husband did I begin to understand what my faith means. That's when I found out that we are saved through grace—that if I accepted Jesus Christ as my savior and surrendered my life to Him, *then* I would go to heaven. I finally figured out He died on the cross for me and for my sins. There is nothing I can do that can be good enough to repay Him for that sacrifice, so I accept Him as my savior.

I finally came to understand these things while I was working as an assistant football coach at Howard College, my alma mater. Howard College was a Baptist school and there were a lot of boys there who were studying to become Baptist ministers. One of them was a young man named Doryl Hall. He was a couple of years younger than I and was studying for the ministry. Doryl would speak at a lot of churches in Alabama, and one day he asked me to join him and give a testimony. I ended up going with him several times. We would drive over to Lincoln or Anniston, and before Doryl would speak to a congregation, I would stand and give a testimony.

After one trip to a church in the summer of 1953, we drove back to Birmingham, and Doryl pulled his car in front of my house. We sat there talking and Doryl told me, "Bobby, we're saved by grace, not by suffering."

Until that moment I thought I just had to be good and live a righteous life to go to heaven. Finally, I'd learned that we're saved by asking for forgiveness and asking Christ to come into our hearts. We don't necessarily deserve it, but Christ has already died on the cross for my sins and your sins.

After that conversation with Doryl in 1953, I realized that God would save me no matter what I had done, because He will forgive our sins. The following Sunday, Ann and I took our kids—only Robyn and Steve had been born by then—to church and when the service was over, Ann and I walked to the front and rededicated ourselves to Christ.

From that day forward, I started following Doryl's example. The first sermon I ever delivered was at Ruhama Baptist, my own church, in 1953. They made me the youth pastor, and I had to deliver the sermon that

Sunday. Even though I was a little nervous, I wrote a sermon and delivered it to the congregation. I've probably given several thousand of them since then. I always felt, as a football coach, I had that responsibility. I always felt that God made me a coach for a couple of reasons: to help kids to understand faith, and to tell others about it when I am asked. I don't go out seeking to speak at churches, but if somebody asks me to do it and I'm available, I will go. I've done it my entire life.

When I speak to a congregation, I try to explain why a football coach is standing behind their pulpit. I ask them, "If you knew the cure for cancer, wouldn't you tell somebody?" If you knew the cure for cancer, you wouldn't keep it a secret. You would write a book or a paper about it and spread the wonderful news. You would share the cure for cancer with the world to stop the death and suffering of millions of people.

That's the reason I speak at churches: I believe that telling people how to live eternally after they die is even more important than telling them about a cure for cancer.

When I was young, my family and I would go down to the Black Warrior River in central Alabama every summer. My daddy and uncle would fish all week. We used cane poles and worms, and it was always a lot of fun. My daddy and uncle would mostly fish off the bank, and whenever they caught a fish, they would throw it up on the bank toward me. It was my job to take the fish off the hook and string it up. As a kid, I waited until I thought the fish were dead because they scared me when they flopped up and down. But as soon as I put the string through the fish's gills and put it back in the water, it would come back to life. The water would start bubbling, and the fish would start swimming again. For the fish to live, it had to be in water. Fish cannot live without water, and man cannot live without God.

There is a void in all of our lives. As a coach, I've dealt with thousands of students over the years, and every one of them has that void. They might try to fill it with alcohol or drugs or sex, but none of that ever works. Until they build a relationship with God, the void is always going to be there.

I always tried to teach my players that the only thing guaranteed in life is their salvation. Winning is not guaranteed. I coached for a long, long time, and the only thing certain about coaching is you are not always going to win. We won a lot of games at Florida State University, but we lost our share of them, too.

Some of my players at FSU might have become All-Americans and first-round draft choices in the NFL draft. They might have signed contracts worth millions of dollars. But all of that meant nothing if they still had that void in their lives. Look at all the wealthy people swindled by Bernie Madoff, who defrauded investors of billions of dollars in the largest Ponzi scheme in history. Those millionaires built big beautiful mansions, owned fancy sports cars, and had millions of dollars saved in their retirement accounts. They thought they had it made. But your house is not guaranteed. An earthquake or a hurricane can destroy it in seconds. You might save a great sum of money, but your life savings are not guaranteed, either. You can lose all your money in a recession, or someone like Bernie Madoff can come along and take all of it. You might develop a fine career, but one day it will be over. I won a lot of football games as a college coach, but my career is now over. You might enjoy great accomplishments, such as winning national championships or winning more than three hundred games, but eventually someone will surpass you. Ever heard of Joe Paterno?

In the end, the only guarantee is salvation through Jesus Christ. When I was growing up, I needed a savior. I was never good enough, and I'm still not good enough.

When I played football at Howard College in the early 1950s, I also played on the school's baseball team and ran track. If you were going to be on scholarship at a small school such as Howard College, you had to play more than one sport. We were playing baseball against Auburn University during my junior season, in 1952. I had never hit a home run in college. No matter how hard I tried, I just could not hit a ball over the fence. Everything I hit seemed to be on the ground, or it was a line drive to the outfield.

During the game against Auburn, I hit a screaming line drive up the middle. I saw the ball fly off the bat, and then I saw it go between the second baseman and the shortstop. I took off running and headed to first base. I started to make my turn toward second base. When I reached second, I looked into the outfield and saw the ball rolling to the fence. The outfielders were still chasing it down, so I took off for third base. I couldn't see the ball anymore, so I knew the third-base coach would tell me to slide, stand up, or run for home plate.

When I finally reached third base, the coach yelled, "Go home, but hurry!"

As I was rounding third base, the center fielder picked up the baseball and threw it to the shortstop. The shortstop fired the ball home. The catcher was crouched down, about a foot in front of home plate, and was squatting near the ground, waiting for the ball. As I made my way toward home, I saw his eyes getting bigger and bigger. I knew that dadgum baseball was about to get there, so I had to take the catcher out. The ball arrived at home plate just as I did. I collided with the catcher, and the ball bounced out of his glove.

The umpire screamed, "Safe!"

I got up and dusted off my jersey. My teammates came out of our dugout to shake my hand and congratulate me. I just could not believe I had finally hit a home run!

But as I was walking back to our dugout, I heard the first baseman yell, "Throw me the ball!"

The catcher threw the baseball to first base. The first baseman stepped on the bag. The first-base umpire yelled, "You're out!"

Wouldn't you know it? I missed first base. I was called out for missing the bag with my foot, and the first home run of my career was taken off the scoreboard. I never hit a home run in my college career.

To me, life is a lot like baseball. Think of first base as Jesus Christ. Second base is all the materialistic things we acquire in life: money, cars, nice clothes, and houses. Third base is all the honors and accolades we earn: being named an All-American, winning the Heisman Trophy, and winning conference and national championships. Home plate is heaven and eternity. If you miss first base and forget to accept Jesus Christ into your heart, then second base and third base don't matter. Without first base, you will never get to home plate, either.

I can remember speaking to a congregation in Georgia several years ago. They asked me to appear on a radio show before I gave my testimony at the church. I was telling that baseball story and was a little long-winded. The radio show cut off right as I was running down the third-base line. I was not able to tell the rest of the story. I went to work the following Monday, and a little old lady called my office. She had heard me telling the story on the radio and asked me one question, "Well, did you score, Coach?"

After accepting Jesus Christ as my savior and trying to follow His path for me every day of my life, I know I am finally headed toward home.

CHAPTER 3

MOTHER HEN

The first time I saw Julia Ann Estock was at a church barbecue. She was fourteen years old and was the prettiest thing I had ever seen. Ann had recently moved to Birmingham and enrolled in Woodlawn High School. She went to our church and sang up in the choir. I always sat in the back row of the church with my buddies, and I would see her up there, singing.

My friends and I would hang out under the streetlamps on the corner across from Ann's house. Ann would come out every night and sweep the sidewalk or something, and one night, I started throwing rocks at her to get her attention. I went over and started talking to her and we really hit it off. She was an A student and was simply gorgeous. We started dating and went together for about two years in high school. We would break up every now and then. She would date someone else, and I would date someone else. But somehow we would always end up back together. I guess that is just the way God wanted it to be.

When I graduated from Woodlawn High in 1949, I really did not know if I was good enough to play football in college. I had played only two seasons at Woodlawn and had been a starter only as a senior because I had been sick or hurt most of the time. College football recruiting was not as big as it is today, and most of the recruiting was done through letters. I can remember only one time when a college football coach came to our high school. He was from the University of Alabama in Tuscaloosa, which, of course, was the school where I really hoped to play.

At that time, recruiting was unlimited, and schools could sign as many freshmen as they wanted. Some players were granted scholarships covering tuition, room, and board. But in probably half of the cases or more, a booster would pay a player's way to college. It was legal to do that back then, and I had a gentleman pay my way to the University of Alabama. His name was Holt Rast Sr., and he worked with my father. His son, Holt Rast Jr., had been a great football player at Alabama and was one of my first heroes. Holt Rast Jr. was an All-American end for the Crimson Tide in 1941 and later served in the U.S. Army, from 1942 to 1946. He was awarded the Purple Heart and the Silver Star after being wounded in action. Holt Rast Jr. later became a state representative in Alabama.

Birmingham was a Crimson Tide city. When I was sick as a child, I spent every Saturday afternoon in the fall listening to the Crimson Tide's football games on the radio. My father took me to Tuscaloosa for a football game at least once every season. As a child, I had a scrapbook filled with newspaper stories and photographs of the Crimson Tide. One of the reasons I was recruited by Alabama was because Malcolm Laney, who had been the head football coach at Woodlawn High School, was an assistant coach for the Crimson Tide. He left the year before I started attending Woodlawn High School, but he was always very friendly to me.

When I left for the University of Alabama in January 1949, I was so homesick and missed Ann so much I could hardly stand it. I didn't own a car, so I would have to take the bus back to Birmingham every weekend to see her. Tuscaloosa was only fifty miles from Birmingham, but I was so lovesick it felt like it took half a day to get there. Every Friday it seemed like that darn bus stopped at every town in the state. I was just so in love with Ann and missed her so much that it really ruined my time at Alabama. I would have married her and brought her to Tuscaloosa with me, but under the rules, getting married would mean losing my scholarship. That was also true at schools such as Auburn, Georgia, and Tennessee, and the restriction didn't change until several years later.

I went through spring practice as a university freshman in 1949 and was beginning to find my way when I made a decision that would change our lives forever.

My roommate at Alabama was a boy named Paul Crumbley. Paul had gone to school at Woodlawn High and was a couple of years older than I was. One night, Paul came into my dormitory room and asked me, "You and Ann aren't together anymore?"

"Of course we are. What do you mean?" I asked him.

"Well, I went home this weekend and saw Ann on a streetcar with Shorty White," Paul told me. "They went to a movie together or something."

Boy, that just killed me. I had played football against Shorty White in high school, when he was going to Phillips High. We always had a good time hanging out together.

I called Ann and she told me what happened. Shorty White had come into the store where she worked and was flirting with her. He found out she was from Woodlawn High School and asked her if she knew Bobby Bowden. She told him I was her boyfriend. She asked Shorty White what he knew about me. Shorty told her that he and I had been down to Panama City Beach, Florida, together the previous summer and that we all went out with some girls at the beach. Ann was so angry she decided she was going to get even with me, so she went to see a movie with Shorty White.

In all honesty, I had actually been to Panama City Beach the summer before I left for school at the University of Alabama. Mort Vasserberg, Aubrey Dickinson, and I had taken a job on a farm about twenty miles north of Birmingham. We had to hoe cotton, hoe corn, and hoe fields. We did that for about three or four days and then we all decided to quit and go to the beach. We all said, "Let's go to Panama City," because that is where kids from Birmingham went when they wanted to go to the beach. We didn't tell anyone about our plans, and we hitchhiked the entire way to Florida.

While we were there, we met a couple of girls from Woodlawn High School. I really did not have much to do with them, but I might have flirted a little. Of course, Ann thought there was much more to it than that, so she was going to make dadgum sure she got even with me.

That incident is really one of the reasons we got married so young. I just could not stand the thought of her on a date with Shorty White. I went home right after that and just dropped everything at Alabama after only one semester.

There was another reason why Ann and I decided to get married at such a young age. We had been together for so long that we were starting to get intimate. When we were married, she was sixteen and I was nineteen. Any parent whose kids marry that young is bound to wonder if pregnancy is the reason. Well, that is not what happened. My mother actually thought that was the case after we were married. I remember her saying to me, "Are ya'll going to have a baby?" I'm sure Ann's mother and both of our fathers had the same fears, but neither Ann nor I believed in premarital sex. That's how we were raised. But despite our religious convictions, we were getting close, boy. You can't help it when a man and a woman love each other the way Ann and I did, and that's one of the reasons why we ran off and got married, on April 1, 1949.

My father and mother had to go to Atlanta for a business meeting that weekend. They took the train to Atlanta, leaving our car at home. Ann and I decided that was our chance. But first I had to run by my buddy's house to borrow some money to get married. I stopped at Dennis Hudson's house, knocked on his window, and borrowed twenty dollars. I swore him to secrecy, asking him to tell no one about our marriage.

We got in the car that Sunday morning and headed for Rising Fawn, Georgia, which is right across the state line. We went there because other people from our high school had run off and gotten married, and they'd all done it in Rising Fawn. I had never been there, but I knew where it was. And because I just could not wait to kiss the bride, I got a speeding ticket in Trussville! That ticket took about half of the twenty I had borrowed because I had to pay the ticket right there. I had only ten dollars left to get us there and back.

We got to Rising Fawn and found out the justice of the peace lived down this long dirt road. We drove to his house and knocked on the front door. He answered the door and was holding a piece of fried chicken. He and his family were inside, eating their Sunday dinner after church. I told him we wanted to get married. He invited us inside and told us he had to finish his dinner first. After he was finished eating, he came back out with his wife. He asked me for the ring. Of course, I had forgotten to buy a wedding ring, so I handed him my high school class ring. He married us right there in his living room. We got the marriage license and headed back to Birmingham.

After we were married, Ann went to stay with her parents, and I went back to my parents' house. About a month later, our secret began to get out. I remember my mother asking me, "Bobby, did you get married?"

"No, no, we did not get married, Mamma," I told her.

"You better not get married, Bobby, because if you do, you'll have to move out," she warned me.

But as soon as my mother finally figured out that Ann and I were actually married, the first question she asked me was, "Bobby, ya'll are going to stay with us, aren't you?"

Of course, our parents thought we were crazy, and no one thought our marriage would last. Ann was still in high school, but the next fall she came to Howard College with me. I had to leave the University of Alabama, so I came home and transferred to Howard. I knew a lot of the players there because many of them were from Woodlawn High School. And of course, I had grown up on the Howard College campus as a child, so it was really like a second home to me.

Leaving the University of Alabama might seem like one of the most difficult decisions of my life, since my dream had always been to play college football for the Crimson Tide. But even if I had stayed at Alabama, become an All-American, and won national championships, none of it would have mattered without Ann in my life. I knew from the very beginning that she was the only woman for me. Paul wrote in 1 Corinthians 13:1–7 that true love cannot be acquired without an act of ultimate self-sacrifice:

If I speak in the tongues of men and of angels, but have not love, I am only a resounding gong or a clanging cymbal. If I have the gift of prophecy and can fathom all mysteries and all knowledge, and if I have a faith that can move mountains, but have not love, I am nothing. If I give all I possess to the poor and surrender my body to the flames, but have not love, I gain nothing.

Love is patient, love is kind. It does not envy, it does not boast, it is not proud. It is not rude, it is not self-seeking, it is not easily angered, it keeps no record of wrongs. Love does not delight in evil but rejoices with the truth. It always protects, always trusts, always hopes, always perseveres.

When we started at Howard College, Ann and I were living with my parents. We went off and got our own apartment one time, but we didn't have any money to pay the bills, so we moved back in with my parents. I was playing football for the Howard team, the Bulldogs, and Ann was one of our cheerleaders. During my first season at Howard, I played half-back on offense for the varsity team.

The first couple of seasons, my team wasn't very good. We went 4–5 in 1949 and 2–8 in 1950. We lost our starting quarterback to an injury, and the coaches decided to give me a try. I ended up starting at quarterback for three seasons. After going 2–3–1 in 1951, we finally turned the corner during my senior season in 1952. We finished 5–4, which was the first winning record at Howard College in a long time. I was named a Little All-American, which was a nice honor for a senior.

I will never forget bumping into Ann on the Howard College campus during my sophomore season in 1950. I was going back to class, and I ran into her walking across the lawn.

She told me, "Bobby, I think I am pregnant."

Sure enough, Ann was pregnant with our daughter, Robyn, who was born in July 1951. Ann dropped out of classes during her pregnancy and then started classes again shortly after Robyn was born. Not long after that, Ann became pregnant with our first son, Steve. He was born in September 1952. Ann dropped out of classes again and started back after Steve was born. We had two children before I even finished college. A few months after Steve was born, Ann became pregnant with our second boy, Tommy. My good friend Hubert Mizell, who was a longtime columnist for the *St. Petersburg Times* and covered many of my seasons at Florida State, liked to joke that it was "three tikes and you're out." We had three children while Ann was attending college, and she never was able to finish school.

By the time Ann and I had moved in with my parents, my older sister,

Marion, had moved out. Marion was about a year and a half older than I was. She was very sweet and a very good piano player. We were very close when we were young. But once she started high school, I did not get to see her as much. Marion went to Howard College, too, and married a football player there. He was going to be a preacher and went off to the Southern Baptist Theological Seminary in Louisville, Kentucky, to study for the ministry, but he ended up going into the real estate business with my father. Marion had six children, just like me. Sadly, Marion died very young, of cancer, at age fifty-eight.

By the time I took my first head coaching position, at South Georgia College, in 1955, Ann and I had three children and one on the way. Robyn and Steve were old enough to attend grammar school, but Tommy and Terry, who was born shortly after we arrived in Douglas, were still very young and spent most of their days at home with Ann. Our first two years at South Georgia, we lived in an old army barracks. Rent was twenty-five dollars per month. After a couple of years, we moved into Powell Hall, which was the dormitory where all the football players lived. We had a downstairs apartment, and it was pretty nice. We lived there and did not have to pay our phone bill or for utilities, so it was a big improvement for us.

Powell Hall was right in the middle of campus, and our children would play on the campus grounds. Terry was only two or three years old, and he would wander up to the Student Center, which was several yards from our apartment. Every time Terry went there, he'd come home and not eat his supper. Ann finally figured out that the students were feeding him.

One day, Ann put a sign on his back that read, "Please do not feed."

Terry came back with a sign on his back that read, "Well fed."

I remember that Terry was always the daring one. Tommy was like me, always very cautious and conservative. One time we came home to find that Terry had somehow climbed up on the roof of the two-story building. I had to go up and bring him down.

After our youngest children, Jeffrey and Ginger, arrived, it became awfully difficult to keep up with six kids. While I was coaching wide receivers at Florida State during the mid-1960s, we would spend Christmas Day at our house and then drive to Birmingham to see our parents the next day. One year, we stopped on the way to have breakfast at a restaurant we liked outside of Prattville. When we finished eating, four-year-old Ginger went to use the restroom. We all left the restaurant, loaded up the car, and headed down the road. About twenty miles down the highway, a patrolman flashed his car's lights behind me, and I pulled my car over to the side of the road.

"Have you left something?" the officer asked me.

We looked around the backseat, and Ginger wasn't there!

When we got back to the restaurant, they had her up on the counter, feeding her candy to keep her happy. She didn't seem bothered in the least.

Because I was on the road coaching and recruiting so much, Ann was often left in charge of disciplining the children. She had a broom and would wear them out if they did anything wrong. But as the kids got older, she would call me whenever something was wrong.

"Bobby, you're going to have to spank Tommy and Steve when you get home because they've been fighting," she would say.

But a lot of times, I would come home from the road and the last thing I wanted to do was punish my kids. Instead, I'd take them in a back bedroom and close the door. "Now, listen," I would tell them. "I'm going to hit this dadgum bed with my belt, and I want you to cry. Make out like I'm whipping you really good."

I would smack the bed with my belt and the kids would start crying and hollering and we would fake out Ann.

I learned this about my wife a long time ago: she is one tough lady. Ann is probably the toughest person in our family. Ann has always wanted me to succeed, and she has always been a driving force behind me. I don't know if I would have accomplished anything or gone anywhere if it had not been for her pushing me. She would always support me in whatever decisions I made. I think one of the reasons why our marriage has lasted so long is that I always made sure to include her in the big decisions. Whether it was leaving Howard College for Florida State or leaving FSU as a young assistant to take an offensive coordinator job at West Virginia, I always made sure Ann had input in making the decision.

More than six decades after two teenagers eloped across state lines, Ann and I are still happily married. We have six grown children, twenty-one grandchildren, and five great-grandchildren. We are as happy now as the day we met.

Even today, I still remember what people said back in 1949: it will never last.

CHAPTER 4

FINDING DIRECTION

In 1955 I was only twenty-five and not much older than most of my players at South Georgia College, a two-year school tucked away in the cotton, peanut, and tobacco fields of Douglas, Georgia. The way I ended up at South Georgia is yet another example of how God had a plan for me all along. But this time my faith would be tested.

Three years earlier, I was nearing the end of my senior season as quarterback at Howard College. I was married with two small children. We had very little money and were still living in my parents' house in East Lake Park. Our daughter, Robyn, was sleeping in a small bed in our room, and our son Steve was sleeping in a crib at the foot of our bed. Ann was pregnant with our third child, Tommy. With a growing family to care for, I did not have a clue about what I was going to do next or what my profession was going to be. I knew I was preparing academically for the coaching and teaching profession, but my dad had a realty business and was hoping I'd join him.

But near the end of my senior season of playing quarterback for the Howard Bulldogs, Earl Gartman asked to see me in his office. Gartman was my head football coach and also worked as the school's athletic director. Coach Gartman told me if I earned my master's degree, he would hire me as an assistant football coach. I agreed to do it, and arrangements were made for me to work on my degree at Peabody College in Nashville, Tennessee, immediately after I graduated from Howard College in January 1953. Peabody was nearly two hundred miles from Birmingham. I would leave for classes early Monday morning and not return home until late Thursday night. It was difficult leaving Ann and the children for so many days, but it was something I had to do to start my coaching career. Since I did not own a car, I would often carpool with other students, or sometimes I would even hitchhike to Nashville.

I earned my master's degree in August 1953 and was hired as an assistant football coach and head track coach at Howard College before the 1953 season. Coach Gartman basically hired me as the team's offensive coordinator, but I also coached the defensive backs. We had a 1–8 record in 1953, which ended up being Coach Gartman's last season as head coach at Howard College.

The following spring, Bill "Cannonball" White returned to Howard College, where he had been head coach in 1940 and 1941. White had just been let go from Sewanee University in Tennessee, and Coach Gartman allowed him to come back to Howard College to coach for one season. White played football at the University of Tennessee and was a disciple of General Robert Neyland, who was one of the great college coaches at the time. Neyland's teams were always known for defense and kicking, and White tried to emulate that formula with his teams.

We were not much better under White, finishing with a 2–7 record during the 1954 season. The highlight in 1954 was opening the season against the National University of Mexico in Mexico City. At the time, I didn't even know they played football south of the border, and we lost the game, 13–6.

White retired as Howard College's football coach after the 1954 season. I expected Coach Gartman to take the job again, but he called me into his office shortly after White stepped down. "Bobby, I'm leaving here," Gartman told me. "I'm going to Austin Peay as head coach. I am going to recommend you for the job here, but I don't think you'll get it. I think they want someone who is more experienced."

Gartman was right. No appeals I made to the new athletic director, James Sharman, or to the president of the college did any good. They both told me the same thing: "You're too young. You're not ready."

Man, I was so upset. So was Ann. They were right, though, because as much as I wanted the job, I was too inexperienced to become a head coach at a school like Howard College.

The school hired Howard Foote as its new head football coach. Howard and I had played football together during my freshman season in 1949 and 1950. He was a successful high school coach in Alabama and knew his football well. He asked me to stay on his staff as offensive coordinator, but I was not sure I could do it. I was still very upset about being passed over for the head coaching job.

I applied for acceptance to Columbia University in New York, where I hoped to earn a doctorate in education. Since I wasn't sure my football coaching career was going to work out, I thought I might become a college professor instead. Columbia University accepted my application, and I even sent the school a monetary deposit for a dormitory room.

But then God intervened again, with an opportunity I never saw coming.

One day shortly after the 1954 season ended, I received a letter from Dr. William Smith, who was president of South Georgia College. Dr. Smith wanted Ann and me to come to the school and interview for the football head coaching position.

"You want to interview me for a head coaching job?" I asked him. "You're dadgum right I'm interested."

Ann and I drove to Douglas the next weekend, and Dr. Smith even interviewed Ann. He really liked her. She was my ace in the hole. She was a beauty queen back in those days. A couple of years later, she entered the Mrs. USA pageant and was named Mrs. South Georgia.

Dr. Smith called me about three days later to offer me the job, and I accepted. I was paid an annual salary of $4,200, which was a $300 raise over what I was making at Howard College. To earn the extra money, I agreed to work as South Georgia College's athletic director and head basketball coach. I had one assistant coach for football, but had no help in basketball. The school did not even have an athletic trainer, equipment manager, or secretary. I was supposed to wear all those hats.

For the life of me, I could not figure out how Dr. Smith even knew my name. I did not learn until several years later that the athletic director at

West Georgia College recommended me for the South Georgia College job. His name was Leven Hazlegrove, and he had played football at Howard College. Hazlegrove had offered me the head coaching position at West Georgia College after my first season as an assistant at Howard. I turned it down because the school did not award scholarships. When the South Georgia College job opened up a year later, Dr. Smith called Hazlegrove, who told him he needed to hire Bobby Bowden.

It was just another example of God watching over me. He had a plan for me all along. It was my job to follow His lead and stay His course.

Many of the players on my first team at South Georgia College in 1955 were veterans who'd served in the Korean War. This was nothing new to me; when I played football at Howard College, many of my teammates were World War II veterans. We had some guys who were thirty-three years old on my Howard College team. At that time, if you were a veteran, the government paid for your college tuition. Veterans were on college football teams across the country, with Uncle Sam footing their bills.

I spent many of my first weeks at South Georgia College trying to raise money to help support the football program. I knew that to recruit better players I had to have more money available in scholarships. I went door-to-door to businesses in Douglas, telling folks that if they could make a small donation it would help cover a player's room, board, and tuition. I probably collected between two thousand dollars and three thousand dollars which was a lot of money then. My fund-raising effort meant that instead of having only eighteen players on scholarship, I could have about thirty players on some type of financial aid.

I was also trying to find ways to make financial ends meet at home. As

South Georgia College's athletic director and head coach of two sports, I was paid for only nine months each year. So for three months, I did not have any money coming into our household. The tobacco industry was still thriving in Georgia at the time, so I worked in a tobacco warehouse during the summer. The job would last for only about a month, but it paid pretty well. I would go to work at about eight o'clock each night and get through around eight o'clock in the morning. All night long, big trucks filled with tobacco would come into the warehouse, and I would weigh the tobacco on the scales. I would write down the weight and give the drivers a receipt. At about two o'clock in the morning, the trucks would stop coming, but I still had to stay on the job.

When the last truck left the warehouse, I would lie down on a big bale of tobacco and fall asleep, with big rats running around on the floor beneath me, until it was time to go home the next morning. A couple of hours later, I would leave for my second job as a lifeguard at Douglas Country Club's swimming pool. I would work as a lifeguard from eleven A.M. until five P.M. and then would finally go home for the day. It was a lot of work during the summer, but it was about the only way I could pay the bills.

To earn extra money at Christmastime, I even took a job with the post office delivering mail. The post office always paid really well during the holiday season. The work lasted for only a couple of weeks, but the extra money always came in handy. The post office in Douglas would give me a cart and load it up with packages every morning. The cart was about the size of a wheelbarrow, and I would go right down the middle of town delivering the mail. I would stop at a store, pick up a package or drop one off, and then head for the next store. The cart had steel wheels and it would make a big ruckus as I pushed it along the concrete sidewalks. One day, I ran into Ann and our four children. She was mortified that her husband was making so much noise and immediately headed for the other side of the street!

By the time the football season rolled around in 1955, I was getting anxious about running my own program. South Georgia College was a perennial powerhouse among junior colleges in the state, but it hit hard times after World War II. The Tigers were very successful under coaches such as Wyatt Posey and Johnny Griffith, who later became head coach at the University of Georgia. But Joe Davis, the coach who preceded me, ran a military-like program, which didn't work for a lot of the ex-veterans. Many of his players quit the team in 1954, so I inherited only eight returning players when I took over.

Needless to say, I was delighted to see sixty players show up for our first day of practice in September 1955. The only problem: more than 80 percent of them were freshmen. Since I had scholarships for only about half of them, I decided to wait until after the first two weeks of practice to announce who would get them. I wanted to find out who would fight the hardest for a scholarship. I did not have many returning players, but the ones who did come back were pretty talented. Ronnie Kelley and Bobby Keys were team captains in 1954. Bobby Keys was a very good offensive lineman, along with Mitchell "Ape" Adams, Stumpy Franklin, Fred Levi, and Milton "Reverend" Cooper.

It seemed like every one of my players had some sort of nickname. Leon "Bull" Smith was one of our better ends. Billy "Stumpy" Franklin

was a five-foot, six-inch guard. Jerome "Blinkey" Barber was a bruising fullback, and Gene "Doodlebug" Edwards was a swift halfback. I
knew how Jimmy "Fats" DePalma earned his moniker; he was one of our
biggest players, at 215 pounds. Arthur "Tiny" Logue was a 315-pound
tackle. He showed up for the first day of camp in 1956 with a trailer full
of weights. He wanted to be Charles Atlas. He quit the team after breaking his nose in practice one day and became our student manager.

To compensate for our lack of experienced players, I often accepted
transfers from four-year universities. We would get players from schools
such as Auburn, Florida State, Georgia, Georgia Tech, and Tennessee.
The players would run into academic problems and their coaches would
ship them to us to get them straightened out.

Vaughn Mancha, who was an All-American lineman at the University
of Alabama and one of my early heroes, was coaching at Florida State
during the 1950s. He called me before my third season at South Georgia
College in 1957 and told me he had a great player for me. His name was
"Big Jim" Patterson, and he was a full-blooded Cherokee. "Big Jim" was
from Henderson, North Carolina. He was about six feet five inches tall
and weighed 240 pounds. At the time that was considered really, really big.

"He's not quite making the grades," Mancha told me. "But he's a good
boy. I promise you, Bobby, you won't have any problems with him. Can
you get him in school up there as soon as possible?"

Jim showed up at South Georgia College a few days later. He was bad.
He had a scar all the way across his chest, and I was afraid to ask him
how he got it. One day in practice, Jim got into a skirmish with one of my
graduate assistants, who was working under Vince Gibson's supervision.

"Jim, you can't talk back to the coaches," I told him. "You have to show respect."

Jim came up to me after practice. He was a very big man, but he stuttered when he talked. Our players called him "Chief" because of his Native American heritage. "Coach, tomorrow on the field, I want you to walk up and hit me right in the jaw," Jim told me. "I just want to show these guys that I will do whatever you say. I want you to hit me as hard as you can."

"Jim, I can't do that," I told him.

Jim was probably not at South Georgia College for two weeks before I received a telephone call from the Coffee County sheriff's office. They had Jim locked up in jail for fighting, and he set a mattress on fire so he could get out. He nearly burned the dadgum jail down! Somehow we worked things out with the sheriff's office and got him back in school.

"Jim, you can't be doing that," I told him. "This is a small town. Everybody in this town knows what everybody else is doing. Now, if you have to fight, go over to the next county!"

About two weeks later, I received a telephone call from the sheriff's office in neighboring Irwin County. Sure enough, they had Jim in jail for fighting. The sheriff told me he needed seven deputies to subdue him. That was kind of how Jim's career went. He was always in trouble, and I couldn't save him.

After Jim nearly got into a fight with Gibson during practice, I had to let Jim go. While I was trying to get him away from campus, I made a mistake I still regret: I lied. I told him I had talked to the coaches at the University of Southern Mississippi and they had a scholarship for him. I told Jim if he could get to Hattiesburg, Mississippi, as soon as possible, they would enroll him in school. Jim believed me and immediately left. I called the coach at Southern Mississippi, but he told me he didn't have any scholarships available.

Things did not work out for Jim at Southern Mississippi, and he called me, wanting to come back to South Georgia College. I felt awful about what I had done, but I just couldn't take him back. And after that, I never again lied or made a false promise to a player.

I didn't hear from Jim again for fifty-two years. Then he called my home in Tallahassee, Florida, in 2009 and spoke with Ann. I called him back the next day. Jim told me he'd changed. Jim was now in a wheelchair and had converted to Christianity and raised kids. Somehow Jim really had turned his life around.

In my first season as head coach at South Georgia College, most of college football was still playing limited substitution rules. Under those rules, a player could come off the field only once during a quarter. If a player left more than once, he could not return to action until the next quarter. The rules made conditioning very important. It also meant that your players had to be very skilled to play offense, defense, and special teams. Although I ended up keeping twenty-eight freshmen on our roster of thirty-six players in 1955, many of them were not typical first-year players. Some of them played football while serving in the military. Homer Sowell, one of our ends, played football for three years while serving on an army base in Alaska.

On October 1, 1955, I made my debut as a college head coach against Middle Georgia College in Cochran, Georgia. Because of injuries, we were starting a freshman quarterback named Roger Wilkinson, who played running back in high school. In fact, our starting lineup included four sophomores and seven freshmen. Fortunately, my concerns about Wilkinson were unfounded. He ran our offense nearly flawlessly, scoring on a fifty-three-yard touchdown run near the end of our 32–12 victory. I could not believe our team came together so fast. My confidence was bolstered even more after our next game, a 25–6 win over West Georgia College at College Field in Douglas. I had coached two games, and my team had won both of them. Life looked pretty good.

But I was given a pretty heavy dose of humility the following week. We were scheduled to play Jones County Junior College in Ellisville, Mississippi. Jones County was ranked among the country's best junior college teams. On top of that, we had to make a four-hundred-mile journey on a team bus my players liked to call the "Blue Goose." I drove the bus to road games, and that was often more of an adventure than the games themselves.

Since our next opponent after Jones County was Troy State Teachers College, I planned our trip around a stop in Troy, Alabama. I decided to leave Sam Mrvos, my only assistant coach at the time, at a hotel there so he could scout Troy State in its game the next day. Troy State was a four-year school, and I figured it would be a much more difficult opponent than a junior college.

Boy, what a mistake that ended up being! I was the only coach left to lead our boys against Jones County. I also made the mistake of letting our players sleep through most of the day, since it was a night game, and they still seemed to be asleep when the game kicked off. We had thirteen turnovers—seven fumbles and six interceptions—and were embarrassed in a 60–13 loss. I still believe that was the worst loss of my coaching career, but I learned a valuable lesson that day. I never overlooked an opponent or looked toward the next game again.

There were only five teams that played in the Georgia Junior College Conference: the South Georgia Tigers, Middle Georgia Wolverines, West Georgia College Braves, Gordon Military College Cadets, and Georgia Military Bulldogs. We played an eight- or nine-game schedule every season, so we faced some of the teams in our conference twice. We filled the rest of our schedule with games against out-of-state junior colleges or B teams from four-year schools such as Florida State and Presbyterian College in South Carolina.

Every season, it seemed like the conference championship would come down to our last game, against Gordon Military College in Barnesville, Georgia. We took a 4–0 record in conference play into the regular-season finale at Gordon Military College in 1955. I was worried before the game because both of our best running backs, Bobby Dixon and Everett Graham, were hurt the week before. We took a 6–0 lead on Ronnie Kelley's short touchdown run in the first half, but then fell behind, 7–6, early in the second half. Kelley scored again to give us a 12–7 lead late in the third quarter. The Cadets tried to mount a comeback a couple of times in the fourth quarter, but our defense stepped up and stopped them. We won the game, 12–7, and claimed the Georgia Junior College Conference championship.

My first season as a football coach was a success. If only my basketball coaching career would have started that well. I was not excited about coaching basketball. I played baseball in high school and college, so I was familiar with the sport. But I never played basketball and knew nothing about it. In addition, I was worried that the basketball season would interfere with football recruiting. We won only one game in my first season as a basketball coach. We were so bad we could not even bring the ball down the court.

So after only one season of coaching basketball, I was so bad, I fired myself. I was the school's athletic director, so I could do it! Sam Mrvos, my football assistant coach, left to take a job at the University of Georgia after the 1955 season. After Sam left, I hired Vince Gibson, who grew up with me in Birmingham and was a heck of an offensive lineman at Florida State. Vince later became the head football coach at Kansas State, Louisville, and Tulane. As soon as Vince came on board, I handed him the keys to our basketball team. I was coaching the baseball team, and Vince started a track program. We ended up winning state championships in baseball, football, golf, and track and field, with Vince and me coaching all the teams.

Before the 1956 football season, we were starting to get some national recognition. The Williamson Rating Board, which ranked junior college football teams, rated us among the top ten teams in the country. I told the local newspaper boys that our team was going to be "big and slow." I actually thought we had a chance to be pretty good, but injuries derailed our team from the start. "Blinkey" Barber broke his right arm, and John Robert O'Neal, a promising young running back, tore cartilage in his knee. Roger Wilkinson, our quarterback, suffered a back injury that sent him to the hospital, and he didn't play again until the following year. We lost our opener to Gordon Military College, 28–13, and had a 2–3 record after five games. But we came back to win our next three games, beating Gordon Military College, 33–6, to share the Georgia Junior College Conference championship with the Cadets.

But in my final season at South Georgia College, in 1958, we lost to Gordon Military College twice and did not win the conference championship. We had a chance to share the title with the Cadets, but they beat us 13–6 in our last game, at College Field. It was the first time we failed to win a title, and I couldn't have known I'd never get a chance to coach my boys again.

The truth is, I never had any intention of leaving South Georgia. Things were going really well and we'd built the football program into one of the best in the state. But then Dr. Smith called me to his office in April 1959. We were getting ready for spring practice, and I had been spending most of my time getting the team ready for a new season.

"Bobby, we're dropping football," Dr. Smith informed me. "We're losing money and we just can't justify fielding a football team any longer." Dr. Smith told me I could stay at the school as athletic director and baseball coach. Naturally, I wanted to be a football coach, but I told him I would probably stay because I did not have anywhere else to go.

But then God intervened in my life again. A few days later, I received a letter from Leslie Stephen Wright, who replaced Major Davis as president of Howard College in 1957. He had just relieved Virgil Ledbetter as the school's football coach after a 1–6–1 season in 1958. Wright wanted me to come to Birmingham to interview for the job. After four years at South Georgia College, my alma mater felt I was ready to be its head coach.

Finding Direction

Howard College offered me the job, and I accepted it for a salary of about $7,500 per season, which was a pretty big raise. But the best news was that Howard College was going to start offering football scholarships again. My alma mater underwent some major changes after moving to a beautiful Colonial-style campus in Homewood, which is only about four miles south of Birmingham. Howard College was working its way to university status, which it would eventually achieve in 1965.

Right when it seemed like my life's ambitions were being toppled again, God intervened and led me in a new direction. South Georgia College was dropping its football program, and it seemed that my football coaching career was over. But then Howard College called, and I got the job I wanted all along. For the second time, I got a job I did not even apply for.

At that moment I began to understand that I was not in control of my future. When I was a sick boy lying in bed, I prayed to God and told Him that if He healed me from rheumatic fever, I would serve Him through football. I promised Him I would go out and speak at churches and be involved in groups like the Fellowship of Christian Athletes.

At that point in my life, I knew God was leading me. It was my job to follow His plan. Stay the course, I told myself, and follow His lead.

Leaving South Georgia College was a painful experience. Even though I was going back home to Birmingham, I did not want to leave the players who meant so much to me. I took thirteen players from South Georgia College with me to Howard College. But over the years, I lost touch with many of the other players I coached in Douglas.

As I was preparing to coach West Virginia in the 1972 Peach Bowl in

Atlanta, I received a phone call from one of my former players at South Georgia. He told me several of them were getting together in Atlanta before the Peach Bowl and invited me to attend a reunion the day before the game. I met them at a hotel, and we reminisced and shared stories of the great times we had together.

In 1987, my former players held a reunion at the Holiday Inn in Douglas, and Ann and I drove up from Tallahassee to attend. As I was checking into the hotel, I was told many of my former players were sitting by the swimming pool out back. I looked out the window and saw a bunch of old men.

"Bobby, they were boys thirty years ago," Ann reminded me.

"No," I told her, "they'll always be my boys."

CHAPTER 5

STAYING THE COURSE

More than any other college football coach, I always admired Paul "Bear" Bryant. He was an All-American end on the University of Alabama's 1934 national championship team, and legend has it that he earned the moniker "Bear" because he agreed to wrestle a captive bear during a circus promotion when he was only thirteen years old. After hearing that story, I knew Bear Bryant must be tough as nails.

After Coach Bryant left Alabama, I followed his early coaching career. He coached one season at the University of Maryland in 1945 and then left for the University of Kentucky, which had never won many football games. But Bryant led the Wildcats to the 1950 Southeastern Conference championship, and then his team upset number-one-ranked Oklahoma in the 1951 Sugar Bowl. It was a shocking victory. Bryant also led Kentucky to appearances in the Orange Bowl and Cotton Bowl, and it did not take me long to figure out that he was a coach I wanted to emulate.

Coach Bryant left Kentucky in 1954 and was named the head coach at Texas A&M University. Before his first season at Texas A&M, Bryant took his boys out to Junction, Texas, for a ten-day training camp. The camp took place in one of the worst droughts and heat waves in Texas history. The temperature topped one hundred degrees on most practice days, but Bryant never backed down. He refused to give his boys water breaks, and they would practice all day long in the stifling heat. It was more like boot camp than football training.

Supposedly, Coach Bryant took three busloads of players to Junction. But when it was time to return to College Station, he needed only one bus to bring his players back. Most of them had quit because the camp was so hard. Gene Stallings, who later became the head coach at the University of Alabama and remains my good friend, played on that Texas A&M team. He told me all the stories about the "Junction Boys," and most of them were hard to believe.

When I was still coaching at South Georgia College in 1958, Coach Bryant was starting his first season as Alabama's coach. I wrote him a letter, asking if he would allow me to come to Tuscaloosa to watch his team practice. I wanted to learn as much as I could about Bryant's coaching methods, and there was not a better way to do it than to see it with my own eyes. Bryant wrote me back and invited me to practice. I planned to travel to Tuscaloosa before the 1959 season, but then I left South Georgia College to become the head coach at Howard College.

I postponed my trip to Tuscaloosa, but I knew what I was going to do before my first season at Howard College, in 1959. I was going to do exactly what Coach Bryant did at Texas A&M. I was going to have my own "Junction Boys" training camp. I was going to take my team out to Cooks Springs, Alabama, about twenty-five miles east of Birmingham. The Cooks Springs Baptist Church camp was up in the hills, and there was a cow pasture there that we could use as our practice field. My camp was going to be pretty rugged, just like the one Coach Bryant had at Texas A&M. If it was good enough for him, it was good enough for me.

Late in the summer of 1959, I wrote a letter to the boys who were going to play on my first team at Howard College:

Do you know football season is nearly upon us? It is hard to realize that in approximately three weeks we will be wearing the togs again. I hope you are as excited about the upcoming football season as I am. I don't even remember being as optimistic over prospects at Howard College as I have been this summer.

I want you to report here in good physical condition so I am enclosing a workout sheet with this letter that I want you to work by. If you will condition yourself gradually to where you can do everything on this sheet each day without excessively weakening yourself, you will be fairly well prepared for our first days of practice. I will keep you going from there.

I have a pleasant surprise for many of you about our first week's practice. We will spend the first seven days at a camp approximately twenty-five miles from Birmingham. At this camp, you will be able to swim, fish, and recreate between practice sessions. This will give each boy a chance to live with his teammates and help us become a closer-knitted team.

Before I close, let me give each of you a bit of advice. Don't report for practice unless you have a "burning desire" to play football for Howard College. If you don't have this desire, we don't need you here.

Also, be sure to report in good physical condition. If you don't, I promise you, you will regret it. Check the workout sheet to see what I mean by fair condition.

If every boy reports that indicated they would do so, with a good attitude and in good condition, we will have a team here that will put Howard College back on the football map <u>soon</u>.

Of course, I did not have a fun-filled summer camp planned for my football team. There would be no campfires or barbecues. I was going to do the same thing Coach Bryant did with the "Junction Boys." Along with that first letter, I attached a workout regimen I wanted my players to follow for the rest of the summer, including:

1. Twenty-five side straddle hops
2. Fifty toe touches; twenty-five with the right hand to left toe and twenty-five with the left hand to right toe
3. Thirty push-ups
4. Fifty sit-ups
5. Forty-yard duckwalk
6. Forty-yard frog hop

By today's standards, I was not asking my players to do very much to prepare themselves for our training camp. Looking back, they probably needed as much help as they could get. But at least all of my boys could walk like a duck and hop like a frog! When they arrived at Cooks Springs, they found a swimming pool covered with slimy green algae. They found a practice field that was really a cow pasture littered with rocks. They found a rustic cabin enclosed by a wire fence and with no air-conditioning. And of course, the boys did not have time for fishing or swimming. They were too busy practicing and sitting in team meetings.

We stayed at Cooks Springs for a week, and I made it pretty tough on them. We went there with forty-seven players, and twenty-two of them quit during training camp. It was not nearly as difficult as the camp that Coach Bryant had in Junction, but it took its toll on my players. Every night I'd hear boys packing up their things and a car driving off. I'd wake up the next morning wondering who had slipped away in the middle of the night. Some of the players who left were pretty good. I really hated to see them leave.

My South Georgia College boys were the keys to my first team at Howard College. I brought thirteen players with me from South Georgia, and most of them ended up being starters at Howard. In fact, all but three of the starters on my first team were transfers from South Georgia. One of the starting ends had transferred from Mississippi State, and the first-team quarterback and the other end were from Birmingham. My quarterback, Joe Milazzo, was a great player. I called him "Golden Arm" because he passed the football so well. Immediately, Joe became the leader of our team.

But the South Georgia boys—players such as guard Bonwell Royal, fullback Carl Sheppard, tackle Richard Finley, end Jimmy Thompson, and running backs Bobby Jackson, George Versprille, and Robert Lairsey—became the backbone of my teams at Howard College. They were already familiar with my program, having spent a year with me in Douglas, where I was able to redshirt them. They practiced with the team at South Georgia College but did not play in our games, so they still had four years of playing eligibility when they transferred to Howard.

One of the players who really made a difference was Bobby Jackson. Bobby was from Mary Persons High School in Forsyth, Georgia, and I believe to this day that he was probably the best all-around player I ever had. At that time you played both offense and defense. Bobby was a great runner and could have been an All-American defensive back. He returned kickoffs and punts and broke a lot of games open with long returns. Bobby later became a football coach at schools such as Florida State, Kansas State, and Tennessee, and coached in the NFL until his retirement.

Seven years after I played my last game as quarterback for Howard College, I was the Bulldogs' head coach, opening the 1959 season against Maryville College in Maryville, Tennessee. We were still learning our way on offense, but I immediately let our boys know I was willing to take some chances and have some fun. We scored our first touchdown on an end-around pass. Milazzo pitched the football to end Don Coleman, who threw a touchdown to Buddy Bozeman. We scored our second touchdown on another trick play: Versprille reached the end zone on a long run off a reverse. We won our first game by a 14–0 score, and my first victory was in the books.

If my players learned anything about me in that first game it was that I was never afraid to call trick plays, even when the outcome was in doubt. We ran a lot of trick plays while I was coaching at South Georgia College, and there was a reason I liked them so much. When I was growing up, I was not very big, but I always played football with older boys. We played touch football in the streets or at the Howard College practice field. I had to use tricks to beat the bigger kids. When I became a head coach, I put a fake punt into my game plan during my first season at South Georgia College. We had a pretty good offense, but our defense wasn't as good. To beat somebody, we always had to score a lot of points. I was going to try to find as many ways to score as I could, and I always loved trying to trick the opponent. I never called them "trick plays," though. To me, they were always "crowd-pleasers," because the folks in the stands loved seeing them.

Fortunately, our offense did not have to score very often during my first season at Howard College. Our defense shut out our first three opponents, and we had five shutouts during a 9–1 season. After Howard had endured five consecutive losing seasons, it felt really good to get my alma mater back on track. We ended the 1959 season playing in the first Textile Bowl, in Fairfax, Alabama, on December 5, 1959. Our opponent was, of all teams, Gordon Military College, which was our nemesis at South Georgia College. Gordon Military was a two-year junior college and was not much of a match for us. Milazzo had one of his best games and threw four touchdown passes, and Vic Baga returned a blocked punt thirty-four yards for a touchdown. We won the game, 52–20, and that was a great way to end my first season.

The following spring, I forged a relationship with Green Bay Packers quarterback Bart Starr, who ended up helping me develop a sophisticated passing game. Bart was raised in Montgomery and played at the University of Alabama. After college, he was a seventeenth-round draft choice in the 1956 NFL draft by the Packers. During Bart's first couple of seasons in Green Bay, he was a backup behind quarterback Babe Parilli, who played for Coach Bryant at the University of Kentucky. In fact, Bart did not play much until Vince Lombardi was hired as the Packers' head coach in 1959.

Under Lombardi, Bart was really beginning to learn a lot about the passing game and seemed headed toward a great career. During the off-season, Bart lived in Birmingham and hosted a radio show. I called Bart one day and asked him if he would like to come to Howard College and talk football with me. We spent most of the day drawing pass plays on a chalkboard in my office, and he shared with me the offense that Lombardi was teaching him.

"You know, why don't you come out to practice today?" I asked him.

At the time, I had only two assistant coaches at Howard College. I hired Virgil Ledbetter, who preceded me as head coach, but he also coached the baseball team in the spring. Walter Barnes also helped me out, but he coached the basketball team. Since Virgil was coaching baseball and Walter was coaching basketball, I attempted to coach the entire football team myself. I would meet with the offensive line at 2:30 P.M. I would practice with them for an hour and have the backs show up at 3:30 P.M. I would work with the backs for an hour, and then the quarterbacks would show up. That's basically how spring practice went.

But Bart had such a great time working with our quarterbacks that first day that he stayed with us the entire spring. I basically turned my quarterbacks and other backs over to him. In the end, Bart really helped me learn a lot about the passing game. When I first started coaching, I focused strictly on the kicking game, running game, and defense. I didn't have our quarterbacks throw five passes in a game if I didn't have to. But Bart really opened my eyes to what we could do with the passing game.

After spring practice, Bart went back to Green Bay and became a star quarterback for the Packers. He led the Packers to NFL championships in 1961 and 1962 and was named most valuable player of the first two Super Bowls, in 1966 and 1967. A few years later, I flew up to Green Bay and met with Bart and Coach Lombardi and learned even more about their passing game.

Looking back at the early years, Bart Starr and Paul Bryant had profound influences on my coaching career. Coach Bryant was always a hero to me. I was so fond of him that I asked him to speak at our awards banquet at Howard College after the 1959 season. I also wrote Bryant a letter the following spring, asking him to hire me as an assistant coach.

"If I hire you, Bobby, I'll have every Baptist in Alabama mad at me," Bryant told me.

It was Bryant's polite way of telling me "no." I continued to go to Tuscaloosa to watch the Crimson Tide practice. I would usually have a graduate assistant coach drive me there. Alabama had a great team, and I watched practice and soaked in as much as I could. Bryant was tough and rugged and always seemed to be smoking a cigarette, and his own tough ways made his kids tough and hard-nosed. We always said his teams were "mean but clean." That was exactly how I wanted my teams to play football.

Before the 1960 season, Bryant sent word to me that he had a few players on his team who were not going to cut it at Alabama. He told me if I would come to Tuscaloosa for practice, he would give me a list of the players so I could see if I wanted any of them on my team. Bryant always sent me to practice with one of his assistant coaches, Hayden Riley, who also worked as Alabama's baseball and basketball coach. His nephew Mike Riley played cornerback at Alabama and later became head coach of the NFL's San Diego Chargers and Oregon State. Coach Bryant, Coach Riley, and I would go to practice and go through his list. I would end up taking five or six of his players every spring, and it would help them and help us.

Every time I went to Alabama, the guy who helped me the most was Gene Stallings. I always arrived in Tuscaloosa a couple of hours before practice started, and Gene and I would sit in his office and talk football. He was very helpful to me; I probably learned more football from Gene than from anyone else.

As Bryant was sending me players, I had to be cautious about not overstocking my roster. Howard College had limited scholarships, and sometimes the money would dry up quickly. During one season, we ran out of money to feed the boys. We did not have the money to pay for a training table, so I went to restaurants around town and asked them to trade our meals for advertising. I called a team meeting and told the boys where they would be eating their meals.

"Joe, you'll be eating at Huddle House," I told them. "Bobby, you'll be eating at Jack's. George, you can head over to the Country Kettle for your meals."

For the rest of the semester, the boys would eat three meals a day at those restaurants. It was difficult for the ones without cars, but at least they weren't hungry. I eventually raised enough money to reinstate our training table.

Armed with a new passing attack at Howard College, we really started playing well and scoring a lot of points. We opened the 1960 season with a 14–0 victory over Maryville College. We beat the University of the South—or Sewanee, as we called it back then—56–0 in the second game. We beat Georgetown College from Kentucky, 41–0. We had an 8–1 record during my second season, in 1960, and were really starting to utilize the passing game well.

There were not a lot of teams on our schedule that were good enough on defense to stop us. In the 1961 opener, we beat Memphis Navy, 60–0. We beat Georgetown College, 64–6, and ended the season with an 80–0 victory over Troy State in Alabama. We finished the 1961 season with a 7–2 record and went 7–2 the next season. In 1962 we even hosted the National University of Mexico and avenged my earlier loss with a 40–0 win.

Unfortunately, I wasn't sure if anyone was noticing our good work. We were playing second fiddle to the University of Alabama, which was always Birmingham's favorite team. I applied for coaching vacancies at bigger schools such as Vanderbilt University and Tulane University, but didn't get much of a response. I wasn't sure if I could move to a bigger school from a place like Howard College, so Ann and I began to wonder if it was time for us to start a different chapter in our lives.

Once again, God answered our prayers. After the 1962 season, I was invited to attend the Touchdown Club of Atlanta's postseason awards dinner. Nearly all of the best coaches in the country attended the event: Paul "Bear" Bryant, Georgia Tech's Bobby Dodd, Auburn's Ralph "Shug" Jordan, LSU's Paul Dietzel, and Clemson's Frank Howard. Every year, the Touchdown Club of Atlanta would have a speaker, and all the famous coaches would sit at one table up front. Usually there were no small-time coaches sitting at that table. But the president of the Touchdown Club of Atlanta was a man named Herb Brown, a graduate of Howard College, and he was determined that his coach was going to have a seat at the front table.

When I arrived at the awards banquet in December 1962, I was sitting next to Bill Peterson, who was the head coach at Florida State University. Vince Gibson, who coached with me at South Georgia College, was working at FSU and told Peterson about me. But I had never met or even talked to Peterson before I sat down at that table.

"Bobby, look, I just lost my wide receivers coach," Peterson told me. "Would you be interested in coming to Florida State?"

I was stunned. Ann and I were talking about leaving Howard College, and now I was getting a completely unexpected job offer. I thought I might have to become an assistant coach or coordinator at a bigger school to get a head coaching job like the one I wanted, and I believed going to FSU might give me that opportunity. Coach Peterson wanted Ann and me to come to Tallahassee to interview, and we decided to do it. When I arrived in Tallahassee, I was met by Vaughn Mancha, who was now the athletic director at Florida State. I met with Coach Peterson, and he offered me the job and a salary of $9,800 per year.

I told Peterson I would think about it, and Ann and I drove back to Birmingham. During the drive home, we decided I would take the job at Florida State. Ann started crying because she really did not want to leave Birmingham. Her parents lived there, and my parents lived there. Birmingham was our home. But we both felt for my career to advance, I would have to leave Howard College.

A few days later, I went to the Birmingham Quarterback Club meeting to hear Texas coach Darrell Royal give a speech. Royal was speaking in Anniston the next day, and I asked him if he would like me to give him a ride. It was a big thrill for me. I was only thirty-two years old and there I was, spending a couple of hours in the car talking with Royal, who would lead the Longhorns to a national championship the very next season, in 1963. While I was listening to Royal speak in Anniston, I received a telephone call from a reporter with the *Birmingham News*.

"Coach Bowden, I hear you're going to leave Howard College for Florida State," the reporter told me.

"Well, yes, that's true," I told him. "I'm going to Florida State."

The next morning, I received a telephone call from Leslie Stephen Wright, the Howard College president. I had not yet told him I was leaving for Florida State, and he was upset because he read about it in the newspaper that morning.

"Bobby, you beat me to it," he told me. "I am supposed to tell the press you are leaving. Next time just tell them 'No comment.'"

I learned a valuable lesson that day about how to handle the media. From that day forward, I kept my mouth closed about job interviews and job offers.

Even though leaving Birmingham was a difficult decision, Ann and I were excited about our new opportunities at FSU. Ann stayed behind to sell our house and let the kids finish school. The entire family moved to Tallahassee that summer, and we started a new chapter in our lives. We had six children by then, and Ann took a job teaching at a church preschool.

I spent three seasons coaching wide receivers at Florida State, from 1963 to 1965. Coach Peterson was running a pro-style passing game at FSU, but no one thought it would work at the college level. The other assistant coaches and I would even sit around and say, "This ain't going to work."

No one thought college players were smart enough to run that kind of sophisticated offense, but Coach Peterson was persistent about it. He spent a lot of time talking to pro coaches about the passing game and was sure it would work in college, too. I think there were only two other college football teams running a pro-style passing game at the time: the Baylor Bears and the Tulsa Golden Hurricane.

Florida State struggled mightily on offense in 1963, finishing with a 4–5–1 record. We didn't even score in three of our games, and we tied Southern Mississippi, 0–0, in a fourth. But the next season, our quarterback Steve Tensi really started to understand offense, and we took off. We had some receivers on that team, such as Fred Biletnikoff, Don Floyd, and Bill "Red" Dawson. We opened the 1964 season with a 14–0 victory over the University of Miami in the Orange Bowl, with Biletnikoff catching two touchdown passes. We won our first five games, including a 17–14 victory over the University of Georgia on the road, after Tensi threw a twenty-yard touchdown pass to Biletnikoff with about six minutes to play.

We lost our only game in 1964 at Virginia Tech, falling to the Hokies, 20–11. We tied the University of Houston, 13–13, but Biletnikoff missed that game because of an injury. He came back at the end of the season, and we beat the University of Florida, 16–7. The Gators were heavy favorites to beat us, but we did a great job slowing down their quarterback, who was some guy named Steve Spurrier. It was the first time FSU ever beat Florida, which sparked a wild celebration in Tallahassee.

After beating the Gators, we were invited to play the University of Oklahoma in the Gator Bowl in Jacksonville, Florida. It was my first big bowl game experience, and I was really excited about facing a traditional power such as the Sooners. Oklahoma was just beginning life without their greatest coach, Bud Wilkinson, who retired after the 1963 season to run for the U.S. Senate. Wilkinson arranged for Gomer Jones, one of his assistant coaches, to replace him as Oklahoma's coach. As expected, the Sooners were not as good under Jones, losing three of their first four games in 1964. But they came back to win five of their last seven games going into the Gator Bowl.

The night before the Gator Bowl, we found out that four of Oklahoma's best players—fullback Jim Grisham, tackle Ralph Neely, halfback Lance Rentzel, and end Wes Skidget—had signed pro football contracts and were ineligible to play in the game. The news really seemed to shake up the Sooners, and we beat them by a 36–19 score. We played in front of the biggest crowd in Gator Bowl history, with more than fifty thousand fans attending the game. Tensi and Biletnikoff really put on a show, hooking up for four touchdowns in their final college game and helping us finish with a 9–1–1 record.

Biletnikoff was probably the finest wide receiver I ever coached. He had tremendous hands and was a great route runner. He was just a very tough football player, too. Fred became FSU's first consensus All-American in 1964 after he caught fifty-seven passes, including eleven for touchdowns. He went to the NFL and became a star receiver with the Oakland Raiders. Fred was inducted into the Pro Football Hall of Fame and the College Football Hall of Fame. Every season, the best wide receiver in college football receives the Biletnikoff Award, which tells you what kind of legacy Fred left at Florida State. In my final season as wide receivers coach at FSU, in 1965, I coached T. K. Wetherell, who would later become the university president, and helped recruit Ron Sellers, who ended up being about as good as Biletnikoff.

The most important thing I learned from Coach Peterson was that a great coach surrounds himself with great assistants. His coaching staffs were always among the best in the country. While I worked under Peterson, his staff included Don James, who would become a great head coach at the University of Washington, and Vince Gibson. Peterson also hired John Coatta, who became head coach at the University of Wisconsin. After I left Florida State in 1965, Peterson hired a young offensive line coach named Joe Gibbs, who won three Super Bowl championships as coach of the NFL's Washington Redskins. Peterson also hired a green linebackers coach named Bill Parcells, who led the New York Giants to two Super Bowl titles.

Coach Peterson taught me that you hire good coaches and good people and let them do their jobs. That was something I tried to emulate throughout my coaching career. I wanted good men, husbands, fathers, and Christians coaching my boys, and I always made sure I let them do their jobs. When I became a head coach, I wanted to make sure I was not an overbearing boss. It was my job to be a chief executive officer and oversee the entire program.

In 1965, FSU slipped to a 4–5–1 record. We lost Tensi and all those great wide receivers, and we just never seemed to find an identity on offense that season. But one of the highlights that year was playing against Alabama and Coach Bryant at Bryant-Denny Stadium in Tuscaloosa. The Crimson Tide was the defending national champion, and the 1965 team was supposed to be even better, with Steve Sloan returning as quarterback. We played Alabama in their homecoming game, and the Tide was coming off a 7–7 tie against Tennessee in Birmingham the week before. We knew the Tide would be motivated to play us, and they were. We played pretty well and only trailed 13–0 at the half. Sloan was hurt in the first half, and Kenny Stabler came off the bench and played really well. Alabama beat us, 21–0, and then beat Nebraska, 39–28, in the Orange Bowl to win a second consecutive national championship.

After three seasons at Florida State, Ann and I were not very happy. I was not getting any breaks, and we felt it was probably time to move somewhere else, as an offensive coordinator. Auburn coach Shug Jordan called and told me he was looking for an offensive coordinator. While it was not an opportunity to work for Coach Bryant at Alabama, it was a chance to go home and be closer to our parents again. I drove up to Auburn and interviewed, and Coach Jordan offered me the job. I told him I would think about it and went back to Tallahassee. A few days later, Jim Carlen called me. Jim was an assistant coach at Georgia Tech and was named the head coach at West Virginia after the 1965 season. He wanted to hire me as his offensive coordinator, but I was not sure I wanted to move my family all the way to Morgantown, West Virginia.

You might think an Alabama boy would take the Auburn job. But my instincts were telling me to go to West Virginia. At the time, West Virginia was not a hot destination for football coaches. The Mountaineers were members of the old Southern Conference, and many of the league's best teams left to form the Atlantic Coast Conference in 1953. West Virginia was left behind, playing against schools such as The Citadel, Davidson, Furman, Richmond, Virginia Tech, and William & Mary. In a lot of ways, it was not big-time football. In my mind, it was not nearly as big as coaching in the Southeastern Conference, at a school such as Auburn.

But for some reason, I felt the opportunities at West Virginia might be better. I thought Coach Jordan would never leave Auburn, and I was intrigued about the possibility of recruiting players from northern states. There were so many great players in states such as Ohio and Pennsylvania, and I thought if I could establish myself as a recruiter in that part of the country, it would only help me when I built a football program of my own.

I prayed about it and asked God for guidance once again. God had provided me with direction until that point in my career, and I was determined to leave my future in His hands. I think that a lot of times, God will test us, but having faith in Him is what gets us through it.

Testing us is part of His plan, and only the strong ones can handle the tough assignments. You have to learn to be tough and get through it. I have always believed that you cannot build character without first facing adversity. I think that all of our strengths are developed by having to fight through difficult times.

A man's reputation is what others say of him; a man's character is what God *knows* about him.

In 1965 I could not have known how much God would test my faith after I moved my family to West Virginia.

CHAPTER 6

TESTED

If there's one thing I've learned in all my years on this earth, it's that God has ways of making His intentions known to us. Sometimes you just need to take a step back to see the big picture. I may not always have realized it at the time, but when I look back over my life, I see the signposts He set along the road I've traveled. That's especially true of my time at West Virginia University.

While I was growing up in Birmingham, the South was segregated. There were Jim Crow laws and separate schools for white students and black students. I still remember seeing the images on television of Birmingham police commissioner Eugene "Bull" Connor and his police officers using high-pressure water hoses and dogs to drive back demonstrators during the civil rights marches of the 1960s. I remember the pain I felt when the Ku Klux Klan bombed the Sixteenth Street Baptist Church in Birmingham with twenty-two sticks of dynamite on September 16, 1963. The explosion killed four little girls: Addie Mae

Collins, Denise McNair, Carole Robertson, and Cynthia Wesley. One of the little girls who died was only eleven years old; the other three were fourteen. My oldest daughter, Robyn, was only twelve at the time. The explosion ripped a hole in the back of the church and blew out all but one stained-glass window. The lone stained-glass window left standing had an image of Jesus Christ leading a group of children. The face of Christ was blown out.

When I left Florida State to become the offensive coordinator for Jim Carlen at West Virginia University in Morgantown in January 1966, I had never played with or coached a nonwhite player. All of my teammates at Woodlawn High School were white. All of my teammates at the University of Alabama and Howard College were white. While I coached at South Georgia College, Howard College, and Florida State, every one of my players was white.

But my mother and father always taught me to treat everyone with respect, whether they were white, black, brown, blue, or red. I never once heard my parents use a derogatory word to describe a nonwhite person. Even though we lived in the Deep South, race was not an issue in the Bowden house.

But not everybody in the South had an open mind. College football teams in the northern states were recruiting African-American players for years, but schools in the South were slow to integrate their teams. In fact, the University of Kentucky was the first school from the Southeastern Conference to integrate its football team, signing Nat Northington to a scholarship in 1967.

Southerners' feelings about race and college football changed forever on September 12, 1970. On that night, Southern California fullback Sam Cunningham, an African American, ran over mighty Alabama's defense in a 42–21 victory at Legion Field in Birmingham. After that loss, Crimson Tide coach Bryant persuaded his administration to finally allow him to recruit black players. Most of the other southern schools started signing African-American players to their rosters the next season.

West Virginia signed its first African-American players in 1963. Guard Roger "Alfie" Alford and tailback Richard "Dick" Leftridge broke the color barrier at West Virginia and were great players. The Mountaineers had four African-American players when I was hired to coach their offense in 1966. Two of the boys were probably the best players on the team: running back Garrett Ford and cornerback John Mallory. Wingback Stephen Edwards and tackle Norman Hill also were black.

I was not sure how African-American players would react to me when I reported for my first spring practice at West Virginia in 1966. I was from Alabama, where there had been so much racial strife, and I had a southern drawl as distinct as the smell of a pine forest. I had never lived north of the Mason-Dixon Line. And to be honest, I never had much interaction with people of a different race.

We owned two cars when I left Florida State for West Virginia. We had a Chevrolet sedan, which was handed down to me by my father, and I purchased a used Pontiac station wagon. Since Ann was staying behind with the children to sell our house in Florida, I left her the station wagon. I drove the Chevrolet to Morgantown and really did not think much about it. But after a couple of days on campus, I woke up to find my Chevy covered with splattered eggs. It took me a couple of days to figure out that students were targeting my car because it had Alabama license plates. Apparently the civil rights struggles in my home state were still fresh in their minds.

I remember the first time I met Garrett Ford. He was probably the best player at West Virginia. They called him "Galaxy" because he ran like a comet. Garrett grew up in Washington, D.C., and was a star running back at DeMatha Catholic High School.

When I met Garrett for the first time, I said, "How ya doin', boy?"

Now, I call everybody "boy." It does not matter if you are eight years old or eighty years old; I am going to call you "boy." My daddy always called me boy.

He would say, "Come here, boy," or "What are you doing, boy?"

That was the way I was raised, and I always called all of my players "boys."

But Garrett didn't like it. Since I was from the South and talked in a way that probably sounded funny to him, I offended him. To try to patch up the misunderstanding, I invited Garrett to my house for dinner later that summer. Garrett had dinner with Ann and me, and he had Tommy and Terry bouncing on his knees. Garrett later told me that was the first time he had been inside a white family's home. I think after that night, he really started to trust me and we developed a very close friendship.

We opened the 1966 season at West Virginia against Duke in Durham, North Carolina. Duke's coaches attended our spring game, so I wanted to try to trick them on the first play. I knew they would not know how dangerous John Mallory was because they had not seen him play offense during spring practice, so on the first play, our quarterback Tom

Digon took the snap and faked a handoff to Garrett, who acted like he was running up the middle. Tom hid the ball, and the defense never saw it. John took off running down the middle of the field and was wide open for a touchdown. It was unbelievable. Unfortunately, our 7–0 lead did not last and we ended up losing the game, 35–14.

We probably scored on the first possession in six games in 1966 because we always used trick plays. We never had much of a chance to win the game, so we would try to surprise them from the start to get momentum. After that, they would just beat the heck out of us. We struggled to a 3–5–2 record in 1966. We lost our starting quarterback during preseason camp. Joe Manchin was supposed to be our quarterback, but he tore up his knee, and the injury ended his career. Joe was elected governor of West Virginia in 2005.

Near the end of my first season with the Mountaineers, we lost to Penn State, 38–6, at home. Penn State's head coach was a young guy named Joe Paterno, who was in his first season. As the offensive coordinator or head coach at West Virginia, I faced Paterno's teams ten times and never beat him. His teams at Penn State just always seemed to be much superior to our teams at West Virginia.

In 1969 we were invited to play against South Carolina in the Peach Bowl in Atlanta. South Carolina was coached by Paul Dietzel and won the 1969 Atlantic Coast Conference championship. The Gamecocks had a very good defense, and I wasn't sure my boys could beat them. I had four weeks to get ready for the bowl game and decided to do something radical. I changed our offense to the wishbone, which I thought would catch South Carolina's coaches completely by surprise. Our wide receivers were not very good, but we had a bunch of good running backs I wanted to utilize as much as possible. I called Darrell Royal at the University of Texas, and he told me the wishbone offense really had only three plays. He explained it to me step-by-step over the phone for the next couple of hours.

When practice started for the bowl game, I went out to the field and drew lines using chalk. I explained to the quarterback where he was supposed to go, told the right halfback where to line up, and told the left halfback where to go. When we arrived in Atlanta a few days before the Peach Bowl, newspaper reporters were allowed to watch our practices. But I made sure we did not practice the wishbone while the newspaper boys were there. We were still practicing with two fullbacks, so no one could figure out the wishbone was coming.

On December 30, I unveiled the wishbone offense at the Peach Bowl, in Georgia Tech's Grant Field. South Carolina's defense didn't know what to do. Eddie Williams ran for 208 yards on 35 carries, which was a school single-game record. Bob Gresham ran for 98 yards, and we ran for 346 yards as a team in a 14–3 victory. It was West Virginia's first victory in a bowl game since 1949, so it was a pretty big achievement for the Mountaineers.

After the Peach Bowl, everybody from West Virginia was really excited. But the assistant coaches and I had been hearing rumors that Coach Carlen might leave for Texas Tech. There were a couple of short newspaper stories written about the possibility of it happening, but Coach Carlen avoided the subject. After Coach Carlen finished addressing the team in the locker room, he called his assistant coaches into the showers.

"Guys, I'm going to Texas Tech," he told us. "If any of ya'll want to go with me, I would love to have you."

Then he pulled me aside and said, "Bobby, I think you can get the West Virginia job."

Immediately, I wanted to find Robert "Red" Brown, the athletic director at West Virginia, and tell him I wanted the job. I knew members of the school's athletic council were in Atlanta, so I thought I should begin lobbying right away.

But 150 miles from Atlanta, my father, Bob Bowden, was dying in a hospital in Birmingham. Daddy suffered a stroke a few weeks earlier that left him paralyzed. He was lying on his deathbed, and I wanted to get home to see him before he died.

Ann and I drove to Birmingham with our children that night, and I received a telephone call from Red Brown the following morning on New Year's Eve 1969.

"Bobby, our athletic council met last night in Atlanta and we want you to be our coach," he told me.

"I'll take it," I said.

That morning, I drove to the hospital to see my father. They were feeding him through a tube, and another machine was providing him with oxygen.

I leaned toward him, kissed his forehead, and whispered in his ear. He could not talk, but he was moving his eyes, so I knew he could hear me.

"Daddy, I got the West Virginia job," I told him.

My father died only a few weeks later, in January 1970. My mother, Sunset Cleckler Bowden, passed away from Alzheimer's disease when she was eighty. I still miss both of them dearly.

When I took over at West Virginia, in 1970, we opened the season by winning our first four games, against William & Mary, Richmond, Virginia Military Institute, and Indiana.

But then we played Duke at Mountaineer Stadium on October 10, 1970. And in that game I made a decision that to this day I still can't believe. We were facing fourth-and-four at Duke's thirty-four-yard line, and I decided we would punt. I wanted to pin the Blue Devils deep in their own territory, but my punter kicked the ball over the goalpost and out of the stadium. It was a call I wouldn't make today, and the fans booed me for it.

West Virginia fans really booed me the next week. We were playing Pittsburgh on the road on October 17, 1970, and that game was always as big as playing Florida when I coached at Florida State. It was really the biggest game that mattered to Mountaineers fans and alumni. In the first half, everything we did seemed to turn into a touchdown. We had a 35–8 lead at halftime, and we were feeling great. In the locker room, everyone was telling me, "We have this game won. Just don't blow it. Don't do anything crazy."

So I came out in the second half and played it conservative, calling very few passes and relying on the running game to run out the clock.

We've got this game won if we just don't make any terrible mistakes, I told myself.

Bowden family, 1940. From left to right: Bob, Sunset, Bobby, and Marion

Bobby and his dog Tiger, 1941

Above: Barrett Elementary School graduation, 1944
Right: Bowden-Bishop Realty Company in Woodlawn

Right: Bobby and Marion, 1945. Middle: Howard College, freshman year, 1949. Bottom left: Bobby and Ann, 1949. Bottom right: Bowden family holiday card, 1956. From top left: Steve, Robyn, Tommy (on Bobby's lap), and Terry (on Ann's lap)

Above: South Georgia College training camp, 1957—Bobby on right, Vince Gibson (holding clipboard), and Bill Meeks (Coffee County High School football coach)

Middle right: At Howard College with Bennie Storey (All-American at Woodlawn High School and Howard College) and James Sharman (athletic director at Howard College), 1959

Above: At South Georgia College with Vince Gibson and Joe Sears (#14) at camp, 1958

Right: Bowden family, 1972. From bottom left: Ginger, Jeff, Terry, Ann, Steve, Robyn, Tommy, and Bobby (in chair)

Above: In Cuba, 1973. Top right: Bobby and Ann outside Pro Shop at Killearn Country Club, 1976. Right: Bobby and Ann, Japan Bowl 1977. Below: First victory over the Florida Gators, 1977

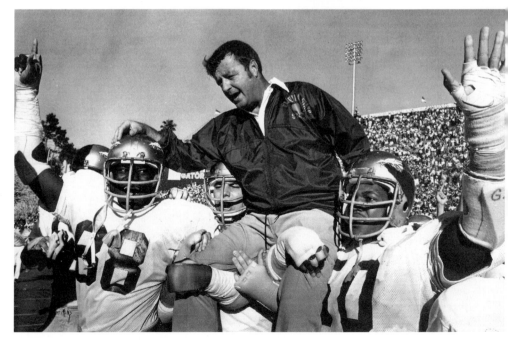

Bowden family, Orange Bowl 1980. On the couch from the left: Janet, Steve, Linda, Tommy, Bobby, Ann, Robyn, Jack. On the floor from the left: Terry, Twila, Ginger, Jeff, and first grandchild Beau (son of Janet and Steve)

Billy Graham talks to the team, 1986

Billy Graham, Jeff, and Bobby, 1986

Bobby with South Georgia buddies, 1990

Right: Bobby with Terry and Tommy at the Orange Bowl (Terry was in his first season as head coach at Auburn and Tommy was his offensive coordinator), 1993. Middle: With President Clinton after the national championship, 1994. Bottom left: Bobby and Ann in Hawaii on the Nike trip, 1992. Bottom right: The first Bowden Bowl and three hundredth career victory, 1999

Top: At the U.S. Capitol with Senator Bob Graham and Senator Connie Mack after the national championship, 2000. Middle left: Bowden family in Panama City, 2000. From left to right: Steve, Terry, Ginger, Bobby, Ann, Robyn, Jeff, and Tommy. Middle right: Bobby Bowden and Jack Lengyel at the College Football Hall of Fame, 2007. Bottom left: Bobby with Bart Starr and Ray Scott

"A Day with the Bowdens" at the University of North Alabama (the very first time that all four Bowden coaches had been together speaking at the same event), 2009

Middle: Bobby making his sons laugh while speaking at the prayer breakfast, July 2009. Bottom left: Bobby and his Bible. Bottom right: Speaking at the University of North Alabama

Well, over the next thirty minutes, I learned a valuable lesson: never sit on the football.

Carl DePasqua, the Pittsburgh coach, was sure his team was just going to get killed in the second half. He took his wide receivers out of the game and put three tight ends on the field. The Panthers were determined to just line up, run the ball, and control the clock so they could keep the score close. But no matter how hard our boys tried, we couldn't stop them. My offense just couldn't get the ball back. Pittsburgh came all the way back and beat us, 36–35.

It was the darkest day of my coaching career. The West Virginia fans were really upset. I had never seen football fans so mad before. A few guys were beating on the door to our locker room, demanding that I come out. I thought they were going to kill me. We had to wait until the fans left the stadium before state troopers could escort me back to the team bus.

It was one of the few times I questioned whether I was a good enough coach to lead my boys to victory.

"Lord, please provide me the strength to overcome this," I prayed.

I got home to Morgantown later that night and found Ann crying on the bed. It was the only time she ever cried about a ball game. I guess she was just sad for me and cracked.

The West Virginia fans doubted me for a long time after that Pittsburgh loss. We came back and won four of our last five games to finish 8–3 in my first season, but the only score the fans remembered was the 36–35 loss at Pittsburgh.

* * *

One thing I will never forget from the 1970 season was the tragic airplane crash involving Marshall University's football team. Marshall University is in Huntington, West Virginia, which is about two hundred miles from Morgantown. West Virginia was the state university and was much bigger than Marshall. Both schools had football teams, but the Thundering Herd and the Mountaineers did not play against each other when I coached the Mountaineers.

On November 14, 1970, we beat Syracuse, 28–19, at Mountaineer Field in Morgantown. Our stadium did not have lights, so we always kicked off at about noon when we played at home. It was a pretty big upset, and we always had boosters and athletic department officials to our house for a party after the games. Later that night, I saw on television that a plane crashed at Huntington Tri-State Airport, near the Marshall University campus.

The Southern Airways DC-9 jet, which was carrying Marshall's football team, crashed into a hillside below the airport. It was a rainy and foggy night, and the pilots had trouble finding the runway. The accident killed all seventy-five on board: thirty-seven players, eight coaches, twenty-five boosters, the pilot, the copilot, two flight attendants, and one other employee of the airline. I had recruited many of the boys who died in the plane crash.

Believe it or not, I was almost on the plane with Marshall's football team. The Thundering Herd fired Charlie Snyder as their coach after a 0–10 season in 1967. Eddie Barrett was the athletic director at Marshall. Eddie had previously worked as the sports information director at West Virginia, and I probably spent more time with Eddie than anyone else during my time in Morgantown. Eddie called me and asked if I was interested in the coaching job at Marshall. I agreed to meet with him, and he drove over from Huntington a couple of days later. To keep our meeting a secret, he drove into our garage, and I closed the door behind him. We met for a couple of hours, and I told him I'd let him know my decision a few days later. In the end, I didn't take the job because I thought I'd get a better opportunity at a bigger school. Marshall didn't have much money to support its football program, and the Thundering Herd was just not winning many games.

Marshall ended up hiring Perry Moss, who was Florida State's head coach for one season in 1959. The Thundering Herd went 0–9–1 in 1968, and then things really went bad. In a desperate attempt to turn the program around, several Marshall boosters brought in 135 high school players from around the country to try out for 35 scholarships before the 1969 season. Marshall ended up committing 144 NCAA violations, which was unheard of at the time. The school was expelled from the Mid-American Conference, and it fired Moss about three weeks before the '69 season started. Offensive line coach Rick Tolley, a Virginia Tech graduate, was promoted to interim head coach. Marshall went 3–7 in 1969, and Tolley came back to coach the next season. He was on the plane that crashed into the hillside in West Virginia. Jack Lengyel, one of my good friends, rebuilt the Marshall football program, along with Red Dawson, who was one of my players when I was an assistant at Florida State.

About ten years later, I had a chance to leave Florida State for Louisiana State University. I was always a big admirer of LSU when I was growing up. The Tigers played in the Southeastern Conference and always seemed to have great teams. Early in the 1979 season, Paul Dietzel, who was LSU's athletic director, called me and said the school was going to replace Charlie McClendon, his football coach. Dietzel said he wanted me to replace McClendon when the season was over.

"You're going to have to turn it down," Dietzel told me. "It's your job if you want it."

Paul told me he would call me every few weeks. It was my fourth season as head coach at FSU, and I was beginning to wonder if we reached a ceiling by winning nine or ten games per season. We finished 8–3 in 1978, but were not even invited to play in a bowl game. The possibility of going to an SEC school was pretty enticing to me at the time.

"When I call, I don't want them to know LSU's athletic director is calling you," Dietzel said. "I'm going to tell your secretary that I'm your brother Paul."

So every couple of weeks, I would get a telephone call from my brother Paul.

But a funny thing happened in 1979. We had a pretty good team coming back. We won our first six games of the season and were ranked number eight in the national polls. I was beginning to think that I might have been wrong about Florida State's chances of playing for a national championship. Our next game was against LSU at Tiger Stadium in Baton Rouge, Louisiana, which is one of the most difficult stadiums to play in college football. Ann and I decided that if Florida State beat LSU on the road, we'd stay in Tallahassee. But if FSU lost to the Tigers, I would take the LSU job.

Wouldn't you know it? We went to Baton Rouge and beat the Tigers by a 24–19 score. I called Paul Dietzel a few days later and told him I was staying at Florida State. I signed a five-year contract extension to remain with the Seminoles.

Dietzel ended up hiring North Carolina State coach Bo Rein, who was considered one of the best young head coaches in the country. Rein played running back for Woody Hayes at Ohio State and was an assistant under Lou Holtz at North Carolina State and under Frank Broyles at Arkansas. After Holtz left North Carolina State to coach the NFL's New York Jets in 1976, the Wolfpack hired Rein to replace him. He led North Carolina State to an Atlantic Coast Conference championship during his last season there, in 1979.

On January 10, 1980, shortly after Rein took the LSU job, he was flying back from a recruiting trip to Shreveport, Louisiana, on a private plane. It was only supposed to be a forty-minute flight, but for whatever reason, air traffic control lost contact with the plane. U.S. National Guard jets later found it over North Carolina and tracked it until it crashed into the Atlantic Ocean. The bodies of Rein and his pilot were never found.

I have always believed that if I had taken Marshall's job in 1968 or LSU's job in 1979, I probably would have died. I didn't know why I'd turned down those jobs; each in its own way was a good alternative to the jobs I had. But something made me decide against them, and I came to understand that this, too, was part of God's plan for me. My faith was being tested. I needed to stay on the path He laid out for me, to follow wherever it led.

CHAPTER 7

THIN ICE

When most people think of the Mason-Dixon Line, they think of it as the divider between North and South. Before the Civil War, it separated freedom and slavery.

But the Mason-Dixon Line was actually drawn by two British astronomers and surveyors, Charles Mason and Jeremiah Dixon, to settle a bloody land dispute before the Revolutionary War. From 1763 to 1767, Mason and Dixon surveyed what are now Delaware, Maryland, Pennsylvania, and West Virginia, attempting to settle a boundary dispute between two wealthy colonial families.

For five years, Mason and Dixon lived in the wilderness, delineating a 233-mile border between Maryland and Delaware, setting huge blocks of limestone along their route to mark the boundary.

When Mason and Dixon reached a point about thirty miles north of Morgantown, West Virginia, they were driven away by hostile

Native Americans. As a result, Morgantown actually lies south of the Mason-Dixon Line.

But for a boy who grew up whistling "Dixie" in the hot, humid summers of Birmingham, Alabama, Morgantown sure didn't feel like a southern town.

Morgantown is about sixty miles south of Pittsburgh, on the banks of the Monongahela River. It receives an annual snowfall of about three feet, depending on where your house sits in the mountains. Even before I moved to West Virginia, I was never known as a very good driver. The icy roads of Morgantown made my daily commutes to the office even more treacherous.

By the end of my third season at West Virginia, I was on pretty thin ice with the Mountaineer fan base, too.

My team went 7–4 in my second season at West Virginia, in 1971, which, of course, did not sit well with many of the school's boosters. We won six of our first seven games, including a 20–9 victory over Pittsburgh in our homecoming game. But Penn State beat us, 35–7, at home and things started to fall apart after that loss. We lost three of our last four games and were not invited to a bowl game.

The next season, we went 8–3 during the regular season and were invited to play North Carolina State in the Peach Bowl. Things were beginning to look better. Lou Holtz was coaching the Wolfpack, and he seemed determined to make my next summer miserable. Lou coached at William & Mary before he went to North Carolina State, and we always beat his teams pretty good. We beat William & Mary, 43–7, in the 1970 opener, and Lou thought I ran up the score by adding a touchdown in the fourth quarter. In fact, he told me as much during our postgame handshake. I never knew the little guy could get so mad. The next season, William & Mary was beating us, 21–7, in the fourth quarter, but we came back and won the game by a 28–23 score. Now Lou was really mad at me.

When Lou left William & Mary for North Carolina State after the 1971 season, I am sure he could not wait to get another chance to play Bobby Bowden and West Virginia. He got his chance in the 1972 Peach Bowl, and he definitely took advantage of it.

On December 29, 1972, we played the Wolfpack in the Peach Bowl at Atlanta-Fulton County Stadium in Atlanta. We took a 13–7 lead at the end of the first quarter, but the Wolfpack came back to take a 14–13 advantage at the half. Then the floodgates opened. North Carolina State scored touchdowns on each of the first five times it had the ball in the second half. We lost the Peach Bowl by a score of 49–13, which was the worst bowl defeat in West Virginia history.

After that loss to North Carolina State, many West Virginia fans believed we lost the game because many of our players broke curfew in Atlanta and were not mentally prepared to play the game. I released a statement through the university to try to clear the air:

> *This might sound crazy, but I'm glad West Virginians are mad at the way we performed in the Peach Bowl. For fourteen thousand people to drive three hundred miles or more and be humiliated would infuriate anyone.*
>
> *I do wish our fans could accept the cold flat fact that we got our tails whipped by an excellent opponent and not try to go around and find behind-the-scenes reasons why we lost. I can assure you my preparations*

and the squad restrictions were the same as the other bowl participants. I can assure you that long hair, mustaches, dress apparel, or training rules in Atlanta didn't lose the game for us.

Living in West Virginia was pretty hard for my family and me after we lost the Peach Bowl. We went 6–5 in 1973 and lost to Pittsburgh by a 35–7 score, which certainly did not help my cause. In fact, we lost four consecutive games in October, including a 62–14 loss to Penn State, which was the worst defeat of my coaching career. The fans were getting pretty upset, but I still had the support of the West Virginia University people, and that really mattered.

University president James G. Harlow and athletic director Leland Byrd told me I would be their coach no matter how things turned out in 1973. I was always grateful for their support and confidence in me. We ended up winning four of our last five games, which took some of the heat off me heading into the summer of 1974.

My 1974 team had seventeen starters coming back, including wide receiver Danny Buggs, who was an All-American. I really thought it was going to be the best team I had at West Virginia. I even went around the state that summer telling everybody we should have a darn good team. I told them the Mountaineers were like a bomb, and we just needed to find an igniter. If we could find a quarterback that season, I thought we had a chance to be pretty good. We were trying to sell season tickets, and I was not afraid to tell people I thought things were going to turn around for us in 1974.

Well, they turned around, all right. We lost our top two quarterbacks and ended up starting Dan Kendra, who was only a freshman and whose son would eventually play for me at Florida State years later. After eight games we had a 2–6 record.

It was getting pretty dadgum unpleasant around campus. Right across the lawn from my office, students hung a sheet out their dormitory window. It read: "Bye-bye, Bobby." I saw that sheet so much I thought it was part of the landscape.

My son Tommy was playing wide receiver on my 1974 team. He read a story in the student newspaper in which the author wrote that Bobby Bowden had to go and that none of my players respected me. For some reason, Tommy cut that editorial out of the newspaper and kept it in his wallet. He was determined to find the author. A couple of weeks later, he learned that the writer lived in one of the fraternity houses on campus. So Tommy and Dave Van Halanger, one of our big offensive tackles, along with a couple of my other players, confronted the boy in his room at the fraternity house.

"Did you write this?" Tommy screamed at him.

The boy was pretty small and was wearing glasses, which were about three inches thick.

"Yes, I did," the boy told Tommy, "but I'll apologize."

Another time, students hung a caricature of me in effigy around campus. Tommy saw the dummy and tried to take it down. A policeman asked him what he was doing.

"I was taking it down because it's not fat enough," Tommy told the policeman. "I was going to make it more plump!"

Some of the threats against me were more serious than others. Upset fans put "Bowden Must Go" signs all over town, and someone put a "For Sale" sign on the front lawn of my home. One fan threw a brick at the front door of our house. Somebody even called the house and threatened to kill me.

But to survive in this profession, I had to learn not to take it personally. I definitely learned how fickle fans can be. You even lose friends during difficult times like that. There were a lot of people who used to invite us to their homes for parties and dinners, but they stopped inviting us after we started losing. At the time, it really hurt me. It was probably the toughest thing my family went through in football.

I told myself, *Bobby, if you ever want to leave, you've got every right in the world to do it.*

I decided that if a better opportunity ever came along, I had a right to take it.

Even though we had a 3–7 record heading into our last game in 1974, I was still being told by the university president, athletic director, and the school's athletic council that my job was safe.

"You're our coach and you're going to stay our coach," they told me.

But to keep my job the next season, I really felt like we needed to win the last game, at Virginia Tech, which was one of our biggest rivals. The Hokies had beaten Florida State, 56–21, in Tallahassee the week before, and had run for more than four hundred yards in the game. Virginia Tech ran a wishbone offense, and Jimmy Sharpe was a really good coach after working for Bear Bryant at Alabama. I just knew my defense would not be able to stop them, especially not with us playing the game in Blacksburg, Virginia.

But my boys came up with several big plays in the game. Marcus Mauney returned an interception ninety-nine yards for a touchdown, and Artie Owens had an eighty-five-yard touchdown run. After falling behind late in the game, we came back and took a 22–21 lead when Kendra threw a ten-yard touchdown pass to Bernie Kirchner with one minute, twenty-eight seconds to play.

Instead of kicking the football deep after we scored, I tried a squib kick so they would not get a long return. The Hokies recovered the football at their thirty-four-yard line. On the next play, one of my boys was penalized fifteen yards for fighting. Virginia Tech picked up another fifteen yards when I was penalized for running onto the field to argue with the officials.

Man, if we lose this game, they're really going to fire me, I thought.

We picked up two more penalties on the drive, and the Hokies moved the ball all the way to our six-yard line with fifteen seconds to go. Virginia Tech sent out Wayne Latimer, who was a pretty steady kicker. We blocked his short field-goal try on his first attempt, but we were called for jumping offside. So they moved the football to our three-yard line, and Latimer tried to make it again. Somehow, he pulled the twenty-yard field goal to the left, and we won the game. I felt like I'd dodged a bullet that day.

I've always felt God's presence during games. But I never felt that God was going to win a game for me. Every coach wants to win games just as badly as I do. I ask Him to help us do our best, but He does not care who wins the game. But I have a feeling God was watching over me pretty closely that day. Looking back, it was probably one of the biggest wins of my career. Even though I had been promised I would be back as

West Virginia's coach the next season, I am not sure if the president and athletic director could have brought me back if we had lost to Virginia Tech. The pressure on them to fire me would have been so intense.

I came back to West Virginia for the 1975 season, and I'm sure a lot of people had low expectations. Most fans probably thought I was a lame-duck coach and it was only a matter of time before I was fired. But I was determined that things were going to change. I rolled up my sleeves and went to work. We had the most intense off-season training program I can remember. I told my players I was finished with losing. They could either get on the train with me or stay behind at the station. I also made three changes to my coaching staff, hiring Paul Moran as wide receivers coach, Mike Working as offensive line coach, and Greg Williams as defensive backs coach.

We opened the 1975 season against Temple. We still had not named a starting quarterback, so we rotated Kendra and Danny Williams during the game. Neither one of the quarterbacks had to throw the ball much, though, because our defense intercepted two passes and returned them for touchdowns. We won the game, 50–7.

The following week, we traveled all the way across the country to play the University of California at Berkeley. The Bears were very good and had a tailback named Chuck Muncie, who would become a star in the NFL. We took a 14–10 lead into the fourth quarter, but California was driving for a go-ahead score late in the quarter. The Bears got as close as our twelve-yard line. Of course, no one believed California coach Mike White was going to attempt a field goal. The Bears lined up to kick a field goal, but they attempted to throw a pass on a trick play instead. Chuck

Braswell knocked the pass down and we scored two more touchdowns for a 28–10 victory.

We beat Boston College, 35–18, the next week and defeated Southern Methodist University, 28–25, in the Cotton Bowl stadium, improving to 4–0. West Virginia moved into the national rankings for the first time since the 1950s, and everybody in Morgantown was really excited. But then we played Penn State but lost, 39–0, to the Nittany Lions. Our star tailback, Artie Owens, was hurt against Penn State and we lost to Tulane, 16–14, in the next game without him.

I knew we had to get things back together quickly or things would head south in a hurry. We beat Virginia Tech, 10–7, in a very difficult win and routed Kent State, 38–13, at home. We had a 6–2 record, but for the 1975 season to be considered a success, my team would have to beat Pittsburgh. The Panthers were nationally ranked after beating Georgia and Syracuse, and Tony Dorsett was one of the great running backs in the country.

On November 8, West Virginia played Pittsburgh at Mountaineer Field. It was one of the most exciting games I ever coached. Even though Pittsburgh had a high-powered offense with Dorsett and quarterback Matt Cavanaugh, the score was tied 0–0 at halftime. Our defense was just playing great. Chuck Klausing, my defensive coordinator, devised a brilliant game plan to slow down Dorsett. The score was tied at 14 going into the fourth quarter, and that was always one of my favorite games because my son Tommy caught a couple of passes to get us into field-goal range at the end. We sent kicker Bill McKenzie on the field to kick a thirty-eight-yard field goal on the final play of the game. McKenzie's kick was good and we won the game, 17–14.

We finished the regular season with an 8–3 record, after beating Richmond and losing to Syracuse in our last two games. West Virginia was invited to play North Carolina State in the Peach Bowl, where we'd lost to the Wolfpack so badly only three years before. I was determined that our poor performance would not be repeated. Instead of taking my team to Atlanta for bowl preparations, we stayed in Clemson, South Carolina. My boys probably were not too excited about spending the week in the country, but I thought it was the environment they needed to stay focused.

We trailed the Wolfpack, 10–6, going into the fourth quarter, but Kendra threw a long pass to Scott MacDonald with about seven minutes left. MacDonald was recruited to West Virginia to play basketball, but we thought he could play wide receiver because of his height and jumping ability. But Scott did not have the surest hands, and I was not certain he would catch the ball after he juggled it at about the fifty-yard line. But Scott hauled in the pass and ran fifty yards for the winning touchdown in a 13–10 victory.

After the game, West Virginia fans were really ecstatic. We finished with a 9–3 record, which was my best season at West Virginia. We avenged the earlier loss to the Wolfpack in Atlanta, and I got some payback with Holtz. Lou and I actually became very good friends and remain close to this day.

A few days after the Peach Bowl, I was in Tampa coaching at a college football all-star game. It was the North against the South, and I was coaching the North team. I guess the game organizers had never heard my accent before. The first night I was in Tampa, I got a telephone call from John Bridgers, who was the athletic director at Florida State. He told me they fired their head coach, Darrell Mudra, and wanted to interview me for the job.

I had already interviewed for the Florida State job twice in the previous six years, and both times FSU hired someone else. The third time, I flew to Tallahassee with Ann to interview with the FSU athletic board after the all-star game. Bridgers told me afterward that I would be offered the job, but I wasn't sure I wanted it. Ann and I discussed it on the flight back to Morgantown, and in the end we decided we would go to Florida State. We figured it would be nice to be closer to our mothers, who were now both widows in Birmingham.

As if I needed convincing that we'd made the right decision, my daughter Robyn and her husband, Jack Hines, picked us up at the airport in Morgantown. Jack drove us back to our house in the middle of an ice storm. As we made our way up a hill, his car started sliding off the road. I got out of the car to help and was wearing a coat and tie. I slipped on the ice and started sliding down the road flat on my face.

I looked up at Ann and yelled, "We're definitely going to Florida State!"

I called Leland Byrd, West Virginia's athletic director, the next morning and told him I was leaving for FSU. He wanted me to stay and even said he would try to set a four-year contract. I had worked with a one-year contract every season I was there. But I decided I wanted to go to Tallahassee, and I really felt like the Lord was leading me there.

If things had not gotten so bad in 1974, I probably would not have left West Virginia because I am always very loyal. I really believe in being loyal. It is not that West Virginia was not loyal to me. The university president, athletic director, and the people who mattered were always very loyal to me. It was the other people. I saw how fickle fans were. They were with you when you were winning, but they forgot you if you were losing. I never liked that part of it. But you know what? It made me develop thick skin, and it made me immune to criticism. For the rest of my career, I really did not care what the critics said. I knew only what was in my heart and that I was trying to do the best job I could. Most important, I was trying to live my life the way God wanted me to live.

But my family and I have very fond memories of West Virginia. My sons Terry and Tommy played football there and graduated with degrees from West Virginia. I have other children who graduated from there. Most of my children still consider West Virginia their home. There are a lot of great people there, and it is a really beautiful place.

I've always believed that if I knew the things I learned at Florida State while I was coaching at West Virginia, we probably would have been much more successful there. It had been my first big head coaching job, and I made plenty of mistakes along the way.

Leaving West Virginia for Florida State in January 1976 was a big moment in my coaching career. But deep in my heart, I knew I would never stay at FSU for long.

Florida State was only going to be a stepping-stone for me.

CHAPTER 8

PROVING GROUND

I must confess that I accepted the Florida State job under false pretenses. When I left West Virginia for FSU in January 1976, I had no intention of staying in Tallahassee for very long. The Florida State program was in disarray and had not been very good in a long time. In the three seasons before I took over, the Seminoles had won four games and lost twenty-nine. It was the post–Vietnam War era, and the university was struggling financially. The school even considered dropping football, just as the University of Tampa had done.

I once said I could think of only two jobs that were worse than coaching at Florida State in 1976: becoming mayor of Atlanta shortly after General William Tecumseh Sherman left town, or being the general who replaced George Custer at the final siege of the Battle of the Little

Big Horn. The Seminoles were that bad. But the weather was nice in Tallahassee, and it was a head coaching job in the South.

"We are not going to stay here for very long," I told Ann. "We'll start making our connections in the South again, and I'll have you back closer to your mamma in no time. Somehow we will end up back in Alabama."

After I saw my team's future schedules, I knew I had to get out of Tallahassee pretty fast. During the 1981 season, the Seminoles would be playing five consecutive road games: at Nebraska, Ohio State, Notre Dame, Pittsburgh, and Louisiana State. You want to talk about Murderers' Row? I knew I had to win enough games in the first few seasons at Florida State to land a better coaching job before the 1981 season rolled around.

On January 12, 1976, Florida State sent a private plane to Morgantown, West Virginia, to pick up Ann and me. I signed a four-year contract to become FSU's new coach and would be paid a salary of $37,500 per season plus a $3,000 expense account, which was about $12,500 more than I earned per season at West Virginia.

I was introduced as FSU's head coach during a news conference in the basement of the old State Capitol building in downtown Tallahassee. I immediately told Seminoles fans what they wanted to hear.

"Florida," I told the crowd. "That's the game we gotta win. There's going to be a common cause—those folks down yonder in Gainesville. I know a lot of you look at me and ask, 'Are you a big-time coach?' I don't know what a big-time coach is. I know I've been hung in effigy. And I know if I beat Florida, I'm a big-time coach."

I didn't know if Florida State could really beat Florida. When I was hired at FSU, the Seminoles had beaten the Gators only twice in eighteen meetings between the schools. I was an assistant coach on Bill Peterson's staff when FSU beat Florida the first time, in 1964. The Seminoles defeated the Gators again in 1967, but lost to them eight straight times before I arrived.

While I was growing up in Alabama, Crimson Tide fans had bumper stickers on their cars that said, "Beat Auburn!" When I coached at West Virginia, Mountaineer fans had stickers that said, "Beat Pitt!" At FSU, they had stickers that said, "Beat Anybody!"

Four days after I was introduced as Florida State's head coach, I met with my players for the first time. I was told by university officials that there had not been much discipline instilled by the former coaching staff and that many of the returning players were struggling in school. The boys needed direction, so I immediately tried to establish the rules of my program.

Gentlemen, let me explain the importance of why we're all here together. First of all, we've got to have a basic understanding of who's in charge around here. There can never be a question of that.

Well, I'm the new guy around here. I'm the head coach. And in the past three years, your Florida State football team has managed to win only four games, and in the meantime, lost twenty-nine. Ya'll have tried it your way, and where did it get you? Nowhere.

More than anything, I wanted to try to instill a sense of pride that should come with playing for a school like Florida State. I wanted the boys to be proud again when they put on their jerseys, helmets, and shoulder pads and played for the Seminoles. I also wanted to make sure they knew it was a privilege—not an entitlement—to play football at Florida State.

> *From now on, it's going to be an honor to wear the garnet jersey and represent Florida State University. We're gonna win again at Florida State. Now, I think we can turn this program around. But, gentlemen, it's going to take a big effort by everyone. We're going to have to push ourselves harder than ever before. We're going to have to make sacrifices, give up individual goals in order to reach a much bigger team goal. But we can do it. We can win at Florida State.*
>
> *Vince Lombardi, the great coach of the Green Bay Packers, once described that glorious feeling that winners have, that feeling that none of you have enjoyed at Florida State. He said, "I firmly believe that man's finest hour, his greatest fulfillment to all he holds dear, is that moment when he has worked his heart out in a good cause and lies exhausted on the field . . . victorious."*
>
> *Yes, we can win. Gentlemen, that will be our goal. That will be the feeling that we all want to achieve—to feel like a winner, to be able to walk around campus with the satisfaction of knowing that, "Yes, we can win." And in order to get that feeling of confidence and to begin winning football games, then things here have to change.*

Even though I was inheriting a team of players of a different generation than the boys I coached at South Georgia College, Howard College, and even at West Virginia, I was going to enforce the same set of rules I had before. The boys would groom their hair, shave their faces, go to class every day, and be encouraged to attend church on Sunday. There would be no smoking, drinking, or drug use among my players.

First of all, we've got to develop a winning attitude and that means self-discipline, because self-discipline wins football games. And that's our goal at Florida State—to win football games. So let's start with the hair. I'm not going to ask you to look like Kojaks, but we are going to keep it neat and we are going to look like football players.

We're also gonna go to class and get up for breakfast. And there's not going to be any room on this team for individuals who've got to drink or smoke. If you do, then you're gonna be gone. Next, we're gonna ask that you attend church regularly and write your mom and dad. It'll mean a lot to them, and more to you over the years.

So, gentlemen, what is sacrifice? It's having a little pride in yourself to not be like the average students. You've gotta outwork them; you've gotta have a desire to excel. Sacrifice also means displaying a winning attitude, looking and acting like an athlete, recognizing the attributes of other students, giving them a pat on the back, shaking their hands, and looking 'em in the eye while doing it. Sacrifice means "yes, sir" and "no, sir" to your supervisors.

But remember, it takes class to come back in the fourth quarter and win, but if we've sacrificed, we can do it.

At the end of my first team speech at FSU, I tried to convince the boys that no matter what, I believed in them. With hard work by all of us, I knew we would start winning football games very soon.

Now, gentlemen, listen up on this final point. We represent a lot of people: our families, our friends back at home, and, very importantly, we represent Florida State University. And as a team, I want to throw this out at you—you're not ordinary. You're not average. You're something special, and I don't want you to ever forget that. And since you are something special, then I know that as a team, we will win.

Gentlemen, we have a tough road ahead, and we've got to be both mentally and physically tough to make it. But if we're prepared in the proper manner, then when the time comes, winning will take care of itself.

After that first meeting, I was beginning to feel a little bit better about the situation I was walking into. Florida State had a lot of good-looking players. I was very impressed when I saw them. I felt really confident in the coaching staff I hired, too. I kept Gene McDowell from the previous FSU staff, and he coached linebackers. I kept Bob Harbison, also from the previous staff, to work with the offensive line, and I promoted Jim Gladden to defensive ends coach. I hired Jack Stanton as my defensive coordinator, and brought in George Haffner from Pittsburgh to work as offensive coordinator and coach the quarterbacks and running backs. I brought two of my assistants from West Virginia: Jerry Bruner, who coached the offensive line, and George Henshaw, who coached the defensive line. I hired Kent Schoolfield, a high school coach from Miami, to coach the wide receivers and tight ends.

My assistant coaches were expected to adhere to an even stricter set of standards than my players. I wanted strong God-fearing men leading my boys. I expected my coaches to lead by example and serve as role models for the boys.

"I won't tolerate a womanizer," I told my coaches. "I won't tolerate a drunk. I won't tolerate a cheater. If you commit any of those offenses, I will fire you."

With the coaching staff I assembled and the players we had coming back, I thought we might produce a winning team at Florida State right away.

I think we can win seven or eight games the first year, I told myself.

It didn't take long to realize that wouldn't be the case in 1976. My first game as head coach at Florida State was against Memphis State at the Liberty Bowl stadium on September 11, 1976. We had four turnovers and eighty-two yards in penalties and looked like a team that was still trying to find its identity under a new coach. We trailed by only 7–3 at halftime, but the Tigers scored two touchdowns in the third quarter. We lost my first game as FSU's head coach, 21–12.

The next game was even worse than the first. We were playing the University of Miami at the Orange Bowl stadium, and I really thought we were going to win. The Hurricanes finished even worse than Florida State in 1975, limping to a 2–8 record. But one of Miami's two victories came against FSU, after the Hurricanes kicked a twenty-nine-yard field goal with thirteen seconds left to win the game, 24–22.

The Hurricanes were much better in 1976. Miami beat us, 47–0, in our second game, but the score could have been 1,000,000–0. Miami scored on nine of its first ten possessions and led by a 31–0 score at halftime. I am sure FSU fans all over the state were thinking, "Same old Seminoles."

The only thing I could think after the Miami game was, *Lord, what have I gotten myself into?*

We were getting ready to play the University of Oklahoma on the road the following week. The Sooners were college football's defending national champions and were ranked number four in the country after two games in 1976. The team was coached by Barry Switzer, and playing the Sooners in Norman, Oklahoma, was never easy. Six days before the game, I decided that we could not win with the team we were putting on the field. So I told my coaches, "We're going to have to go with the young guys. If we're going to get beat, let's get beat with these freshmen. We're going to take our licks with them this year and get ready for four years down the road, when they're all seniors."

We recruited a very good freshman class in 1976. Jimmy Jordan was a strong-armed quarterback from Leon High School in Tallahassee, and Kurt Unglaub was Jimmy's favorite receiver there. Mark Lyles was a big, strong running back from Buffalo, New York. I wanted Mark so badly I hired his high school coach, Nick Kish, as a graduate assistant on my coaching staff.

Against the mighty Oklahoma Sooners, we started seven freshmen: Unglaub and Jackie Flowers as wide receivers, Mike Good on the offensive line, Lyles at fullback, Scott Warren and Walter Carter on the defensive line, and Dave Cappelen was already starting as our kicker. We also decided that we were going to rotate Jordan with quarterback Jimmy Black as much as we could.

We went to Oklahoma and had a 6–3 lead after the first quarter. The Oklahoma crowd was shocked. The Sooners came back and beat us by a 24–9 score, but I was really proud of my boys for their effort. I think the young guys earned a lot of confidence in the game and were starting to believe they could play against anyone.

We came back and beat Kansas State, 20–10, at home on October 2, 1976, which was my very first victory at Florida State. The next week, we upset Boston College by a 28–9 score on the road. The Eagles were ranked number thirteen in the national polls, but we recovered four of their fumbles and returned one sixty-five yards for a touchdown.

By then, folks around Tallahassee were finally getting pretty excited about Florida State football. We played Florida at home on October 16, 1976, and more than forty-two thousand fans packed into Doak Campbell Stadium. The Gators were ranked number twelve in the country and had seven players who would later play in the NFL. It was supposed to be one of their best teams.

Florida jumped on us, 10–0, in the first quarter, but my boys kept fighting. We came back and took a 23–20 lead on Jimmy Black's two-yard touchdown run in the third quarter. After the Gators scored two touchdowns to go ahead by a 33–23 score, Black was sacked and came out of the game with a concussion. I put Jimmy Jordan into the game, hoping he could give our offense a spark. Jimmy led us down the field for a field goal with about five minutes to go, and then put us back in position to score in the final seconds. We had the ball first-and-goal at Florida's nine-yard line with seven seconds to play. Jimmy dropped back and threw for fullback Jeff Leggett at the goal line.

Jimmy overthrew him by about six inches and we lost the game, 33–26.

We might have lost the Florida game on the scoreboard, but it was probably the biggest moral victory of my career. Our performance let the Gators know that they were not just going to run over Florida State anymore. We lost to Auburn and Clemson in the next two games, dropping our record to 2–6 after eight games, but I thought we were playing pretty well.

Things started to turn around for Florida State in the ninth game of 1976, when we hosted Southern Mississippi on November 6. We trailed the Golden Eagles, 27–10, going into the fourth quarter, but then we scored twenty points in about seven minutes; Rudy Thomas, who was one of our seniors, scored three touchdowns in the fourth quarter. His last touchdown was ninety-five yards, after he caught a short pass from Jimmy Black and scored with about four minutes to go. We won the game, 30–27.

The next week we played at North Texas State in Denton, Texas. The game was almost canceled because of a snowstorm. Most of my boys had never seen snow before. It was eighty degrees in Florida when we left on Friday, and we woke up Saturday morning in Texas with about five inches of snow on the ground. The winds were howling off the Oklahoma plains, and it was just frigid. North Texas State did not want to cancel the game because it was homecoming, so I sent my equipment manager Frank DeBord out to buy every pair of gloves and long underwear he could find.

We went to Fouts Field to play the game, and you couldn't even see the field, just the goalposts. The officials took orange highway cones and put them at the corners of the end zone. Then they put cones every ten yards to mark the field. We were going to play the dadgum game in the snow, which I had never done before.

"Boys, just go out and have a good time," I told my team before the game. "I don't know how to play in this stuff, either."

Somehow, Jimmy Black figured out a way to throw the football in the snow. I guess he figured if he could get the football to his receivers, North Texas's defensive backs would have a hard time running them down in the snow. He threw a nine-yard touchdown to Ed Beckman and a ninety-one-yard touchdown to Kurt Unglaub. We had a 13–7 lead in the fourth quarter, but the Mean Green came back and scored two touchdowns to take a 20–13 lead going into the fourth quarter. Both teams blocked a punt to score.

We got the football back with about five minutes to go, and I don't know how Jimmy Black did it, but he started rolling out and hitting passes. Jeff Leggett scored on a seven-yard run to cut North Texas's lead to 20–19, and I decided we were going to go for two points and a victory. We could not kick the ball in the snow anyway, but I did not want the game to end in a tie after we'd been freezing to death for three hours. I called a halfback pass, and Larry Keys threw a two-point conversion pass to Unglaub to win the game, 21–20.

We ended the 1976 season against Virginia Tech at Doak Campbell Stadium on November 20. We were trailing, 21–14, in the fourth quarter, but Jimmy Jordan came off the bench and threw a thirty-three-yard touchdown pass to Jackie Flowers to make it 21–20. I decided to go for two points again, but we didn't get it and still trailed by one point on the scoreboard. The Hokies were driving deep into our territory with about six minutes to go. They were on our four-yard line and all they had to do was kneel down and they would win the game. But Virginia Tech fumbled at our four-yard line, and Aaron Carter recovered the football for us. On the very next play, Jordan threw a ninety-six-yard touchdown to Unglaub to win the game, 28–21.

I believe that the final three games of the 1976 season were really important for us. We came from behind in the fourth quarter to win each of those games. We felt like the kids were beginning to realize that if they would fight for sixty minutes, we could win some dadgum games. Most of our best players were only freshmen, and I thought they would become our backbone during the next three seasons.

But to beat Florida and consistently win football games, I knew we had to find a player who would make our defense better in a hurry. I found that kind of player in Warner Robins, Georgia. His name was Ron Simmons, and he might have been the most important player we ever signed at Florida State. Ron had a rare combination of size and speed. He could bench-press five hundred pounds in high school, and not many players in college or the NFL could accomplish that feat during the 1970s. Ron was strong as an ox, was built like Superman, and could run like a gazelle on the field.

The University of Georgia was trying to sign Simmons to a football scholarship, too. But I had a secret weapon in Ron's hometown. Billy "Stumpy" Franklin played guard on my teams at South Georgia College during the 1950s. Billy owned a battery store in Warner Robins and hired Ron to work there when he was in high school. Every year, Ron worked for Billy. Billy was kind of like a father to him. Billy wanted Ron to go to Florida State and play for me, and I thought we had a pretty good chance of getting him.

But then the Bulldogs played the worst trick on me. Mike Cavan was a star quarterback at Georgia from 1968 to 1970, and he was a heck of a recruiter as an assistant coach for the Bulldogs. About two weeks before national signing day in 1977, Ron Simmons announced he was going to attend Florida State. His announcement really caused a shock wave in Georgia. I think the governor of Georgia and everybody called Ron, asking him why he was going to Florida State. But Ron liked me and he really believed Billy's promise that I would take care of him. Ron just felt like we were being honest with him.

On the Friday night before national signing day, Cavan persuaded a television station in Georgia to report that I was taking the head coaching job at the University of Mississippi. Ken Cooper was struggling as the Rebels' coach, and there was some speculation that he might be fired. Ron was at a high school basketball game that night, and when he heard the news that I was leaving Florida State, he just went crazy. He called me at home.

"You lied to me!" Ron told me. "You lied to me! You told me you were going to coach me at Florida State."

I told him the story was not true, but we had to win him back all over again. We signed a lot of great players in Ron's recruiting class. Guys such as Monk Bonasorte, Bobby Butler, Reggie Herring, Paul Piurowski (whose son Caz would end up playing for me at FSU), and Rick Stockstill really helped us turn things around over the next few seasons.

Ron was a linebacker in high school, but we made him the nose guard on our defensive line. Immediately, he made our defense much better. I have often said that the 1977 season was my favorite season of all time. We went 9–2 during the regular season, losing to Miami, 23–17, and then to San Diego State, 41–16. We beat Auburn for the first time and came from behind to beat Virginia Tech again.

In the final game of the 1977 season, we played Florida on the road. We had played the Gators pretty close the year before, but I am not sure anybody thought we could beat them in Gainesville. Wally Woodham and Jimmy Jordan were sharing snaps at quarterback, and both of them just lit up the Florida defense. They combined to throw for four touchdowns, and Roger Overby caught three of them. We won the game, 37–9. The victory ended a nine-game losing streak to the Gators.

When we came back to Tallahassee that night, our fans were so excited they didn't know what to do. We came up Interstate 75 from Gainesville, and then came across Interstate 10. We exited onto Highway 90 so we could drive to the stadium, and there were walls and walls of cars pulled over on the side of the highway. The caravan took us right to Doak Campbell Stadium, where about ten thousand people were waiting inside for an impromptu pep rally. It was really unbelievable and was one of the greatest nights of my life.

By finishing 9–2, 1977 became the first time Florida State had won nine games in a regular season, and we were invited to play Texas Tech in the Tangerine Bowl in Orlando, Florida. Larry Key returned a kickoff ninety-three yards for a touchdown, and Jimmy Jordan threw three touchdown passes in a 40–17 victory over the Red Raiders. We won ten games in 1977, which is not something I ever thought we could do at Florida State.

We had an 8–3 record in 1978, but we weren't invited to play in a bowl game. Our people learned that you have to campaign to play in a bowl game, so Florida State formed a bowl committee. We had one person in charge of the Orange Bowl, one in charge of the Gator Bowl, one in charge of the Fiesta Bowl, and so on. It was their job to campaign for FSU. We wanted to make sure that we were never left out of a bowl game again when we deserved to play in one.

Fortunately, we didn't have to worry about being snubbed in 1979. I felt really good about the team we had coming back because all of the freshmen we played in 1976 were now seniors. We had been building toward 1979 for four years.

In our first team meeting, on January 8, I laid out the blueprint for what I hoped would become a championship team.

"Men, I hope we recruited boys who want to be champions," I told them.

I told our players there were three objectives for the 1979 season: to finish undefeated, to be ranked in the top ten of the national polls, and to win a major bowl game. After three seasons at Florida State, I really believed we had the talent, leadership, and depth to accomplish those goals.

"We have the physical ingredients in this room," I told my players. "We have veterans who have been to war and won. We have more depth and we have a senior base, which is always key. We recruited excellent freshmen to help you, and we have all our kickers back. Our defense will be the key this coming season."

But I made sure I warned my players about the things that could spoil the 1979 season.

"You must have a good, positive attitude and morale," I told them. "You must improve physically with the best off-season program we've ever had. You have the full confidence and support of the coaching staff, but there are some things you can do that would hurt us. You must go to study hall and to class. We need everyone in this room to win a championship, and if you're not in school, you can't help us. You must be obedient and not misbehave. Do not become involved in drugs or cause public disturbances."

I drew a basket of apples on the chalkboard. I filled in one of the apples with chalk, illustrating that it was rotten.

"If one apple goes bad," I told my team, "they all go bad. It's like cancer. We have to stick together."

After three seasons at Florida State, I was beginning to believe we had the stuff to win.

CHAPTER 9

NO PLACE LIKE HOME

As Florida State embarked on the 1979 football season, I was looking two years into the future. I still could not come to grips with the schedule my team would face in 1981. We were going to play five consecutive road games against many of college football's traditional powers. It would require road trips to five different states, and would cover more than four thousand miles.

Florida State fans later came up with a catchphrase for that grueling five-week stretch of road games, at Nebraska, Ohio State, Notre Dame, Pittsburgh, and Louisiana State.

They called it "Octoberfest."

But our future schedule did not look very festive to me. In fact, it looked more like my funeral.

College football teams have an inherent advantage when they play home games, and my team was no different. Florida State fans were beginning to believe that the Seminoles could win every week, and more than forty-five thousand of them flocked to Doak Campbell Stadium for each home game. Sometimes the crowd support even willed my boys to victory. It is just easier playing home games than road games. Players sleep in their own beds the night before the game, they dress in their own locker room, and they play in familiar surroundings. And it doesn't hurt when the crowd is cheering for you instead of cheering against you.

In 1978, FSU started what I believe is the best tradition in all of college football. Before we played Oklahoma State in the 1978 home opener, a student riding a horse led my team from a stadium tunnel. The rider was named after Seminole Indian chief Osceola; the Appaloosa horse was named Renegade. From then on, no FSU home game started until Renegade charged down the field, and Osceola planted a flaming spear at midfield.

In 1979, Florida State was building a home-field advantage. Tallahassee was even beginning to feel like home for Ann and me. It just took a few bumps in the road to make us realize it.

Our senior-laden team played Southern Mississippi in our season opener, on September 8, 1979. It was probably the closest we came to getting beaten during the regular season, and we probably should have lost the game. We just could not make a first down. We trailed by a 14–3 deficit going into the fourth quarter. But with about eleven minutes to go, Monk Bonasorte blocked a punt. We recovered the football at the Golden Eagles' fifteen-yard line. Three plays later, Jimmy Jordan threw an eight-yard touchdown to Jackie Flowers to make it 14–9. Our defense stopped Southern Miss on its next possession, and then Gary Henry returned a punt sixty-five yards for a touchdown. We made a two-point conversion to win the game, 17–14. It was the kind of comeback you often see from championship teams, and I was beginning to think we were that kind of team.

We really didn't have much trouble during our next five games, beating Arizona State, Miami, Virginia Tech, Louisville, and Mississippi State. We had a 6–0 record and a ten-game winning streak going back to the 1978 season. We were ranked number eight in the national polls, and excitement around Florida State football was probably at an all-time high.

At that point, Louisiana State University's interest in me was really heating up. LSU athletic director Paul Dietzel—or my "brother Paul," as he liked to tell my secretary when he called—was contacting me every week. Paul told me he already had approval from the Louisiana governor to hire me as the Tigers' coach, once Charlie McClendon departed. But Ann and I were beginning to believe that we might be able to build something special at Florida State. I only needed a victory over a team like LSU to convince me it could happen.

"We're undefeated and they've already lost two games," I told Ann before the game. "If we can't beat the Tigers, I think we need to take the LSU job because that means this program will never be as good."

We played LSU at Tiger Stadium on October 27, 1979. Playing the Tigers at Death Valley was never easy, especially at night, after the Cajuns had all day to lather up for the game at their tailgates outside the stadium. Earlier that week, I told the media our trip to LSU was "the biggest football game in FSU history." ABC-TV decided to broadcast the game to most of the country, which was really a break for us because the game kicked off in the afternoon. There were representatives from nine bowl games in attendance, so I wanted to make sure my boys put on a good show. But as soon as we arrived at Tiger Stadium, I was hounded by newspaper reporters, who wanted to know if I was going to come to LSU after the season. I was worried the situation might become a distraction for my team.

We fell behind the Tigers 13–7 in the second quarter, but then Jordan threw a fifty-three-yard touchdown to Hardis Johnson to give us a 14–13 lead. I surprised a lot of people by starting Jimmy over Wally Woodham, who started every game during our ten-game winning streak. Jimmy had a stronger arm than Wally, but was also apt to take more chances in the passing game. Jimmy more than justified my decision by throwing for 312 yards and three touchdowns against the Tigers. We still had only a one-point lead going into the fourth quarter, but then Jimmy threw a forty-yard touchdown to Jackie Flowers to make it 21–13. We added a field goal late in the game and held on for a 24–19 victory.

On the flight back to Tallahassee, Ann and I decided that we would stay at Florida State. I called Dietzel the next day and withdrew my name from consideration for his pending job opening. We won our last four regular-season games, beating Florida for the third straight time, and finished with a perfect 11–0 record. We accepted an invitation to play in the Orange Bowl only a few hours before we defeated Memphis State, 66–17, at home on November 17, 1979.

In the Orange Bowl, we ended up playing Oklahoma, the Big Eight Conference champion. The Sooners had a quarterback named J. C. Watts, who was really dangerous running the football in the wishbone offense. His actual name was Julius Caesar Watts Jr., and he sure played like a conqueror. I heard J.C. preach at a Baptist church before the Orange Bowl. We both gave a testimony that Sunday and I left that church thinking, "Boy, if he plays as well as he preaches, we're going to get killed!"

We took a 7–0 lead in the Orange Bowl on Michael Whiting's one-yard touchdown run. We had a chance to score again a few minutes later, after Bobby Butler blocked a punt. But we fumbled a snap on a field-goal try and never had a chance to kick the ball. A short time later, Watts took off for a sixty-one-yard touchdown run. After Jordan threw an interception, Oklahoma scored again to take a 14–7 lead. The Sooners ended up winning the Orange Bowl, 24–7. Watts ran for 127 yards, and Billy Sims ran for 164 yards and one touchdown. Sims was one of the best running backs I ever coached against.

Oklahoma was just a much better football team than Florida State in 1979. But it still was very important for my team to play in the Orange Bowl because FSU had never played in such a high-profile game before. We finished sixth in the final Associated Press Top 25 poll, which was the highest the Seminoles had ever finished a season.

Much to everyone's surprise, FSU was right back in the national championship hunt the next season, in 1980. We had to replace all the great seniors who had left, but Ron Simmons was back on defense and guys such as Monk Bonasorte, Bobby Butler, Reggie Herring, and Paul Piurowski developed into great defensive players. We had a dominating offensive line led by Greg Futch, Ken Lanier, and Mark Macek. Rick Stockstill was taking over at quarterback, and Sam Platt was a very capable running back.

As long as we found the leadership we had the previous season, there was no reason we could not win as many games in 1980. We opened the 1980 season at LSU and won, 16–0, spoiling the debut of Jerry Stovall, whom Dietzel had hired as his head coach. We had shut out our first two opponents after beating Louisville, 52–0. Our defense was just so dominant with Simmons anchoring the middle of the line.

We lost one game during the 1980 regular season, falling to the University of Miami by a 10–9 score at the Orange Bowl stadium in our fourth game. We had played East Carolina the week before, winning, 63–7, but we lost our top two centers during that game. Gil Wesley was our starting center and tore up his knee; John Madden, who would later become my son-in-law, was his backup and sprained his ankle in the fourth quarter.

We went to play Miami the following week and fumbled the snap seven times because we had a guard playing center. We lost two fumbles and did not play very well, but we still had a chance to beat the Hurricanes. Miami scored its only touchdown on a fluke play right before halftime. The Hurricanes had third-and-eighteen at their forty-yard line, and Jim Kelly threw a bomb into the end zone. We were penalized for pass interference, and Miami was given the ball at our one-yard line. I still watch replays of that pass from time to time—the highlights are on old film reels—and I still don't think it was pass interference. But the official's opinion was the only one that mattered, and Miami scored on a one-yard run right before the half.

We trailed 10–3 going into the fourth quarter, but Stockstill threw an eleven-yard touchdown to Sam Childers to make it 10–9 with thirty-nine seconds to play. Once again, I decided to go for two points and the victory. Stockstill dropped back to pass and threw into the end zone for Phil Williams, who was open across the middle. But Jim Burt, Miami's nose guard, jumped in the way and the pass hit him right in the face mask. We lost the game by that 10–9 score.

After the Miami game, we didn't know what we were going to do about replacing our center. We were getting ready to play at the University of Nebraska. I knew we couldn't have a guard playing center again, or we wouldn't have a chance at even staying close with the number-three-ranked Cornhuskers. I told the coaches in our Sunday night meeting that we had two centers on the freshman team: a scholarship player from Cincinnati and a walk-on player from Savannah, Georgia.

"Look at the boy from Cincinnati and the boy from Savannah," I told my coaches. "Work both of them in practice all week. Whichever one can snap the ball to the quarterback without fumbling is going to start against Nebraska."

The walk-on was a boy named Jerry Coleman. He came to me before the season and told me he wanted to redshirt, which meant he would practice with the team but not play in games. Since he wouldn't play in games, he would still have four years of eligibility left when the season ended.

When Jerry asked me to redshirt, I thought, *What the heck does he want to redshirt for? He's never going to get on the field.*

Jerry probably did not weigh two hundred pounds, but he told me he always wanted to play for Florida State, and that made a lasting impression on me.

The day before we left for Nebraska, George Henshaw, my offensive coordinator, walked into my office.

"Coach Bowden, the walk-on never misses a snap," George told me. "He can't block a shadow, but he's perfect on the snaps. The other boy is fumbling a bunch."

I called Jerry into my office later that day.

"Son, you're going to have to start against Nebraska," I told him. "They have an All-American nose guard, but just don't botch the snap!"

Jerry's eyes got really big, and I could tell he was very excited. I was scared to death. I almost sent his mother flowers before we even played the game.

We played the Cornhuskers at Memorial Stadium in Lincoln, Nebraska, on October 4. I was afraid we were going to get beaten. As a coach, you do not like to think your team does not have a chance to win a game, but nobody beat the Cornhuskers in Lincoln back then. About an hour before the game, somebody knocked on the door to our locker room. It was Nebraska coach Tom Osborne. He just wanted to make sure we had everything we needed. I was really touched by Tom's gesture, and it showed me what kind of man he is. Tom and I share very much the same beliefs and values, so we became close friends over the years.

For whatever reason, my boys had a lot of confidence playing at Nebraska, even after we fell behind by a 14–0 score in the first half. Bill Capece, our kicker, made a thirty-two-yard field goal right before halftime, which cut the Cornhuskers' lead to 14–3. We came out in the second half and kicked another field goal, and then Platt scored on a six-yard touchdown run to make it 14–12. Capece kicked two more field goals to give us an 18–14 lead, and Memorial Stadium was about as quiet as a funeral parlor.

But Nebraska's offense started driving down the field late in the game, and Jeff Quinn, their quarterback, was completing everything he threw. The Cornhuskers had the ball at our three-yard line with ten seconds to play, and Quinn rolled out for another pass. But Piurowski chased him down and knocked the football loose, and Garry Futch recovered the fumble for us.

More than any other victory, I think beating Nebraska on the road probably put Florida State on the map. We'd beaten some pretty good teams in the past, and had even gone undefeated during the regular season in 1979. But beating a program such as Nebraska's in its own stadium told people that the Seminoles were a team that had to be taken seriously. Before that game, I don't think a lot of people had even heard of Florida State. We were well known enough to people in the South, but not all over the country.

After we upset the Cornhuskers, people everywhere were asking, "Who's Florida State?"

I know the Nebraska fans thought we were pretty good. They gave us a standing ovation as we left the field. I never saw a gesture like that from opposing fans again. I learned that day that Nebraska fans had just as much class as their coach.

We beat Pittsburgh, 36–22, at home the following week. They might have been the best team I ever coached against. Dan Marino was the quarterback; Russ Grimm and Mark May, two future NFL Hall of Famers, played on the offensive line; and Hugh Green was among the most dominant defensive linemen in college football history. Three decades later, I am still trying to figure out how we beat them.

We ended the 1980 regular season by beating Florida for the fourth consecutive time, after Stockstill threw two touchdown passes to Hardis Johnson in the second half of a 17–13 victory. We finished the regular season with a 10–1 record and were invited to play Oklahoma in the Orange Bowl for the second season in a row.

A few weeks before we played the Sooners in the 1981 Orange Bowl, I was contacted by Auburn officials about replacing Doug Barfield, who resigned after the 1980 season. My mother's brother was the president of a bank in Childersburg, Alabama, and he was pretty close to some of the big Auburn boosters. They were working through my uncle to contact me, and I agreed to meet Auburn officials at my uncle's home about a week before Christmas Day. I met with them for a couple of hours and listened to what they had to say. I drove back to Tallahassee after the meeting, unsure what I would do.

Since we were going to the Orange Bowl to play in the biggest game in Florida State history, I wanted to make sure that no one found out I was talking to Auburn. I did not want my boys distracted while they were preparing to play the Sooners. A couple of days before Christmas,

I received a telephone call from Harry Philpott, who was the president of Auburn University. He wanted me to come to Auburn and coach the football team.

"Look, I can't take this job," I told him. "I just signed a five-year contract extension, and I'll have to pay Florida State $750,000 if I leave."

"Well, resign from your job and we'll fight it in court," Philpott told me.

"I don't think I can do that," I told him. "Look, I'm getting ready to go play Oklahoma in the Orange Bowl. I don't want this situation distracting my team. Why don't you just hire Pat Dye from Wyoming? He coached with Bear Bryant and he knows everything Bear does. If you want to beat Alabama, go hire somebody who knows how to beat Bear."

Auburn did hire Dye, and he led them to four Southeastern Conference championships in twelve seasons.

If my team could beat Oklahoma in the Orange Bowl, we had a chance to win the 1980 national championship. Georgia was ranked number one in the country, and we were ranked number two heading into the bowl games. The Bulldogs were playing Notre Dame in the Sugar Bowl in New Orleans. If the Fighting Irish beat Georgia on New Year's Day 1981, and we defeated Oklahoma later that night, we would be crowned national champions. We watched the Sugar Bowl at our hotel before leaving for the Orange Bowl. Georgia's sensational freshman running back, Herschel Walker, scored two touchdowns, and the Bulldogs won the Sugar Bowl, 17–10.

My boys weren't deflated by Georgia's victory. We put up a much better fight against Oklahoma the second time. Early in the fourth quarter, Oklahoma botched its snap on a punt. Butler recovered the football in the end zone for a touchdown, and we took a 17–10 lead. Oklahoma gave us every chance to win the game, fumbling seven times and losing five of them.

But Watts engineered a methodical last-minute drive, throwing an eleven-yard touchdown to Steve Rhodes and a two-point conversion pass to Steve Valora with one minute, twenty-seven seconds to play. We lost the Orange Bowl, 18–17. I really believe Watts was one of the best big-game performers I ever faced. He made great decisions running the wishbone and was a tremendous leader on and off the field. It was no surprise to me that he later became a Baptist layman and four-term U.S. congressman.

After we lost to Oklahoma in the Orange Bowl for a second time, I wasn't sure we'd ever get that close to winning a national championship again. I knew we had the resources and the talent to win national titles at Florida State, but there is always so much luck involved. You usually have to win every one of your games, and you have to hope that other teams don't win all of theirs.

Heading into the 1981 season, I was not concerned about winning a national championship. I was only worried about surviving "Octoberfest," the five-week stretch of road games I had been dreading for years. Octoberfest actually did not end up being so bad. We lost at Nebraska, 34–14. But we won the next week at Ohio State, 36–27, and then beat Notre Dame, 19–13, in South Bend, Indiana. Dan Devine had resigned as the Fighting Irish's head coach after losing to Georgia in the Sugar Bowl, and Notre Dame had replaced him with Gerry Faust, a high school coach from Cincinnati. Stockstill threw two touchdown passes against the Fighting

Irish, including the game winner with fewer than eight minutes to go.

We had to play at Pittsburgh the next week. Dan Marino was back for his junior season, and I'm sure he wanted to get some revenge for what happened in Tallahassee the year before. The Panthers were just as good as they were in 1980 and beat us, 42–14. We finished Octoberfest by winning against LSU, 38–14. We beat Western Carolina, 56–31, in our eighth game to improve our record to 6–2. We went 3–2 during Octoberfest, but it really took its toll on my boys. They were just tired and beat up after traveling to so many games and playing so many difficult opponents.

We ended the 1981 season with a three-game losing streak. We played at Florida in the regular-season finale, and the winner of the game was going to be invited to play West Virginia in the Peach Bowl in Atlanta. I wasn't sure how I felt about playing my former team, but it didn't matter. Florida beat us, 35–3, in Gainesville, ending our four-game winning streak against the Gators.

The next five seasons ended up being an adjustment period for us. The University of Florida hired Charley Pell as its coach in 1979, and we really had problems recruiting against them. The Gators seemed to be getting the best high school players in the state. Florida ended up being placed on NCAA probation for recruiting violations, and Pell was fired three games into the 1984 season. That incident really seemed to change the momentum in the state of Florida.

We never had a bad season from 1982 to 1986. We had a winning record and went to a bowl game every year. But we seemed to get our momentum back in 1985, after we signed what we called our "Solid

Gold" recruiting class. That class included many of our best players at Florida State, including cornerback Deion Sanders, quarterback Peter Tom Willis, nose tackle Odell Haggins, running back Sammie Smith, and guard Pat Tomberlin.

We finished 9–3 in 1985 and defeated Oklahoma State, 34–23, in the Gator Bowl in Jacksonville, Florida. The next season, we finished 7–4–1, but played another difficult schedule. We lost at Nebraska, 34–17, and fell at Michigan, 20–18. We were upset by Florida, 17–13, in the regular-season finale, but were still invited to play against Indiana University in the All-American Bowl in my hometown of Birmingham.

Needless to say, I was pretty excited about going home again. I had not coached a game in Birmingham since leaving Howard College in 1962. On New Year's Eve 1986, the day we were going to play Indiana at Legion Field, Ray Perkins announced he was leaving the University of Alabama to become coach and general manager of the NFL's Tampa Bay Buccaneers. Word had already been circulating about the possibility of Perkins leaving Alabama, and many of my friends around the state were calling me and trying to persuade me to take the job.

After we beat the Hoosiers, 27–13, in the bowl game, reporters asked me if I was interested in coaching the Crimson Tide.

"Alabama's got to decide who Alabama will hire," I told them.

Another reporter asked me how long it would take me to consider an Alabama offer. "Like that," I said, while snapping my fingers.

The newspapers reported that I would leave Florida State at the drop of a hat, which was not really the case. Later that night, I received more telephone calls from influential people at Alabama, asking me if

I would be interested in replacing Perkins. Of course I was interested, but I did not want to interview for the job. I was perfectly happy at Florida State, after pouring my heart and soul into building a program for eleven years. But it was no secret that Alabama was my favorite team as a child, and when I was younger I always dreamed about coaching the Crimson Tide.

"Bobby, we want you to be our coach," they all told me. "The president wants to talk to you."

I told every one of them the same thing: "I don't want an interview. I will talk to the president if he offers me the job. But I am not applying for a job, and I am not interviewing for a job. I have a good job, and I am not looking for a different one. But if they offer me the job, I will be glad to talk to them."

Ann and I stayed in Birmingham an extra night. The next day, Dr. Gaylon McCollough, the starting center on Alabama's 1964 national championship team and a renowned plastic surgeon, called me and told me that Alabama president Joab Langston Thomas wanted to meet with me in Birmingham.

This is great, I thought. *I'm getting called back home. They're going to offer me the job.*

But I assumed too much. Gaylon picked me up that night and we went to a building in downtown Birmingham and walked into a conference room on the third floor. I thought I was going to meet with only President Thomas and a couple of the more influential boosters. But there were eighteen people sitting at a table when I walked in the room. They had a bunch of faculty members in the room, even a couple of ladies.

What are they doing? I thought. *They'll never be able to keep this meeting a secret.*

I sat there as they interviewed me.

Walter Lewis, who was one of the first African-American quarterbacks at Alabama, asked me how I felt about starting a minority quarterback.

"I already coached one at West Virginia," I told him. "It would not bother me."

During that interview, I tried to play the role of Paul "Bear" Bryant, the legendary Crimson Tide coach, as best as I could. I told them we would have grueling training camps and would play a physical brand of football. I told them my players would be fundamentally sound and "mean but clean," just like Coach Bryant's players were. I told them I'd do exactly what Coach Bryant did at Alabama.

After about an hour, President Thomas finally said, "Okay, let's break it up."

I got up and walked toward him to shake his hand. "Thank you for coming, Bobby," he told me.

I left, and the only thing I could think was, *They didn't offer me the dadgum job!*

Ann and I flew back to Tallahassee. When we drove down the street in front of our house, there were TV cameras all over our front yard. The media caught wind of my meeting in Birmingham, and many of the TV stations in Florida were already reporting that I was leaving for Alabama. Ann and I drove around the block, trying to think of what I was going to say. We didn't even know how we were going to get into our house.

I did the only thing I know how to do: I told the truth. "Nobody has offered me the Alabama job," I told the reporters. "I have not applied for the job. I will not go chasing after it. I've got a job, and I'm very happy here."

A few hours later, President Thomas called me from Alabama. "Bobby, we're going to hire Bill Curry," he said.

I could not believe it. I thought sure as heck they were going to offer me the job. Apparently when I told them I'd do exactly what Coach Bryant did at Alabama, that wasn't what they wanted to hear. President Thomas had wanted to hear "Ivy League." I talked too much about football, and how we had to win this championship and play in that bowl game, and how they were going to have to give me this and give me that.

I was really heartbroken. I'd been so confident about getting the job that when I went to a pep rally the night before the All-American Bowl, I was sitting there nearly in tears, because I didn't know how I was going to tell all the FSU people that I was leaving for Alabama. Of course, the way things turned out, I wouldn't have to.

The coach Alabama hired, Bill Curry, played football at Georgia Tech and was an all-pro center in the NFL. He was the head coach at his alma mater before going to Alabama, leading the Yellow Jackets to a 31–43–4 record in seven seasons. It was not a popular hire in Alabama.

Curry resigned as Alabama's coach after the 1989 season. He had a 26–10 record in three seasons but never beat Auburn, which is really important when you're the coach of the Crimson Tide. A few days later, I was at Los Angeles International Airport, waiting for a flight to Tokyo to coach in the Japan Bowl, a college football all-star game. I was paged over the loudspeaker, and they told me I had a long-distance telephone call. It was Garry Neil Drummond, who was a University of Alabama trustee and one of the school's biggest financial supporters.

"Bobby, we want you to come coach at Alabama," Garry told me. "Money is not an issue."

I got on the plane and flew to Tokyo. Alabama athletic director Cecil "Hootie" Ingram called me at my hotel the next day. He was the athletic director at Florida State for nine years before returning to Tuscaloosa, where he was born and raised.

"Bobby, you know I always wanted you to coach Alabama," Hootie told me.

"Well, let me think about it," I told him.

Ann was with me, and we talked about the situation. About an hour later, I called my attorney and told him to call Hootie. "Tell him that it's too late," I said. "I'm going to stay with Florida State."

I was sixty years old. By that time, I felt like FSU was my school. The University of Alabama was Bear Bryant's school. No matter what I could have done as Alabama's coach, it still would have been Coach Bryant's program. I could never have topped his accomplishments there. I always felt like Florida State was where God wanted me to be. When I didn't get the Alabama job the first time, I looked at it like, "Well, God must not want it to be." I was upset about it, but I believed it was God's will. He had a direction for me, just like He always has.

I received offers from other schools through the years, but I always told them I was not interested. Only once did I seriously consider coaching in the NFL. After the 1986 season, the Atlanta Falcons were thinking about changing head coaches. I secretly met with Falcons owner

Rankin Smith and a few of his executives at his plantation in Thomasville, Georgia. Oddly enough, his farm was called Seminole. We kept talking and they even sent their chief scout to Hawaii to be with me while I coached in the Hula Bowl, another college all-star game. We kept talking about the possibility, but I did not want to leave FSU. The Falcons hired Marion Campbell to replace Dan Henning. I never told anyone about the Falcons' interest in me because I like to protect people and they never actually said, "Hey, we want you to be our coach."

I always felt like I was better suited to coach college athletes than professional athletes. Ten years ago in Miami, Dan Marino asked me during a game of golf, "Why didn't you ever go into pro football?" I told him I didn't think I could motivate professional athletes. I could motivate college boys, but money is what motivates the pro players. To this day, I've never really wanted to coach pro ball.

I believed God had a destination for me, anyhow. It was Florida State. It was home. And I was about to find out there was nowhere else like it in college football.

CHAPTER 10

WHERE IS PABLO?

Pablo Lopez was an offensive tackle on our teams in the mid-1980s. Pablo grew up in a tough neighborhood in Miami, but was really starting to come into his own by his junior season, in 1986. He was a big boy, probably six feet four inches and 280 pounds. He was a star player at South Miami High School, where he played with Mike Shula, who later was the University of Alabama's quarterback and the Crimson Tide's head coach. Pablo was inconsistent during his first couple of seasons at Florida State, but I thought he had the potential to play in the National Football League.

Pablo was always a free spirit and was one of the most popular players on our team. He always had a great attitude and made jokes and pulled pranks on his teammates. But off the field, Pablo was starting to find direction in his life. He had a baby girl and married his girlfriend. He was starting to become a man.

Only four days after Pablo was married, he was murdered on the Florida State campus.

September 13, 1986, was one of the worst days of my life. It was the week after our second game in 1986, and we did not have a game that Saturday. I released the boys after practice on Friday, and most of them went home for the weekend. But Pablo injured his shoulder in our 34–17 loss at Nebraska the week before, so he stayed in Tallahassee to receive medical treatment.

On Friday night, Pablo watched television with three of his teammates in their off-campus apartment. Later that night, they attended a fraternity dance at Montgomery Gymnasium. Someone pulled a fire alarm during the dance, so everybody in the gym was evacuated into the parking lot. Police later told me that Pablo and another man argued after someone kicked the car Pablo was riding in. They argued for a while, and the man left and went to a friend's house. He came back with a shotgun and found Pablo.

"You're not going to shoot me," Pablo told him.

The man shot Pablo in the stomach. He died before the ambulance reached Tallahassee Memorial Regional Medical Center.

The police called me at about 1:30 A.M., and it was the sort of call you never want to receive as a football coach or a father. When your phone rings that early in the morning, you know one of your boys did something to get into trouble. I will never forget the scene I saw in the hospital. Most of our players were there, and they had not yet been told that Pablo was dead.

Ken Smith, our team chaplain, and I pulled all of the boys into the hospital's chapel. "Boys, Pablo is gone," I told them.

Immediately, many of my boys started wailing. They were on the floor kicking and screaming, and punching walls. It was complete chaos. I had never seen anyone react to death like that before. Fred Jones, one of our linebackers, played with Pablo in high school and was his college roommate. Fred was so overcome with grief he had to be treated at the hospital.

The next day, I called a team meeting. The boys filed into our meeting room, where each of them had an assigned seat. When the meeting started, Pablo's seat was obviously empty.

"Where is Pablo?" I asked my boys. "I know where Pablo is. He's in heaven, because I know Pablo was saved. Through the blood of Christ, he was saved and will spend eternity with Him. Where will you spend eternity when you die? Will you go to heaven with Pablo?"

I told the boys my office door was open if any of them wanted to talk to me about salvation. Many of my players came to talk to me. So did my quarterbacks coach, Mark Richt, who is now head coach at the University of Georgia. Mark accepted Christ as his Lord and savior that day. He has been deeply committed to Christ ever since.

Later that day, I had to pick up Pablo's mother and wife from the airport in Tallahassee. I spoke at his funeral a couple of days later.

"I've been coaching for about thirty-four years, and in those thirty-four years, I've had about three boys called," I said. "It seems to me that God only seems to call the ones that are ready."

When I talked to my boys about salvation, I often read them John 11:25–26:

Jesus said to her, "I am the resurrection and the life. He who believes in me will live, even though he dies; and whoever lives and believes in me will never die. Do you believe this?"

Throughout my coaching career, I felt it was my purpose to share my religious beliefs with my players. I promised God when I was a little boy that if He cured me of rheumatic fever, I would serve Him through coaching. I believed God's purpose for me on this earth was to nurture young men physically, mentally, and spiritually. I believed my job was to make faith available to those boys. I didn't beat them over the head with it, but I made it available to them. I told them, "Boys, this is what I believe. You don't have to believe what I believe, but this is the way it is. I hope and pray that you believe it, too."

Twice a year, I took my boys to church in Tallahassee. One Sunday, we would go to a predominantly white church and another weekend we would go to a predominantly African-American church. I always wrote their parents a letter before the season, letting them know what we were going to do. I told them that if they did not want their son to attend church, they could contact me and let me know. In thirty-four years of coaching at Florida State, only one of my players' parents asked that their son be excused from church service. Going to church was not a require-ment; it was completely voluntary.

When I recruited a young man, I told his parents, "When your boy comes to Florida State, you are out of the picture. You are hundreds of miles away, and your boy is on his own for the very first time. While he's in my hands, I'm going to do my best to do your job. I know you want your son to go to class. I know you want your son to stay out of trouble. I know you want your son to go to church. I am going to try to pick up right where you leave off. Is that okay?"

When I was young I went to church because my mamma and daddy made me go. When I went off to college, I went because I knew my par-ents wanted me to go. I just tried to fulfill the parents' roles while their boys were at college, and I really tried to point the boys in the right direc-tion. Our team chaplain, Clint Purvis, had Bible study during the week. We had a team chapel. We had a devotional before every coaching staff meeting. I had Christians speak to our teams before games. One time, Billy Graham spoke to my team before one of his revivals at Florida State.

But I never used a boy's religious beliefs against him. If he was good enough to play, he was going to play. I coached boys who were Baptist, Methodist, Protestant, and Catholic. I coached boys who were Muslim. I coached boys who were Jewish. On my team I had one Jewish boy whose older brother was a rabbi. I never forced my beliefs on any of them, and I believe they appreciated me for that. Faith is a personal thing, and it's every person's right to believe what they want to believe.

Shortly after I was named coach at West Virginia University in 1970,

I started recruiting a young man named Artie Owens. He was one of the fastest running backs I ever saw play. Artie was born in Montgomery, Alabama, but his family moved to Pennsylvania when he was a child. As a senior at Stroudsburg High School, Artie broke state records with 41 rushing touchdowns and 2,061 rushing yards. I had to have him. Every school in the country was trying to recruit Artie, but he ended up signing to play for the Mountaineers.

Even before Artie signed with West Virginia, I knew he was an atheist. He did not believe in God. Before every game, I would gather my players in the locker room and say a pregame prayer. I would always say, "If anyone does not believe in prayer, you do not have to participate. You can go stand in the tunnel and wait for us to go out on the field."

Before Artie's first game at West Virginia in 1972, he walked out of the locker room while we prayed. The next game, Artie did the same thing. By about the fourth or fifth game, I guess Artie got tired of leaving. He stayed in the locker room and listened to our prayer, and before long he was a Christian. Artie played five years in the NFL before retiring and now helps mentally handicapped adults in Pennsylvania.

You would not believe the number of boys who called me back after twenty or thirty years and told me, "Coach, I'm glad you shared the word with us." You would not believe how many of my boys serve as pastors and ministers.

There are probably a lot of people who believe I should not have been talking to my boys about religion. The American Civil Liberties Union never came to Florida State to complain about me teaching my boys about Christ and faith. I always waited for them to come and complain, but they never did. If they had complained about it, it just would have driven me underground. I would have done it without anyone knowing about it. Teaching my boys about faith meant that much to me, and I would not have cared if they fired me for doing it. I just would have said, "Boys, meet me in the basement."

The first assistant coach I hired at West Virginia University in 1970 was Chuck Klausing, who was head coach at Indiana University of Pennsylvania. Later Chuck became head coach of Carnegie Mellon University in Pittsburgh. He was a former marine and spent nearly forty years coaching football. A few years ago, Chuck and I were having a conversation about our problems in society today.

"Bobby, the boys have not changed," Chuck told me. "The parents have changed. Parents have quit raising their kids."

Chuck was right. Kids are raised differently now from when I was growing up. Too many children are neglected today, on too many levels. They're not shielded enough from negative influences. Mass media assault them with conflicting messages. Too many kids come from broken homes, or grow up without involved, guiding parents. I think boys who get into gangs do it because they so desperately want to be part of a family. That's where football can help them, and I witnessed it happen many times during my coaching career.

Todd Williams was an offensive lineman on my Florida State teams from 1999 to 2002. Todd's mother abandoned him when he was ten years old. Todd never knew his father, who was shot and killed in the streets when Todd was young. Todd was raised by his grandmother, Joyce James, in Bradenton, Florida. When his grandmother died of complications from diabetes in 1993, Todd was basically an orphan. The state planned to put him in a foster home, so Todd ran away. He slept on the streets in Bradenton and later moved to Miami, where the streets were a lot more dangerous. To survive, Todd stole women's purses and stripped cars to sell the parts at salvage yards. He was arrested a few times and was sentenced to a juvenile correctional facility. Finally, Todd decided he had to turn his life around. Before his grandmother died, Todd promised her he would graduate from high school and make something of himself.

Todd moved back to Bradenton and moved into an apartment on his own. To pay the bills, Todd worked in a grocery store after school. He enrolled at Bradenton Southeast High School and started making good grades. At six feet five inches and three hundred pounds, Todd was an enormous prospect. He eventually became a starting guard for us and was named All-Atlantic Coast Conference. He graduated from Florida State with academic degrees in criminal justice and sociology, and was named the NCAA's Inspirational Athlete of the Year during his senior season, in 2002.

During Todd's senior season, he gave a devotional to our team after parents' weekend. He told his teammates how envious he was after seeing their parents at the game the week before.

"I always wondered what it would feel like to have my mom and dad sitting in the stands cheering for me," Todd told his teammates. "I always wondered what it would feel like to see them wearing my jersey. I will never know. You guys don't know how lucky you are."

When Todd walked across the field at Doak Campbell Stadium to be honored on Senior Day against the University of Florida in 2002, he was escorted by many of the people who became his family. Clay Shiver, one of my former offensive linemen, who became Todd's mentor, walked him across the field, along with Clint Purvis. The woman who managed the apartment complex where Todd lived in Bradenton and mentored him was there, along with the pastors of the churches Todd attended.

Todd Williams and boys like him made it difficult for me to retire from coaching. I knew there were thousands of lost boys on the streets. I knew it was my job to help as many as I could. We had many players like Todd Williams on our Florida State teams.

Darnell Dockett was only thirteen years old when he found his mother murdered in 1994. Darnell and his older sister spent the night at their grandfather's home in Decatur, Georgia, one night, and when they walked into their mother's house the next morning, she was lying in a pool of blood in the hallway. Darnell's mother had a history of drug abuse, and the police never solved who killed her. Darnell was estranged from his father, who was dying of pancreatic cancer. Darnell's uncle, Kevin Dockett, took him into his home in Maryland, and Darnell tried to test him nearly every day. The boy just seemed to be filled with rage at times, and he was placed in special education classes because of his behavioral problems. But after administrators threatened to kick Darnell out of school, he turned his life around.

We signed Darnell to play on the defensive line for us in 1999. He wanted to play defensive end, but we thought he was better suited to play tackle. He was so upset about it he wanted to transfer to another school. When Darnell called his uncle in Maryland, Kevin Dockett told him he could not come home. Darnell had some problems at Florida

State, including being suspended from playing in the 2002 Sugar Bowl for accepting improper benefits. But after what Darnell went through as a child, what boy would not have problems? Darnell ended up setting a Florida State record with sixty-five tackles for loss during his career. He really became a dominant player for us, and was drafted in the third round by the Arizona Cardinals in the 2004 NFL draft.

Before Darnell's senior season, in 2003, he gave a devotional to his teammates. "I have one regret in life," Darnell told them. "I never told my mamma I loved her."

Darnell looked at Michael Boulware, one of our star linebackers.

"You have great parents," Darnell told Michael. "I want you to call them and tell them you love them. If you don't have a cell phone, you can use mine. Just please tell them that you love them. Please do it for me."

Greg Jones was a bruising running back for Florida State from 2000 to 2003. He was raised in Beaufort, South Carolina, by his grandmother Evelyn Middleton, who died of cancer when Greg was a junior in high school. Greg's mother lived in Virginia and his father lived in New York, so he was basically left to care for himself. Greg did not react well to his grandmother's death and started to skip classes and stay out late at night. But Greg turned things around during his senior season of high school and was one of the most heavily recruited players in the country.

Greg surprised a lot of his teammates when he delivered his first devotional before a game.

"You know what it is like to not be wanted?" Jones asked them. "When I was four months old, my mamma didn't want me. My daddy didn't want me. They basically threw me away to my grandmother, and left it up to her to raise me. When I was in high school, my grandmother died. God took away the only person who wanted me."

I tried to make every one of my players feel like they were wanted and loved. In more than half a century of coaching, I saw many cases in which football brought structure and a sense of family to a boy's life. The boys come to school now and they might look different from the boys I coached fifty years ago at South Georgia College and Howard College. But they are still the same boys I coached five decades ago. They just need someone to give them direction. That's why I always believed my job was to make them better athletes, better students, and better people. It was my hope that when they left me, they were going to become better fathers, husbands, and men.

CHAPTER 11

WIDE RIGHT

I was excited about the direction of the Florida State football program in 1987. We were coming off a 7–4–1 record in 1986, and now that the possibility of leaving Florida State for Alabama was in the rearview mirror, I was really anticipating the season. Most of the highly regarded freshmen we signed in 1985 were juniors, and it was time for them to step up to the plate. I knew players such as running back Sammie Smith and cornerback Deion Sanders were as good as anybody, but it was time for them to deliver. With nine starters coming back on both offense and defense, there were no more excuses at Florida State.

In our first team meeting, on August 11, 1987, I talked to the boys about what it would take for them to compete for a national championship. "You win championships when you decide as a team to play together and pay a price," I told them.

What kind of price would they have to pay? I told them what they would have to do:

- Make good grades and go to class.

- Project a positive image in the community and stay out of trouble.

- Stay away from drugs and alcohol.

- Excel in our strength and conditioning program.

- Play disciplined football on the field and follow coaches' instructions.

- Play and practice even with pain and not let nagging injuries keep you out of action.

- Block, tackle, and take care of the fundamentals of football.

- Play with enthusiasm and encourage your teammates.

- Win the fourth quarter and never quit.

Near the end of that first meeting, I drew a wall of stone on the chalkboard. I illustrated a wall built of larger stones and smaller ones. "You might be a pebble," I told my players. "You might be a rock. You might be a boulder. But we can't build a wall without every one of you."

In many ways that analogy reminded me of one of the first Bible songs I sang as a child.

> *Joshua fit the battle of Jericho*
> *Jericho, Jericho*
> *Joshua fit the battle of Jericho*
> *The walls come tumblin' down, Hallelujah*

In Sunday school we learned that God appeared before Joshua as he was leading his Israelite army in their conquest of Canaan. God ordered

Joshua to march his expansive army around the city once every six days, with seven priests carrying rams' horns in front of the ark. On the seventh day, the army was to march around Jericho seven times as the priests sounded their horns. And after Joshua ordered his army to shout, the walls of Jericho crumbled to the ground. Joshua's army charged into the city and destroyed it.

The Battle of Jericho is one of my favorite Bible stories because it teaches us that if we believe in God's will and have faith in Him, He will lead us into battle. Joshua was obedient and followed God's commands, and the Israelites were able to topple a fortress that was believed to be impenetrable. But the story also teaches us that no matter how thick we build walls, they can crumble if we do not have faith in God.

Would my boys have faith in each other heading into the 1987 season? Would they be willing to pay the price required to win a national championship? I was about to find out. Even though Florida State was still an independent, I believed we played in the most difficult conference in America—the state of Florida. From 1983 to 2009, Miami, FSU, and the University of Florida combined to win ten national championships. That's one about every three years. The University of Miami became a powerhouse under Howard Schnellenberger in the early 1980s, winning its first national championship, in 1983. Jimmy Johnson replaced Schnellenberger before the 1984 season, and nearly led the Hurricanes to another national title, in 1986. Miami was undefeated and ranked number one in the country when it lost to number two Penn State, 14–10, in the Fiesta Bowl at the end of the 1986 season. With a great defense led by All-American defensive back Bennie Blades and defensive end Daniel

Stubbs coming back, the Hurricanes would be difficult to beat again in 1987.

Going into the 1987 season, Florida State had a two-game losing streak against Miami. We had a six-game losing streak against Florida. We beat the Gators four of the first five times I coached against them. I was naive enough to think there was nothing hard about playing Florida. It was going to be easy, right? But then we just could not find a way to beat the Gators from 1981 to 1986, losing in close games and routs along the way.

When Ann and I had the 1987 senior class to our house for a barbecue a couple of weeks before the season opener, linebackers Paul McGowan and Terry Warren showed up with their hair cut into Mohawks. I told them if we finished the 1987 season with an undefeated record, I would do the same. Before our season opener against Texas Tech on September 5, 1987, I told my boys, "Make it come true. I want it to happen."

For the first month of the season, Ann was getting a little worried. She didn't want her husband coming home with a Mohawk. We blew out our first four opponents, scoring at least thirty points each against Texas Tech, East Carolina, Memphis State, and Michigan State. Our defense was playing really well, too. I hired Mickey Andrews as our defensive coordinator before the 1984 season, after Jack Stanton left to work for the NFL's Atlanta Falcons. Mickey played for Coach Bear Bryant at the University of Alabama and really knew how to win. Mickey won two national championships as a player at Alabama, and led Livingston College in Alabama to a small-school national title as its head coach. Mickey would become one of my closest confidants and an even closer friend.

We played Miami in our fifth game of the 1987 season, on October 3,

1987. Miami was ranked number three in the country; we were ranked number four. I really thought playing Miami was a litmus test for us. If we could beat Miami at home, it would prove we were finally on the same level with the Hurricanes. I told the media that week, "They've played for the national championship before. They've been in the top ten all along. We're here for the first time in almost ten years. This is where we find out if we belong here."

Of course, those Miami teams had a real swagger about them. I loved the way the Hurricanes played with so much enthusiasm, but I really started tightening things up at Florida State in 1987. I did not want anything to prevent us from being as good as we could be. I banned earrings, muscle shirts, and hats from the locker room. I was so strict Deion Sanders told the *Washington Post* I would probably have them wearing "double-breasted suits with a Bible in [their] hands." I wanted our boys to look like football players and act like gentlemen.

In our locker room at Doak Campbell Stadium before the game, I told our players Miami intimidated Florida and Arkansas in its first two games. The Hurricanes blasted the number-twenty-ranked Gators, 31–4, and then crushed number-ten-ranked Arkansas, 51–7, on the road three weeks later. Jimmy Johnson did not hold anything back against Arkansas, his alma mater. "Are you going to let them intimidate you?" I asked my boys. "Everybody says Miami has the best defense in the country. But I think our defense is better."

There was probably more future NFL talent on the field against Miami in 1987 than in any other game I coached. I told Paul McGowan he had to play better than George Mira Jr., Miami's star linebacker. I told Deion and our other defensive backs they had to cover receivers better than Miami's secondary did. I told Terry Warren and Shelton Thompson they had to rush Miami quarterback Steve Walsh better than Stubbs rushed our quarterback Danny McManus. "We have to intimidate Walsh," I told our defense. "If we don't, he will hurt us."

For nearly three quarters, we turned the tables on the Hurricanes and intimidated them. We had a 10–3 lead at halftime, and then blocked a punt and returned it for a touchdown. We kicked another field goal for a 19–3 lead. But things went downhill from there. We lost, 26–25. Miami finished 12–0 and won the 1987 national championship, beating Oklahoma, 20–14, in the Orange Bowl. We won the rest of our games, defeating Nebraska, 31–28, in the Fiesta Bowl, and finished 11–1 and ranked number two in the country in the final polls.

A couple of weeks after we beat the Cornhuskers in the Fiesta Bowl, we had our first team meeting of the 1988 season. I told the team we were probably going to be ranked number one in most of the preseason polls. I warned my players of the consequences that came with being so highly regarded. "Never before has an FSU squad entered the season with so much expectation," I told them. "We are going to face the most demanding pressure ever. We will be under the media's eye every minute. The national media will be waiting for us to screw up. Do not give Miami bulletin-board material this summer!"

We were opening the 1988 season against the Hurricanes, the defending national champions, at the Orange Bowl stadium. Miami had beaten us three consecutive times. I didn't want to give the Hurricanes any added motivation when they played us. Late in the summer, Ann and I traveled to Europe. While I was away, a Florida State booster came up with what he thought was a great idea. He got my players together, and they decided to produce a rap video, kind of like the "Super Bowl Shuffle" the Chicago Bears made during their Super Bowl–winning season in 1985. When I came home from Europe, the boys wanted me to appear in the video. But I wanted no part of it. I could have killed it right there, but I was afraid I might ruin team morale. Besides, I had other things to worry about. Deion Sanders left Tallahassee to play minor-league baseball in the New York Yankees' farm system, and when he came back he had to pass an algebra course in summer school to remain eligible. And the NCAA sent some of its investigators to Tallahassee to look into some alleged rules violations that were not true, but that became a distraction nonetheless.

The kids were very excited about the video, so I let them do it. When I saw the video, the dadgum thing was about four minutes long. The lyrics went something like this:

> *We are the Seminoles of Florida State,*
> *We know we're good; some say we're great.*
> *Our goal is simple—best in the land,*
> *Rockin' to the beat of the Marching Chiefs Band.*
> *On Saturday night, we'll show our stuff,*
> *We'll show the nation how we're tough.*

I didn't like the video. Deion and Odell Haggins had big roles in it, and both of our quarterbacks, Chip Ferguson and Peter Tom Willis, appeared in the video as well. After watching some of my boys rap in the thing, I thought it might actually have been better if I participated. I was terrified of it. I just knew Jimmy Johnson was down in Miami playing the video in his team's locker room every minute of every day, because when we went to the Orange Bowl to open the season, Miami beat us, 31–0. We couldn't do anything right. Ferguson threw two interceptions. Sammie was held to only six rushing yards. Walsh threw all over our defense. They just killed us on national TV, and it was embarrassing. Our number one ranking lasted all of sixty minutes.

We came back and beat Southern Mississippi, 49–13, at home the next week, and then traveled to play Clemson at Death Valley in Clemson, South Carolina, on September 17, 1988. The Tigers were ranked number three in the country; we fell to number ten after losing so badly at Miami two weeks earlier. We really needed something good to happen against Clemson to turn our season around. We took a 21–14 lead into the fourth quarter, but Clemson tied the score at 21 on Tracy Johnson's nineteen-yard touchdown run with two minutes, thirty-two seconds left.

Clemson kicked off to us, and our offense couldn't do much of anything. We faced fourth-and-four at our twenty-one-yard line with one minute, thirty-three seconds to play. Any sane coach in the country would have punted the football and hoped his defense made a stop to have the game end in a tie. But Clemson had momentum and I wanted someone to win the game. I called a play we installed in practice earlier in the year. It was called "puntrooski," and I'm not sure I called a more risky play in all my years of coaching.

We sent punter Tim Corlew onto the field, and he lined up like he was going to punt. But center David Whittington snapped the football to Dayne Williams, who was one of our blocking backs. Williams took one step forward, hunched over, and placed the football between the legs of LeRoy Butler. Corlew jumped high into the air, trying to convince the Clemson defense the snap sailed over his head. Williams waited a second and took off running to his right, with a wall of blockers in front of him. But Butler had the football and, fortunately for us, he was all alone. LeRoy ran seventy-eight yards down the left sideline before he was tackled at Clemson's one-yard line. We scored a touchdown a couple of plays later, but officials ruled the twenty-five-second clock had not started and took the touchdown off the scoreboard. Richie Andrews kicked a nineteen-yard field goal to win the game, 24–21.

More than any other play, "puntrooski" probably earned me the moniker "riverboat gambler," which is what a lot of people called me back then. But I actually stole the play from Jerry Claiborne, who coached at Virginia Tech. When I was an assistant at Florida State in 1965, Jerry ran the play against us two times. I used it a couple of times in a running formation at West Virginia, but never tried it in a punt formation before we played Clemson. Clint Ledbetter, who was one of our graduate assistants in 1988, ran the play when he played at Arkansas State. He had film of the "puntrooski" and showed it to us.

Beating Clemson really turned our season around in 1988. We won every game after losing at Miami and finished with an 11–1 record. We beat Florida for the second season in a row, after losing six games in a row to the Gators, and defeated Auburn, 13–7, in the Sugar Bowl. We finished the season ranked number three in the country, behind national champion Notre Dame and number two Miami.

I was very concerned about the upcoming season in 1989. We lost three starting offensive linemen and were replacing them with two sophomores and a freshman. We lost three starting defensive backs, including Sanders, who was the fifth pick in the 1989 NFL draft by the Atlanta Falcons. Deion was one of the best pure athletes I ever coached. Bob Harbison, our offensive line coach, recruited Deion out of Fort Myers, Florida. Bob said he was the best defensive prospect he ever saw, and Bob was a pretty good judge of talent. Deion was a great player as soon as he arrived on campus. He started as a freshman as our nickel back and would go into the game when we played five defensive backs. Then his career really took off.

During Deion's sophomore season, in 1987, he played on the FSU baseball team as an outfielder and ran sprints for the track-and-field team. During one weekend, he played in a baseball doubleheader in the Metro Conference tournament, and then he went and ran a leg of the four-hundred-meter relay race and the one-hundred- and two-hundred-yard dash at the conference track-and-field meet, winning each event. He went back to the baseball game and had the game-winning hit in the championship game. In 1992, Deion played with the Atlanta Falcons and Atlanta Braves on consecutive days. He was just an unbelievable athlete, and going into the 1989 season I was not sure how we were going to replace him.

I learned in our 1989 opener against Southern Mississippi that it was not going to be easy. We played the Golden Eagles at the Gator Bowl stadium in Jacksonville, Florida, on September 2, 1989. Southern Miss had a quarterback named Brett Favre. We had already played against Favre twice, beating his teams 61–10 in 1987 and 49–13 in 1988.

We were ranked number six in the country in the preseason and were heavy favorites to beat Southern Miss. But Favre threw a two-yard touchdown pass to tight end Anthony Davis with twenty-three seconds left to beat us by a 30–26 score. Of course, everybody says Favre beat us, and he did hurt us that day. But the guy who really hurt us was a freshman named Timmy Smith. Southern Miss had a player who led the country in kickoff returns in 1988. We were determined we were not going to kick the ball to him. So we kept kicking it to Timmy Smith after we scored, and he kept bringing the football back to our forty-yard line. Favre would have a short field to work with, and he kept matching us score for score. If we would have kicked the ball out of bounds, we probably would have won the game.

We played Clemson in Tallahassee the next week and lost, 34–23. We were 0–2, and everybody in Tallahassee thought the sky was falling. If we had won one of those first two games, we probably would have won the national championship in 1989. Why? We finally beat Miami.

We played the Hurricanes at Doak Campbell Stadium on October 28, 1989. Miami was ranked number two in the country, and we had climbed our way back up to sixth after winning five games in a row. Miami had a thirteen-game winning streak and had won forty-eight of its previous forty-nine regular-season games. Obviously the Hurricanes were very difficult to beat. But during the summer before the 1989 season, I told the FSU booster groups I spoke to that I wouldn't lose to Jimmy Johnson again. Of course, Johnson left Miami for the NFL's Dallas Cowboys after the 1988 season and was replaced by Dennis Erickson.

We seemed to be more relaxed before we played Miami in 1989. I know I was more relaxed. When my players and assistant coaches looked for me to deliver a pregame speech, I was sleeping in a chair in front of the chalkboard. No one wanted to wake me up. I did not have to say much to get my boys ready to play. I read them two postgame quotes from Miami players after the Hurricanes whipped us 31–0 in 1988. "Our third-stringers could have put up a better game," Miami defensive lineman Willis Peguese told the *Miami Herald*. "I felt Florida State quit after the first series."

Added Hurricanes cornerback Roland Smith: "Florida State can be easily intimidated."

My boys were even more motivated to play the Hurricanes after Miami's players tried to stop Chief Osceola and Renegade from galloping to midfield to plant a flaming spear in the turf during pregame warm-ups. They took out their anger on Miami's offense. Our defense intercepted freshman quarterback Gino Torretta four times. Linebacker Kirk Carruthers intercepted two passes and recovered a Miami fumble at our one-yard line. Dexter Carter ran for 142 yards and we won the game, 24–10.

The Hurricanes still ended up winning the 1989 national championship, finishing 11–1 and defeating Alabama, 33–25, in the Sugar Bowl. We won our last ten games, including a 41–17 victory over Nebraska in the Fiesta Bowl, and finished 10–2.

Miami got its revenge against us the next season, pulling off a 31–22 upset at the Orange Bowl stadium on October 6, 1990. The Hurricanes had two good backs, Leonard Conley and Stephen McGuire, and our defense could not stop either of them. The Hurricanes ran for 334 yards and really whipped us. We were ranked number two in the country before that loss. Adding salt to the wounds, number one Notre Dame lost to Stanford, 36–31, on the same day. We lost at Auburn, 20–17, two weeks later and were knocked out of the national championship race. We beat Penn State, 24–17, in the Blockbuster Bowl and finished 10–2.

When I met with my team before the 1991 season, I wanted to make sure they knew I was not obsessed with winning a national championship. By then the media were starting to say and write that I had "Bo Schembechler Syndrome." Bo was a great coach at the University of Michigan, leading the Wolverines to nearly two hundred victories in twenty-one seasons, but he never led them to a national championship. In 1991, Tom Osborne had been the head coach at the University of Nebraska for nearly two decades, but still had not won a national title. Of course, Tom would win at least a share of three national championships before he retired. But heading into the 1991 season, everybody was saying Tom and I were the best coaches never to have won a championship. Everybody else believed I could not lead my team to victory in a big game when it really mattered. They all said, "He can't win the big one."

I wanted to win a title badly, but I wasn't consumed by it. "I am frustrated over not winning a national championship," I told my players during a team meeting on August 6, 1991. "I am not obsessed with it, but I would like to win one before I am done. When will we win a national championship? When our players realize it is within their realm of potential. When they are willing to pay the price it takes."

We opened the 1991 season ranked number one in the country again. I wanted to make sure my team did not make the same mistakes we made in 1988. We were overconfident and cocky in '88, and I was determined it would not happen again. At the time, I told the media it was a case of putting on too much perfume. "It's okay to smell like perfume," I said. "But in 1988 we took a bath in it."

There were plenty of reasons to be excited about Florida State football in 1991. Our quarterback Casey Weldon was a Heisman Trophy candidate. We had two great running backs, Edgar Bennett and Amp Lee, and Terrell Buckley was one of the best defensive backs I ever coached. Carruthers and Marvin Jones, our two great linebackers, were both coming back.

We opened the 1991 season against Brigham Young University in the Disneyland Pigskin Classic in Anaheim, California. The Cougars were led by quarterback Ty Detmer, who won the Heisman Trophy as a junior in 1990. BYU was a formidable opponent to start the season, and I wanted to make sure my boys knew it. "They say we can't do it," I told my team before the game. "They say Florida State will fall on its face again. But do you know why we're going to win? Our seniors won't let us lose!"

Weldon, one of our seniors, had one of his best games against BYU. He completed twenty-one of twenty-eight passes for 268 yards with two touchdowns and really outplayed Detmer in our 44–28 victory. Bennett, another senior, ran for 101 yards with three touchdowns. We played at Michigan in our fifth game, and Buckley intercepted a pass and returned it forty yards for a touchdown on the second play of the game. Casey threw two touchdowns in the second half, and we beat the number-three-ranked Wolverines, 51–31, in front of a crowd of 106,145 fans at Michigan Stadium. We won our first ten games, and few of the games were very close. We trailed Louisiana State 16–14 going into the fourth quarter at Tiger Stadium on October 26, but we scored two touchdowns in the fourth quarter to win, 27–16.

I do not think I ever coached in a more anticipated game than against Miami on November 16, 1991. Since early in the summer, fans across the country had been circling the game on their calendars. We were ranked number one in the country the entire season and had a sixteen-game winning streak; the Hurricanes were ranked number two and had won fifteen games in a row. It was the twenty-sixth matchup of number one vs. number two in college football history, but the first time since number one Purdue beat number two Notre Dame in 1966 that teams from the same state played in such a game. When I first started coaching at Florida State, we could not give away tickets to the Miami game. No one wanted to see it. In fact, Schnellenberger and I had to act like circus promoters to drum up interest. Schnellenberger flew to Tallahassee in 1982 and we staged a weigh-in like boxers before a heavyweight bout. The following year, Howard flew to Tallahassee and we stood in a boxing ring wearing gloves to promote the game. There just was not a lot of interest in the state.

Of course, that changed during the late 1980s and early 1990s, when it seemed we were playing the Hurricanes for a national championship every season. Florida State's sports information department issued 550 media credentials for the 1991 game at Doak Campbell Stadium. You could not find a ticket anywhere. The twenty-five-dollar tickets were being scalped for as much as five hundred dollars, which was unheard of at the time. I had friends calling me every day looking for tickets. A citrus grower in Florida even offered me oranges and grapefruits for the rest of my life if I could find him a pair of tickets.

The 1991 game against Miami was being billed as the "Game of the Century," and it certainly lived up to its hype. Our defense was dominant in the first half against Miami. We sacked Torretta six times and forced him to throw two interceptions inside our fifteen-yard line. Our fans were going nuts, but I was concerned standing on the sideline. We missed a couple of chances to score touchdowns in the second half and settled for short field goals. Instead of leading the Hurricanes by a comfortable margin, we had a 16–7 lead early in the fourth quarter. Miami's Carlos Huerta kicked a forty-five-yard field goal to make the score 16–10 with about ten minutes to play. Late in the game, Torretta completed a fourth-down pass to Horace Copeland for a first down at our twelve-yard line. Miami fullback Larry Jones ran for a one-yard touchdown three plays later, and Huerta's extra-point kick gave Miami a 17–16 lead with three minutes, one second to play.

On the sideline, my boys were still confident we were going to win the game. Weldon did a great job leading our offense down the field. We moved the ball inside Miami's twenty-yard line with less than one minute to play. But we were out of time-outs, so I sent Gerry Thomas on the field to kick a thirty-four-yard field goal. With twenty-nine seconds to play, I heard Gerry's foot hit the ball. I heard our fans roar. I thought the field goal was good. "Hey, didn't we get that?" I yelled.

"Naw, we missed it," somebody said.

"What the heck happened?" I asked.

Wide Right

The ball had sailed inches to the right of the goalpost's uprights. The kick was wide right.

I think I was in a state of disbelief. Once again, Miami took away our national championship. The 1991 game hurt worse than all the previous losses to the Hurricanes because my boys did everything right. They were focused, worked hard, and stayed together as a team. The following Monday, I met with my seniors. According to my notes from the meeting, I told them "it was time to put up or shut up." I still thought we had a chance to play for a national championship if we beat Florida in our regular-season finale and won our bowl game.

"After the next two games, the 1991 team will be either the best team in Florida State history or the most disappointing team in school history," I told them. "Why are we different today than we were two weeks ago? We're ranked number three instead of number one, but we're still as talented as we were two weeks ago. Our confidence and spirit have to remain intact. Can you inspire this team to play its hardest? Will you finish your careers as Florida State's best team or its biggest letdown?"

The Gators, who won their first SEC championship in their second season under Steve Spurrier in 1991, beat us by a 14–9 score in Gainesville. We finished 11–2 after beating Texas A&M, 10–2, in the Cotton Bowl on New Year's Day 1992. Miami won the 1991 national championship, finishing 12–0, and defeating Nebraska, 22–0, in the Orange Bowl.

Florida State joined the Atlantic Coast Conference in 1992 and we won every game but one: Miami. We were ranked number three and Miami was ranked number two when we played in the Orange Bowl stadium on October 3. Tamarick Vanover, one of the best freshmen we ever had, returned the opening kickoff ninety-four yards for a touchdown. We had a 7–0 lead after only sixteen seconds. But the game turned into a defensive slugfest, with both teams struggling to score points. We fell behind, 17–16, in the fourth quarter, and then gave up a safety on a special-teams mistake that gave Miami a 19–16 lead. Our quarterback Charlie Ward put together a great two-minute drive in the final seconds. But on the final play, Dan Mowery missed a thirty-nine-yard field goal wide right—how else?—and we lost the game. We finished 11–1 after beating Nebraska, 27–14, in the Orange Bowl.

I am not going to lie: losing to Miami year after year was frustrating. As good as our teams were, we still had not won a national championship, primarily because we kept losing to the Hurricanes on missed kicks. I used to get mad because no other contender was playing Miami, but I still had to play the Hurricanes every year. Notre Dame quit playing them. Florida quit playing them. Penn State quit playing them. But Miami was still on my schedule every season, and it was always the game that made or broke our season. At one point I said, "When I die, they'll put on my tombstone, 'At least he played Miami.'"

It really felt like the Miami Hurricanes were a wall standing between Florida State and a national championship. But before long, that wall, too, would come tumblin' down.

CHAPTER 12

UNSEEN EYES

The night before every football game, we gathered our players in our locker room, or in the conference room of a hotel if we were playing on the road. We met for an hour or so, talking about the keys on offense, defense, and special teams. More important, someone delivered a devotional at the start of the meeting. Sometimes I delivered it, but oftentimes one of my players, coaches, or team chaplains talked about something important to them.

One of the devotionals I often liked to tell our players was a story I heard many years ago. It was about Lou Little, who was a famous football coach at Columbia University in New York from 1930 to 1956. He led Columbia to a victory in the 1934 Rose Bowl over Stanford University and coached the famous novelist Jack Kerouac and Sid Luckman, who was a great T-formation quarterback for the Chicago Bears during the 1940s.

Little also coached at Georgetown University in Washington, D.C., from 1924 to 1929. There, he coached a defensive tackle who probably weighed two hundred pounds, which was very big back in those days. Little worked with the boy every day, but the young man just did not get any better. But the boy was persistent, worked hard, and had a great attitude. In fact, the boy never missed a practice in his four seasons on the team. Three or four days before the boy's final game at Georgetown, Little received a telegram that informed him the boy's father had died. Little had seen the boy walking with his father. "Son, I am sorry," Little told him. "But your father passed away. Go home and take care of your family. We'll try to win this game for you."

That Saturday, Little walked into his team's locker room and was surprised to see the boy standing there. "Coach, you have to start me," the boy said.

"Son, you have never been a starter," Little told him. "This is the championship game. I cannot take that kind of risk today."

"Coach, I have to do this for my father," the boy pleaded. "Just put me in for the first play and then you can take me out of the game."

Little was overcome with sympathy. How could he not grant the boy his wish? So he put the boy in the starting lineup, and the boy ran down the field to cover the game's opening kickoff. He tackled the player returning the kick so hard he nearly knocked him into the first row of seats. The boy jumped up and ran to the sideline just like he promised his coach he would do, but Little motioned to him to stay in the game.

During the rest of the afternoon, the boy played like he was possessed. He led Georgetown's team in tackles and delivered big hit after big hit. Georgetown won the game and claimed a conference championship.

Little pulled the boy aside during the team's celebration in its locker room. "Son, what in the world got into you today?" Little asked him. "You've never played like that before. You've never shown that much desire in four years."

"Coach, you know my father died," the boy said. "You know my father was blind. Today was the first time he could see me play."

I met Little at a coaches' convention in Washington, D.C., during the late 1960s. I asked him if that story was true, and he told me it was. After watching Warrick Dunn play at Florida State for four seasons, I can only imagine he played as hard and with as much passion as that boy at Georgetown University for the same reason. Warrick had someone watching over him, too.

We recruited Warrick while he was a senior at Catholic High School in Baton Rouge, Louisiana. On January 7, 1993—about a month before Warrick signed a scholarship to play football at Florida State—his mother was murdered while escorting a grocery store manager to a bank to make a night deposit. Betty Dunn Somers, a corporal in the Baton Rouge police department, was thirty-six. Two days after his eighteenth birthday, Warrick and his grandmother were left to raise his five siblings.

After Warrick left for college, his brothers and sisters moved in with his grandmother, Willie Wheeler. I was not sure how Warrick would react to being away from his family. He was still dealing with the grief of losing his mother. But Warrick became a roommate with Charlie Ward, our quarterback, and that was the best thing that could have happened to Warrick. Both were very quiet and very much alike. Charlie is from Thomasville, Georgia, which is just across the state line from Tallahassee, and his parents adopted Warrick in many ways.

Warrick was a quarterback and a defensive back in high school. We recruited him to play defense, but Warrick wanted to play running back. He was pretty small, only about five feet nine inches and 173 pounds, and we weren't sure he could take the punishment of running the ball some twenty times a game. But his mother wanted him to attend Florida State, so he was going to sign a national letter of intent to play for us. "Warrick, we have all the running backs we can take," I told him. "If you come to Florida State, you have to play defense. Will you do that?"

"Yes, Coach Bowden," Warrick told me. "But will you promise me you will at least give me a chance to play running back?"

"I'll give you a chance to run the ball," I said. "But if it comes down to it, you have to agree to play defense."

We opened preseason camp in August 1993, and Warrick was playing defense. Before one of our scrimmages, Warrick came to me and reminded me of my promise to let him try out at running back. So we put him on offense, and no one could tackle him. After that day, Warrick was a running back for the rest of his career, and I am not sure we ever had a better runner at Florida State. Warrick will always be one of my favorite players. From time to time, he came to my office and talked about one of his brothers or sisters getting into trouble or having problems in school. "Coach, what should I do?" he asked me. I always told him to go home and get it straightened out. He drove all the way to Baton Rouge, worked things out with his family, and then came back to Florida State. It was just so much for a nineteen-year-old boy to handle, but Warrick never complained and helped his grandmother raise his brothers and sisters well.

After Warrick left Florida State, he played for the Tampa Bay Buccaneers and Atlanta Falcons and became one of the NFL's best running backs. More important, he became one of the NFL's best ambassadors. He established the Warrick Dunn Foundation and Homes for the Holidays, which have provided financial assistance for many single mothers to buy houses for their families. He was named NFL Man of the Year and was honored by former president Bill Clinton for his charitable work. I do not know if I have ever been more proud of one of my former players.

I have said this many times: Florida State would never have won the 1993 national championship without Warrick. It was almost as if Warrick was the missing piece to the puzzle. We had a great defense coming back, and I expected great things from Charlie Ward during his senior season, in 1993. Charlie was a tremendous athlete and starred on Florida State's basketball team before becoming our starting quarterback. I was so confident Charlie was going to win the Heisman Trophy as college football's best player that I told Rob Wilson, our sports information director, not to even launch a campaign for him. "We'll just mess it up," I said. "Charlie is going to win the thing on his own."

It did not look that way one year earlier. Like most of our quarterbacks, Charlie waited until his junior season to become a starter. He replaced Casey Weldon as the starter in 1992, and Charlie really struggled during his first few games. He threw four interceptions in our 1992 opener, against Duke. He threw four more interceptions against Clemson the next game. Charlie was such a good runner we thought we could utilize the option with him, so we had him under center working out of an I-formation. But we later found out that when Charlie dropped back to pass and turned his shoulders, he could not see down the field very well. He could not read what the defense was doing.

But when we put him in the shotgun for our hurry-up, two-minute offense late in the first half or late in a game, he always played much better. "If the boy is better in the shotgun, why don't we just leave him in the shotgun?" I asked Mark Richt, our offensive coordinator.

We played at Georgia Tech two weeks later, and it looked like we were going to lose again. We trailed, 21–7, going into the fourth quarter. I told Mark to put Charlie in the shotgun for the rest of the game because we were going to throw the ball on every down. Immediately, Charlie led us down the field, and William Floyd ran for a one-yard touchdown to make it 21–14. After Georgia Tech kicked a field goal to take a 24–14 lead, Charlie took us back down the field and ran for a five-yard touchdown to make it 24–20 with three minutes, twenty seconds to play. We got the football back by recovering an onside kick, and Charlie took us right back down the field again. He threw a seventeen-yard touchdown pass to Kez McCorvey to give us a 27–24 lead with one minute, forty-eight seconds left. Our defense added a safety in the final seconds and we won the game, 29–24.

The following week, we won our first Atlantic Coast Conference championship by beating the University of Virginia, 13–3, on the road. A week later, we unveiled our "fast break" offense against the University of Maryland at Doak Campbell Stadium on November 7, 1992. It was pretty fast, too. With Charlie working out of the shotgun on every play, we scored six touchdowns in the first half and led, 42–7, at halftime. We passed for 424 yards and ran for 434 yards against the Terrapins. We scored seventy points against Tulane University the next week and beat Florida, 45–24, in our regular-season finale. After beating the University of Nebraska, 27–14, in the Orange Bowl on New Year's Day 1993, I was really excited about our offense going into the 1993 season. After throwing fifteen interceptions in the first eight games in 1992, Charlie threw only three in the last four games. No one could slow him down.

When I met with our 1993 team for the first time that spring, I told them if we had eliminated one play from each of the previous four seasons, we would have won a national championship every year. "We have to take care of the little things," I told them. "We have to have perfect execution. There is absolutely no room for error. There is only one thing left to win: a national championship. We have accomplished everything else."

I thought we might have the country's best offense going into the 1993 season, but I was not as optimistic about our defense. We were going to have to replace most of our starters, including linebacker Marvin Jones, who left school after his junior season in 1992. Marvin won the Butkus Award as the country's top linebacker and was the fourth pick by the New York Jets in the 1993 NFL draft. We also lost defensive linemen Carl Simpson and Dan Footman and linebacker Reggie Freeman, who were second-round choices in the NFL draft. And we had to replace both starting safeties, John Davis and Leon Fowler, and Sterling Palmer, another starting linebacker. I nearly lost Mickey Andrews, our defensive coordinator, after he interviewed for the head coaching job at the

University of Houston. I was disappointed Mickey did not get the job, but I was very happy to have him back at Florida State.

We were ranked number one in the country by almost every college football poll heading into the 1993 season. I always preferred that my teams start somewhere in the top five, but I thought there was added pressure that came with being number one. Every opponent was going to play its best game against you, and you felt like you were walking into every stadium with a bull's-eye on your back. A number-one ranking also brings a lot of media attention and interview requests, which might become distractions if your team does not handle the spotlight well. Of course, one of the big story lines going into the preseason in 1993 was if Bobby Bowden would finally win a national championship. I was not consumed by winning a national championship, but I certainly wanted to win a title before I retired.

In an interview with Craig Barnes of the *Fort Lauderdale Sun Sentinel* a couple of weeks before the 1993 season, I tried to explain my feelings about not having won a national championship. "If I left the game tomorrow, it's something that would be missing from my résumé, but my faith tells me there are things in life more important than a national championship," I told him. "I'd like to have it for Florida State, for all the boys who have played for me, and for all the people who have supported our program through the years. I'm aware the near-misses have been more frustrating to others than to me, but they shouldn't think I don't want it. Naturally, I want it, and our intensity to pursue it won't be reduced until we get it."

I believed our 1993 team was talented enough and experienced enough to compete for a national championship. But we had to fill many holes on defense and had to stay healthy. During the first week of preseason camp, we lost three players to season-ending knee injuries. Cornerback Corey Fuller, safety Steve Gilmer, and running back Tiger McMillon were lost for the season, and I didn't think we could afford to lose any of them at the time. The good news: Charlie Ward looked sharp after undergoing surgery to clean up his left, nonthrowing shoulder during the off-season. The surgery did not seem to affect Charlie at all, and I was really happy with the way he was practicing.

We opened the 1993 season against the University of Kansas in the Kickoff Classic at Giants Stadium in East Rutherford, New Jersey. We were an overwhelming favorite in the game, but I wanted to see how our defense would play and if our new kicker could handle game-type pressure. After "Wide Right I" and "Wide Right II" against the University of Miami, I was determined that we would not lose another game on a missed field goal. Before the 1993 season, we signed Scott Bentley of Aurora, Colorado, who was the most highly recruited kicker in the country. Scott kicked a fifty-eight-yard field goal in high school, but it came in the high altitude of the Rocky Mountains. He even appeared on the cover of *Sports Illustrated* with actor Burt Reynolds, a former Florida State player, before the season started. Because of our kicking problems of the past, Scott was facing enormous pressure. Scott suffered a hip injury and pulled his groin during preseason camp, so I was very anxious to see him kick.

Our defense and kicking game were certainly up to the challenge in a 42–0 victory over the Jayhawks. Charlie threw only twenty-six passes in the game, and we unveiled our "Kentucky Derby" offense, in which the second-string players would take the field for the first play of possessions. The first string would return for the second play, and I thought it was a way for us to develop more experienced depth. We used three running backs in the game, and Sean Jackson, Marquette Smith, and Warrick Dunn all ran well. Our rebuilt defense threw a shutout and stopped Kansas's offense on eight consecutive plays from our two-yard line in the strangest goal-line stand I ever saw. We jumped offside on three plays, giving Kansas a first down each time. But we turned the Jayhawks away on fourth-and-goal from our one-yard line and then drove ninety-nine yards for a touchdown. Bentley did not attempt a field goal, but he made six extra-point kicks and showed a very strong leg on kickoffs. Overall, I did not have much to complain about in our opener.

Two days before we played Duke, in our second game, I left practice and flew to Auburn, Alabama. I wanted to see my son Terry coach his first game as Auburn's coach. I even did my weekly radio call-in show from the Auburn campus. I was there to watch Terry direct the Tigers to a 16–12 victory over the University of Mississippi at Jordan-Hare Stadium. Auburn ended up finishing 11–0 in his first season, but the Tigers were not eligible to play in a bowl game because of NCAA violations committed by the previous coaching staff. Auburn finished fourth in the final Associated Press Top 25 poll.

We beat Duke, 45–7, on the road in a game that was delayed about twenty minutes because of lightning. Our offense played well in a mud pit, with Charlie throwing for 272 yards, with two touchdowns. But Bentley missed the first field-goal attempt of his career. Worse, he missed the kick wide right after he promised me he always missed them left. Scott also missed three extra points in the game, but I could only hope his problems resulted from the poor playing conditions.

The 1993 team had the best start to a season of any of my squads at Florida State. We beat Clemson, 57–0, in our third game, handing the Tigers their worst defeat since 1931. Our star linebacker Derrick Brooks blocked a punt to set up a touchdown and returned a fumble eighty-three yards for another score. Things were going so well that even when backup quarterback Danny Kanell mistakenly lined up under a guard—instead of the center—to take the snap, he just moved over and threw a seventy-eight-yard touchdown pass to tight end Lonnie Johnson.

We beat North Carolina, 33–7, in our fourth game and shut out Georgia Tech, 51–0, at Doak Campbell Stadium in our fifth game. We were ranked number one in the country, with a 5–0 record, outscoring our opponents by a combined total of 228–14. Some media members started calling us the "greatest team in college football history." Of course, I knew it would take only one loss to knock us out of the national championship race. And I knew which team was coming up next on our schedule: Miami, our long-time nemesis. The Hurricanes had beaten us three straight times and in six of the previous seven seasons. Miami had won three national championships since 1987, and we were still seeking our first title. Predictably, the game was getting a lot of attention across the country.

"It's the Super Bowl of college football," Miami defensive lineman Dwayne Johnson told the *Chicago Tribune* days before the 1993 game. "It's the Wrestlemania of wrestling. The Riddick Bowe/Evander Holyfield of boxing. It's big."

It was certainly a heavyweight fight between two great college foot-ball teams. Miami had not lost a regular-season game since 1990. We had a 69–9 record since the start of the 1987 season, with five of those losses coming against the Hurricanes. Miami had eliminated us from the national championship race five times in seven seasons and upset us when we were ranked number one in the country in 1988 and 1991. The national media believed the Hurricanes had a psychological edge over us; I believed the Hurricanes had a lot of great players when we lost to them in the past. "We can't intimidate them," I told the media that week. "But they can't intimidate us, either."

The night before the game, I talked to our team about having the "will" to win. "How will you react when adversity strikes?" I asked my players. "Will you shake it off and play harder?" I told our offensive line the key to the game was blocking Miami's defensive line. With great players like Warren Sapp, Pat Riley, Darren Krein, and Johnson, who would later become the Hollywood actor "The Rock," the Hurricanes were good enough to disrupt our offense and harass Charlie in the back-field. "We can't let Miami do what it did in 1991," I told my team. "They beat us at home and cost us a national championship. This is the 1993 Florida State team. This team is better!"

On October 9, 1993, we hosted the number-three-ranked Hurricanes at Doak Campbell Stadium in what would become one of the most memorable games in Florida State history. On the third play from scrim-mage, Sean Jackson cut back near the line of scrimmage and ran sixty-nine yards for a touchdown to give us a 7–0 lead. Miami came back to tie the score at 7–7 on Frank Costa's six-yard touchdown pass to Donnell

Bennett. On our next series, we faced third-and-ten from our twenty-eight-yard line. But Charlie broke out of the pocket and rolled to his right before firing a seventy-two-yard touchdown pass to Matt Frier to give us a 14–7 lead. Later in the second quarter, we added a wrinkle by putting Warrick next to Charlie in the backfield. Our center Clay Shiver snapped the ball directly to Warrick, and he picked up a huge first down. Charlie scored on a two-yard touchdown run to give us a 21–7 lead at halftime.

Our defense dominated Miami in the second half. We held the Hurricanes to only one hundred yards of offense, and they managed only a twenty-three-yard field goal after halftime. Devin Bush, one of our safeties, intercepted a pass and returned it forty yards for a touchdown with about five minutes to play. We won the game, 28–10. Finally, we beat the Hurricanes and kept our national championship dreams intact. Beating Miami was a huge relief, but we still had seven games to play. I did not want my boys to believe the Hurricanes were our only obstacle. "If we put all of our eggs in one basket, we're barking up the wrong tree," I told them. "You don't win a national championship in the middle of the year."

Before we played the University of Virginia at home the next week, I told my players about the Bible story of Paul the Apostle and Silas being imprisoned. During their first night in jail, Paul and Silas prayed and sang hymns to God. Suddenly an earthquake shook the prison, and the doors to the cell in which Paul and Silas were being held swung wide open. The chains that bound them to the prison floor were broken. The prison guard was so terrified he drew his sword to commit suicide because he believed Paul and Silas escaped. "Don't harm yourself!" Paul shouted. "We're still here." The jailer found a torch to see them and fell trembling at their feet. I read my players Acts 16:30–31:

> *He then brought them out and asked, "Sirs, what must I do to be saved?"*
> *They replied, "Believe in the Lord Jesus, and you will be saved—you and*
> *your household."*

"Boys, there is only one loving God," I told my players. "Your sins will find you out. You must ask Him for forgiveness and He will forgive you. If there's anything you're guilty about doing this week, ask God for forgiveness."

I wanted to make sure my boys were focused on the rest of the season and did not have something weighing on their hearts and minds. I wanted them to know that God forgives all sinners. Every one of us breaks commandments and makes mistakes, because no one is perfect, which is why Jesus died on the cross for us.

I was concerned about how my players would react after playing such an emotional and physically grueling game against Miami. Virginia was unbeaten and nationally ranked. But we jumped on the Cavaliers early in the game, after Vanover caught a short pass and ran eighty-six yards for a touchdown early in the first quarter. Charlie threw three touchdowns and ran for another score in the game. We led, 30–0, at halftime and won the game, 40–14.

The next Monday, I warned my players about not looking ahead to our upcoming game against the University of Notre Dame in three weeks. The Fighting Irish were undefeated, and our road game against them was looming as large as playing Miami. But unless we beat Wake Forest and Maryland the next two weeks, it would not matter. "What will be our place in history?" I asked the boys. "Can you go down as the best team ever? Don't lose to Wake Forest or forget about it!" I made each of my boys make a pledge that they would not talk about playing Notre Dame during the next two weeks.

We beat Wake Forest, 54–0, at Doak Campbell Stadium on October 30, 1993, and defeated Maryland, 49–20, the next week to improve our record to 9–0. Charlie sat out the Maryland game because of a rib injury, but I knew he would be ready to play against Notre Dame. "Charlie Ward will go, unless a train runs over him," I told the media. I knew Charlie would be ready to go. There was nothing that could keep him off the field at Notre Dame because he was too fierce a competitor.

The hype surrounding the Notre Dame game in 1993 was probably more intense than any other game I coached. It was even bigger than all of our games against Miami because the Fighting Irish were involved. Notre Dame has more tradition than any other college football program in the country. The Catholic school in South Bend, Indiana, produced seven Heisman Trophy winners and won eleven national championships. When Florida State was still an all-girls school in the 1930s and 1940s, the Fighting Irish were as popular as the New York Yankees across the country. Notre Dame has the "Golden Dome" and "Touchdown Jesus," the mosaic mural on the side of Hesburgh Library, which you can see from the stands of Notre Dame Stadium. Notre Dame's sports information department issued 750 media credentials for the game, and ESPN sent its "GameDay" TV show to campus. The South Bend post office even issued a special edition postmark commemorating the latest "Game of the Century."

To be honest, I wasn't too concerned about my boys becoming overwhelmed by playing at Notre Dame. My 1981 team beat the Fighting Irish, 19–13, in South Bend. Most of my boys had never even heard of "the Four Horsemen," "the Gipper," Knute Rockne, Ara Parseghian, Paul Hornung, and all the other Notre Dame legends. Really, about the only thing they knew about Notre Dame at the time was a former walk-on player named Rudy Ruettiger, who was the inspiration for the 1993 film *Rudy*. A lot of my boys even went to see the movie at theaters in Tallahassee the week before our game against the Fighting Irish.

My beliefs about my players being ignorant of Notre Dame's traditions were confirmed when Kez McCorvey referred to its legendary coach as "Rock Knutne." Derrick Brooks even told the media about the famous "Three Horsemen" of Notre Dame. The last thing I wanted was our players' off-the-cuff comments to wake up the echoes in South Bend. "I appreciate what Notre Dame has accomplished, but those old guys don't play anymore," McKorvey told the media. "You can't win with mojo or magic. Joe Montana isn't going to put on the pads and win for them."

Montana, who played at Notre Dame during the 1970s and won four Super Bowl rings with the San Francisco 49ers, was not coming back to quarterback the Fighting Irish. But as well as we played in the first nine games, I knew Notre Dame was more than capable of beating us. In addition, Lou Holtz was now coaching the Fighting Irish, and he always seemed to rise to the occasion in big games. The Irish were big and strong and were led by offensive tackle Aaron Taylor and defensive tackle Bryant Young, two future NFL all-pro players.

The night before the game, I delivered a devotional at our hotel in South Bend. I talked to my players about boxer Evander Holyfield, who became the heavyweight champion of the world six days earlier when he defeated Riddick Bowe in a bout at an outdoor arena at Caesar's Palace in Las Vegas. Holyfield, who professed to be a born-again Christian, thanked God in his postfight news conference. "God gave me the strength and I had the courage," Holyfield said. "I can do all things through Christ, Who strengthened me." I told my players that they should not be ashamed to profess their faith, because that is what the Bible teaches us to do.

I read my players Romans 10:9–10:

That if you confess with your mouth, "Jesus is Lord," and believe in your heart that God raised him from the dead, you will be saved. For it is with your heart that you believe and are justified, and it is with your mouth that you confess and are saved.

When I awoke in South Bend on the morning of November 13, 1993, I thought we had caught a break. There was definitely an autumn chill in the air, but it was not the frigid temperatures I feared would greet us. Also, there was not a hint of rain. If I thought anything might slow us down that day it was cold weather and a muddy track. I thought we were faster than Notre Dame, but I worried about their size and strong running game. Before the game, I told our defensive linemen we had to outquick Notre Dame's mammoth offensive line. I told our linebackers and safeties that we could not arm-tackle running backs Lee Becton and Jeff Burris. "We have to gang-tackle them and pound them for four quarters," I said. "They can take over the game. We have to swarm like bees!"

Looking back now, the game might have started too easily for us. We took the opening kickoff and marched eighty-nine yards for a touchdown, with Charlie throwing a twelve-yard touchdown pass to Kevin Knox. But Notre Dame answered and tied the score at 7–7 after Adrian Jarrell surprised us with a thirty-two-yard touchdown run off a reverse. The Fighting Irish took a 14–7 lead on Becton's twenty-six-yard touchdown run, and then Charlie threw a pass into the wind that was intercepted at our twenty-three-yard line. Notre Dame needed only four plays to score and took a 21–7 lead on Burris's six-yard touchdown run. I was very concerned on the sideline. Notre Dame's offensive line was pushing us around up front, and we were doing a very poor job of tackling. I tried to express my concerns to our team at halftime.

Notre Dame kicked a forty-seven-yard field goal early in the third quarter to make the score 24–7, but my boys were not finished. Charlie threw a pass in the left flat for Warrick, and he scored a six-yard touchdown to cut Notre Dame's lead to 24–14. Bentley kicked a twenty-four-yard field goal to cut our deficit to 24–17, but our defense could not stop Notre Dame's offense. With about seven minutes to go, Burris ran for an eleven-yard touchdown to give the Irish a 31–17 advantage. Most teams would have quit at that point, but my boys had the hearts of champions. With about two and a half minutes to play, we had fourth-and-goal from their twenty-yard line. Charlie threw into the back of the end zone, but he did not see safety Brian Magee. Fortunately, Magee tipped the ball right into McCorvey's hands, and his touchdown cut Notre Dame's lead to 31–24 with two minutes, twenty-six seconds to play.

We tried an onside kick to get the ball back, but it was not successful, and Notre Dame recovered. Our defense came up with a huge stop and forced the Irish to punt. They had to punt into a strong wind, and after only a five-yard punt, we took over at our thirty-seven-yard line with fifty-one seconds to play. Charlie drove us all the way to Notre Dame's fourteen-yard line in the final seconds. His first pass was knocked down at the line of scrimmage. On second down, he threw a pass to Warrick near the goal line, but cornerback Shawn Wooden knocked it down. Our comeback came up fourteen yards short of the end zone, and we lost the game, 31–24.

Losing to Notre Dame was devastating, but I knew we still might have a chance to play for a national championship. As long as we stayed in the top two spots in the Bowl Coalition poll, which was established in 1992 to match up the top two teams in the country in the same bowl game, there was a good chance we would play the Fighting Irish again. Notre Dame had only one game left, against Boston College the next week. We still had to play North Carolina State at home and Florida on the road. When the polls were released the day after our loss to Notre Dame, we were number two, behind the Fighting Irish. We still had a puncher's chance with two games to go.

Before we played the Wolfpack on Senior Day at Doak Campbell Stadium on November 20, 1993, I talked to my players about overcoming their disappointment of losing to Notre Dame. "We must take out our frustrations on N.C. State," I told them. "Play every down like it's your last. Do you want another shot at Notre Dame? We have to play like we're still the best team in the country!"

I did not have to worry about my players' motivation against the Wolfpack. About two hours before we played N.C. State, Boston College stunned number-one-ranked Notre Dame, 41–39, on a last-second field goal at Notre Dame Stadium. The Fighting Irish nearly rallied from a twenty-one-point deficit in the fourth quarter and actually took a 39–38 lead with one minute, nine seconds to play. But the Eagles drove right back down the field, and kicked the winning field goal in the same end zone where Charlie's pass was batted down the week before. David Gordon, the Boston College kicker, would have been elected mayor of Tallahassee in a landslide vote that day. My boys responded by beating the Wolfpack by a 62–3 score, handing them their worst loss in half a decade.

When the college football polls were released the next day, they were split. Florida State was ranked number one in the Associated Press writers' poll; Nebraska was number one in the CNN/*USA Today* coaches' poll. The Bowl Coalition poll, which combined the two popular votes, had the Cornhuskers ranked first, and we were second. I was still elated, though, because we only had to beat Florida to play Nebraska for the national championship.

Beating the number-seven-ranked Gators would not be easy, though. Florida had won twenty-three consecutive games at the Swamp and had never lost there under Steve Spurrier, who took over as its coach before the 1990 season. The Gators had already won a second straight

Southeastern Conference East Division title and were getting ready to play Alabama for the SEC championship. Their only loss was a 38–35 defeat at Auburn. The Gators' offense was just as potent as our attack, averaging 42.3 points per game. Florida quarterback Danny Wuerffel had thrown twenty-one touchdown passes to set a national record for freshmen. Obviously, fans of the schools really did not like each other very much, and we had played some big games against the Gators in the past. But the 1993 regular-season finale was easily the biggest contest in the rivalry to that point. "I don't believe this game has ever meant more," I told the media that week. "There just hasn't been one that's meant more than this one."

The night before we played the Gators in Gainesville on November 27, 1993, I did not have to tell my players what was at stake. They knew if we beat the Gators, there was a very good chance we were going to play Nebraska in the Orange Bowl in Miami for the national championship. "Can we beat them in the Swamp?" I asked my boys. "No one thinks we can. But everyone in this room knows we're going to do it. Win or lose, we must keep our poise. No taunting. No trash talking. It's all business."

In front of 85,507 fans at the Swamp, the largest crowd ever to watch a college football game in the state of Florida, my boys played the first three quarters with poise and precision. Charlie was spectacular in a performance that probably won him the Heisman Trophy. He completed thirty-eight of fifty-three passes for 446 yards with four touchdowns. We took a 13–7 lead at halftime, and then Charlie threw two touchdowns to McCorvey in the third quarter to give us a 27–7 lead going into the fourth.

But Florida scored two touchdowns in the fourth quarter to cut our lead to 27–21 with five minutes, fifty-eight seconds to play. We faced third-and-ten from our twenty-one-yard line. Charlie faked a handoff to Warrick, and then rolled to his left to avoid a sack by defensive tackle Ellis Johnson. Charlie lofted a soft pass to Warrick, who made linebacker Ed Robinson miss a tackle. When Warrick turned up the field, there was no one in front of him. He ran seventy-nine yards for a touchdown and put the game out of reach. We won the game, 33–21.

As we drove back to Tallahassee that night, I didn't know how the polls would turn out the next day. I just knew my boys could not have done anything more to impress the voters. Nebraska was undefeated. So were West Virginia, my former team, and Auburn, which was ineligible to play in a bowl game because of NCAA probation. But my son Terry accomplished something I had never done: his team finished a season with an unbeaten record. West Virginia coach Don Nehlen was really lobbying for the Mountaineers to play Nebraska in the Orange Bowl because his team was undefeated. I didn't blame him for lobbying, but West Virginia did not play our schedule, either. We played games against six nationally ranked opponents, including Miami and Notre Dame, which were ranked number three and number two, respectively, when we played them. West Virginia fans even sent postcards to sportswriters and broadcasters around the country trying to rally support for the Mountaineers.

When the polls were released the next day, I was relieved to see us ranked number two in the Bowl Coalition poll. Nebraska was number one in the coaches' poll, followed by Florida State and West Virginia. But we were ranked number one in the Associated Press poll, followed by the Cornhuskers and the Mountaineers. A week later, when a final poll was released after the SEC championship game, the Orange Bowl game was finalized. We were playing Nebraska for the national championship.

I was always very fond of Nebraska coach Tom Osborne. We spent some time together during the off-season, and I spoke in Lincoln, Nebraska, a few times at Fellowship of Christian Athletes events and for other civic groups. Tom was one of the best coaches in the country and always did things the right way. Like me, Tom had never won a national championship. Going into the Orange Bowl, Tom had 206 career victories and I had 238. Tom came close to winning a national championship in 1983, but the Cornhuskers lost to Miami, 31–30, in the Orange Bowl, after Turner Gill's two-point conversion pass fell incomplete in the final seconds. One of us was finally going to win a championship ring, and the other coach would begin the quest for a title again the next season.

Las Vegas oddsmakers did not make my job any easier by declaring us a seventeen-point favorite in the Orange Bowl. That really seemed to inspire the Cornhuskers, who were ranked number one and undefeated. But Nebraska had lost six consecutive bowl games and had not beaten a top-ten-ranked team since 1987, so I guess a lot of people figured we would win in a rout. I took my team to Miami knowing we were walking into a fierce battle. "It inspires the other team," I told the media. "It infuriates the other team. I wish we were a seventeen-point underdog. I know I could get my kids mad about that."

After we arrived in Miami a week before the game, I tried to keep my players relaxed. I did not want them to know how badly I wanted to win a national championship, but it was eating me up inside. After waiting so long, I was finally becoming consumed about winning a title. I admitted it publicly before we played the Hurricanes. "Obsessed," I told a reporter when he asked me how much I thought about winning a national title. "It's ruining my trip down here. We've never played in a game that comes down to everything. If we win it, we'll win a national championship of some kind. For me to say I'm not thinking about it wouldn't be right. I think about it more than ever."

When we gathered the boys at our hotel on New Year's Eve 1993, I talked to them about having peace of mind. I wanted to make sure they wiped everything else from their minds and concentrated solely on playing Nebraska. I quoted Philippians 4:13 from the New International Version:

I can do everything through him who gives me strength.

I needed all the strength I could muster in the final seconds of the Orange Bowl on New Year's Day 1994. Our offense really struggled against Nebraska's defense in the first half. We trailed, 7–6, at the half, but then Charlie threw a one-yard touchdown to fullback William Floyd on our opening possession of the second half to give us a 12–7 lead. Bentley kicked a thirty-nine-yard field goal late in the quarter to make the score 15–7. But Nebraska came back early in the fourth quarter, with Lawrence Phillips running for a twelve-yard touchdown to cut our lead to 15–13. We gave the football back to Nebraska with four minutes, thirty-nine seconds to play. Tommie Frazier, the Cornhuskers' great option quarterback, drove them from their twenty-yard line to our four-yard line. Our defense stopped Nebraska on three consecutive runs, forcing Byron

Bennett to kick a twenty-seven-yard field goal, which gave Nebraska a 16–15 advantage with one minute, sixteen seconds to go.

Nebraska's ensuing kickoff went out of bounds, so we started our final drive at our thirty-five-yard line. Charlie was sensational running our two-minute offense, and we were helped by two fifteen-yard penalties against the Cornhuskers. We drove to Nebraska's five-yard line, and Bentley kicked a twenty-two-yard field goal to give us an 18–16 lead with twenty-one seconds to go. We were penalized fifteen yards for an unsportsmanlike conduct penalty after Scott's field goal, so Nebraska took possession at its forty-three-yard line with fourteen seconds remaining. Frazier's first pass was incomplete, leaving seven seconds on the clock. But he completed his second pass to tight end Trumane Bell down the middle. Bell was tackled at our twenty-eight-yard line, and I thought the game was over. The scoreboard clock showed time expired. My boys soaked me with a Gatorade cooler full of ice water. I ran onto the field to find Tom to shake his hand, and I was immediately swarmed by my players and many of our fans. It was complete chaos.

When I met Coach Osborne in the middle of the field, one of the officials came back and told us there was actually one second left in the game because Nebraska called a time-out before the clock expired. "Are you kidding me?" I asked. "Where is the ball at?" The official told me the ball was at our thirty-three-yard line. I did not think the Cornhuskers' kicker could make it from that far away. But then the official came back and said, "Coach, we made a mistake. The ball is on the twenty-eight-yard line." Dadgumit, now the kick was within his distance. The only thing I could think was, "Geez, we just aren't meant to win it."

I could barely stand to watch as Bennett lined up for the last-second, forty-five-yard field goal attempt. But I watched it and watched it and the ball sailed left of the upright. Finally we'd won our first national championship. After all those darn wide rights, Nebraska had a wide left. After all those missed kicks, we won a championship because someone else missed a kick.

I am not going to lie; it was a relief to get the monkey off my back. If I had never won a national championship, I still would have been satisfied with my career when I retired. I think winning a title was more important to my players, fans, and alumni than it was to me. I never made football my god and I never let my desire to win a championship become more important than the things that really mattered to me: my faith, my family, my players, and my coaches. Every time I took the field, I was more concerned about the score He is keeping "up there."

I have always known there were unseen eyes watching me.

CHAPTER 13

SECOND CHANCES

Throughout my coaching career, I was always known as a "second chance" coach. Kicking a boy off my team or taking away his scholarship was often my last resort when it came to discipline. I just did not want to throw a boy back on the streets with no structure or direction in his life. I was ridiculed for being that way, because some people believed I was too soft when it came to discipline. Most of the time, fans wanted a public hanging when one of my boys made a mistake. But other people commended me for it because I was able to help so many boys over the years. I was a boy myself one time. If people had not forgiven me for some of the things I did when I was younger, I never would have made it in life. When I was coaching my boys, I knew what a lot of them were going through. Many of them came from broken homes and had not been taught the difference between right and wrong. I knew some of the temptations they were facing being away from home for the first time. If they made mistakes, I was going to save them if I could. And I really did not care what anyone else thought about it.

About four months after Florida State won its first national championship, I called my players together for a meeting on April 12, 1994. I wanted to warn my boys about outside influences that could tear apart the fabric of our team. I talked to my boys about alcohol, drugs, sex, sports agents, and the importance of staying out of trouble. I was elated to finally have won a national championship ring, but I also knew that being a champion brought increased scrutiny from the media.

"If you were in danger of being killed, would you not expect me to warn you?" I asked my players. "I would expect you to warn me. If you were driving down a road and the bridge was out and there was some guy there telling you stop, wouldn't you stop? That is the way it is with disobeying God and breaking His commandments. I'm telling you this because I do not want to see you go over that cliff."

I was not naive enough to believe that some of my players were not having premarital sex. These days, it seems like very few people believe that a man and a woman should wait until they are husband and wife to have sex. That was one of the reasons why Ann and I were married so young. I tried to explain to my players that sexual activity with anyone other than your wife was a sin and it broke one of God's commandments. And I talked to my players only about abstinence. I don't believe in telling them safe sex is acceptable. I believe that in God's eyes, safe sex is wrong, too, unless it is with your spouse.

"Adultery and fornication are sins," I warned my boys. "Having a child

196

out of wedlock is completely irresponsible. If you are guilty of doing it, don't do it anymore. Repent of your sins."

I read my players two verses from the Bible. The first verse was Proverbs 28:13:

He who conceals his sins does not prosper,
But whoever confesses and renounces them finds mercy.

I also read them John 1:8–9:

If we claim to be without sin, we deceive ourselves and the truth is not in us. If we confess our sins, he is faithful and just and will forgive us our sins and purify us from all unrighteousness.

I told our boys we were living in a fishbowl and that everything we did was being watched closely by others. We could not make mistakes; we had to go to class; and we had to be good citizens. I knew my boys were not perfect—no one is perfect—but I wanted to make sure they understood the consequences of doing something wrong.

About a month later, many of my worst fears as a football coach were realized. On May 16, 1994, *Sports Illustrated* published a story that detailed a shopping spree seven of my players made at a Foot Locker sporting goods store at Governor's Square Mall in Tallahassee. The shopping spree was paid for by a local man who was working as a "runner" for an unlicensed sports agent in Las Vegas. What my boys did was against NCAA rules; what the agent did was against Florida state laws. It was against the law in Florida for sports agents to offer improper benefits to student-athletes who had remaining college eligibility. The agent could be tried and imprisoned for breaking the state's sports agent laws.

The episode was really embarrassing. I had worked so hard to make sure my program had a clean image when it came to NCAA rules. We had never been accused of breaking them, a fact I was very proud of. But the Foot Locker episode not only launched an NCAA investigation but also threatened the college eligibility of my players. As a coach, you always fear something like that will happen. There's no way to monitor more than one hundred players every single day, but you try to educate them about NCAA rules and warn them about the dangers of certain sports agents as much as possible. Of course, immediately after it happened *Sports Illustrated* tried to find out if I or any of my coaches knew about the shopping spree. I knew nothing about the incident until *Sports Illustrated* sent a reporter to campus to ask me about it months after the incident.

We spent the next few months answering a lot of questions. Florida State officials hired an outside law firm to launch an internal investigation, which found that neither I nor my coaches were aware of the incident. A year later, Florida State was placed on one year's probation by the NCAA, but the punishment really was not that severe. We still were allowed to participate in bowl games and have our games broadcast on TV. And the NCAA probation did not affect our 1993 national championship, either. Four of my players were suspended for multiple games during the 1994 season for participating in the shopping spree.

When I met with my team before the 1994 season, I told them the incident was water under the bridge as far as I was concerned. I was not proud of my boys' actions, but I was going to afford them a chance to redeem themselves. "We have to look ahead and forget the past," I told them. "But we must learn from our mistakes."

There were a lot of ways to discipline players short of kicking them off my team. I could take a young man's scholarship away for a semester and make him pay for his books and tuition. I could take away his dormitory room and make him pay rent for an apartment. I could take away the training table and make him pay for his own food. I could make him run up and down stadium steps every morning for a month. There are a lot of ways to discipline kids, just as there is more than one way to skin a cat. But if a boy messed up again after getting a second chance, I usually had to let him go. Sometimes a young man would make a terrible mistake, and I could not always help him. If his mistake involved law enforcement and jail and things such as that, I could not help my boys all the time.

One of the boys I could not save was Roosevelt Snipes, who was a running back on our teams in 1983 and 1984. In all of my years of coaching, I do not know if we ever had a better running back. Roosevelt was probably as fast as Deion Sanders and had balance like Warrick Dunn. Roosevelt was like a cat. You could throw him up in the air and he would always land on his feet. He was just a tremendously talented player. Roosevelt signed a scholarship to play football for us after his senior season at Sarasota High School in Florida in 1981. But he failed to qualify academically, so he spent the 1981 and 1982 seasons playing at Coffeyville Junior College in Coffeyville, Kansas. His junior-college coach also coached Mike Rozier, who became a great running back at the University of Nebraska. The coach told me Roosevelt was a more explosive running back than Rozier, and I had no doubt after watching him practice for the first time.

Roosevelt made an immediate impact for us during the 1983 season. He ran for more than 600 yards with four touchdowns playing behind Greg Allen. Roosevelt ran for more than 100 yards in four games and nearly helped us upset number-ten-ranked Auburn University at Jordan-Hare Stadium in Auburn, Alabama, on October 1, 1983. He ran 82 yards for a touchdown, but officials said he stepped out of bounds after gaining only 35 yards. We lost the game by a 27–24 score. Roosevelt was even better in his second season, in 1984, running for 754 yards with six touchdowns. I really thought he had a bright future going into the 1985 season.

But Roosevelt had a lot of problems. He just did not like going to class, and I had to suspend him and revoke his scholarship in May 1985. I told him if he made good grades during summer school, I would consider letting him return to the team before the 1985 season. But midway through summer school, Roosevelt dropped out of classes and went back home to Sarasota. He was drafted in the 1985 NFL supplemental draft by the San Francisco 49ers, and they offered him a $500,000 contract. But the 49ers cut him during training camp after he tested positive for cocaine.

Less than a year later, Roosevelt robbed a convenience store in Sarasota every day for three days. He was not the smartest criminal, either. Before one of the robberies, he placed a telephone call to Larry Strom, a Florida State booster, who lived in Sarasota. I guess Roosevelt thought he would have an alibi since he was talking on the phone at the time of the robbery.

The only problem: Roosevelt made the call from a pay phone in the convenience store's parking lot.

Roosevelt had a drug problem and was arrested for selling crack cocaine to an undercover police officer in West Palm Beach, Florida. In 1989, he was arrested for robbing a hotel in Sarasota. We tried to help him get straightened out, but he just never turned his life around. Roosevelt served a seven-year prison sentence from 1992 to 1999. Less than three months after Roosevelt was released, he was arrested again for cocaine possession and was sent back to prison for three more years. He went back to jail again in 2004 on another robbery charge. Roosevelt is currently serving a fourteen-year prison sentence at Polk Correctional Institution in Polk City, Florida. He is scheduled to be released on March 4, 2018, when he will be fifty-six years old. By that time, Roosevelt will have spent nearly half of his life incarcerated.

I still receive a letter from Roosevelt about once a year. I sent him a Bible a few times and have tried to encourage him to turn his life around. Even when he gets out of prison, there will still be time for him to accomplish something in his life. I have tried to explain to him that God forgives all sinners. I know Roosevelt is not proud of how he has lived his life, but if he asks God for forgiveness, he could be saved. His life is not over.

Sammie Smith was another former player who found trouble after leaving Florida State. Sammie was raised in Apopka, Florida, which is near Orlando, and the town has produced several blue-chip college football prospects. Sammie was lucky because he had great parents who really steered him in the right direction when he was young. His mother was a teacher, and his father worked in a packing plant. Sammie was a fabulous running back at Apopka High School, and we were involved in a fierce recruiting battle with Miami, Michigan, Ohio State, and Southern California to sign him. In the end, he chose to play at Florida State because he wanted his parents to be able to see his games.

Sammie really made an immediate impact for us. I rarely saw running backs with his combination of size and speed. He ran for 611 yards with four touchdowns in his first full season, in 1986. The next season, he ran for 1,230 yards, a single-season total that still ranked second-best in Florida State history going into the 2010 season. When he was a junior, Sammie dislocated his shoulder and his production slipped to 577 yards in 1988. After that season, Sammie became the first junior in Florida State history to leave school early and declare his intentions to enter the NFL draft. During predraft workouts, Sammie ran the 40-yard dash in 4.32 seconds, which was unheard of for a running back who weighed nearly 225 pounds. The Miami Dolphins selected him with the ninth pick in the 1989 NFL draft, and Sammie signed a contract worth $2.5 million.

But Sammie never reached his potential in the NFL. He had problems fumbling the football, and the media and fans criticized him for it harshly. After Sammie fumbled going into the end zone against the Houston Oilers late in the 1991 season, the fans really turned on him. He was traded to the Denver Broncos the next season, and he played in only three games before he underwent surgery for a torn abdominal muscle. Sammie's NFL career was over.

Sammie returned to Apopka and started a small construction

company. He was building houses in his hometown, and things really seemed to be going well for him. He got married and had a daughter. But on September 14, 1995, Sammie was arrested on federal drug charges. According to law-enforcement officials, Sammie was trafficking cocaine. I was shocked. Sammie pleaded guilty to two charges of possession and distribution of cocaine and was sentenced to seven years in prison. Before our game against Central Florida at Doak Campbell Stadium on October 23, 1995, I talked to my boys about Sammie. "Money is the root of all evil," I told them. "God still loves Sammie Smith. But he is going to pay a price for disobeying God's commandments. He still can be saved. He has to tell the Lord, 'I am a sinner. Please forgive me and come into my heart.' Sammie must repent."

Sammie made a terrible error in judgment, but he owned up to his mistake and served his time. While Sammie was imprisoned, he made a videotape for us from jail in which he told our players about the mistakes he made and warned them about the dangers of drugs. After Sammie was released from prison, he started his own courier company and has done well for himself. From time to time he would return to Florida State and talk to my boys about the dangers of drugs and alcohol.

I never went on the recruiting trail looking to sign troubled players. We took some boys who had academic issues and minor behavioral problems, but we always recruited the same players everyone else did. I once told a civic group that my administration always asked me why I recruited so many academically challenged players. "If I went out and only signed A students, we would not need academic counselors, would we?" I told them.

But during the summer of 1995, I received a lot of criticism for taking wide receiver Randy Moss. Randy was a *Parade Magazine* All-American at Dupont High School in Rand, West Virginia. He was the state's two-time basketball player of the year and was one of the best track-and-field performers in the country. We tried to recruit Randy out of high school, but he signed with Notre Dame because he said it was always his dream to play for the Fighting Irish. Less than two months after Randy signed a national letter of intent with Notre Dame in February 1995, he was arrested for his involvement in a fight at school. Police said the incident was racially motivated, and Randy was charged with a felony. The charge was eventually reduced to a misdemeanor, but Notre Dame still rejected Randy's application for admission.

Later that summer, Notre Dame coach Lou Holtz called me and recommended I try to recruit Randy. Lou told me he recommended three schools to Randy's mother, and Florida State was one of them. At the time, I did not think offering Randy a scholarship was a smart thing to do. I knew we would take a lot of criticism from the media, and we had just put the Foot Locker episode behind us. But I made some telephone calls and talked to people who knew Randy best. I talked to his mother, his high school football coach, his attorney, and people who mentored him in West Virginia. I talked to my athletic director and university president about the possibility of taking him. Our athletic director, Dave Hart, said I could take him as long as Randy redshirted his freshman season and did well in classes.

I offered Randy a scholarship, and he enrolled in classes at Florida State during the summer of 1995. As I expected, the media backlash was pretty severe. I tried to explain my decision to Bob Harig, a columnist with the *St. Petersburg Times* in Florida. "I think if people will take my record in forty years of coaching and see the boys I've given second chances to, I don't think they will show me a long list of guys who didn't pan out," I told him. "Some kids need a dadgum break. I'm not one of those guys who has tried to build my program by recruiting problem players. But there are times when you have to take a second look. I think a lot of it is from people who are jealous they don't have him. I know criticism is coming. I expect it. But if I can't take criticism, I might as well get out of coaching."

Randy did well during his redshirt freshman season, when he practiced with our team but did not play in games. He was going to class and staying out of trouble. In our spring game in 1996, Randy caught a fifty-six-yard touchdown pass, and my coaches were really excited about his potential. But on May 23, 1996, I dismissed Randy from the team before he ever played in a game at Florida State. A week earlier, while at home in West Virginia for the summer, he admitted to smoking marijuana, which was a violation of his probation in West Virginia. "I went to bat for Randy, because I earnestly believed in him," I said in a statement released by our sports information department. "But he chose to again break the law. It is my hope that he has learned from all of this."

A West Virginia judged sentenced Randy to one year in jail. The judge allowed him to take classes at West Virginia University during the daytime and spend his nights in jail in a work-release program. After more than two months in jail, Randy was released for good behavior. He enrolled at Marshall University in Huntington, West Virginia, where he became one of the best wide receivers in college football history. During his sophomore season, in 1997, Randy set an NCAA record with twenty-five touchdown catches and was named an All-American. Of course, he became one of the NFL's most productive wide receivers in twelve seasons with the Minnesota Vikings, Oakland Raiders, and New England Patriots.

I think a lot of times we forget as a society that college football players are still young men. With the media attention the sport gets nowadays, everything they do is magnified. My boys were not perfect, and a fair share of them made mistakes along the way. But they're still boys. If I had a player do something wrong for the first time, I was going to give him a second chance if I could. I learned a long time ago that if I wanted to be popular with everyone else, I would have just kicked those players off the team when they messed up. But I never took that approach. I was a second-chance coach. My God is a second-chance Father.

CHAPTER 14

TRANSFUSION

One of my favorite devotionals I told our team is a touching story about two young children living in Southeast Asia during the Vietnam War. A little girl was hurt and needed a blood transfusion to save her life. They couldn't find an adult with the same type of blood in her village, so they had to draw blood from her twelve-year-old brother. Doctors asked the boy, "Are you willing to give blood to your sister to save her life?"

The little boy said he would do anything to save her. As the doctor started to put a needle into the boy's arm, the little boy started to cry. "Why are you crying?" the doctor asked him.

"Will it hurt when I die?" the little boy asked.

The little boy really thought he was going to die by giving blood to his sister, but he loved her so much he was willing to die for her. I often asked my players what kind of sacrifices they were willing to make for their teammates. They were only playing a game, and football is never a matter of life and death, but would they make the sacrifices necessary to become a champion? Would they put aside personal glory for the success of the team?

During the 1990s, I found that winning a second national championship was as difficult as winning the first title, in 1993. We lost to Miami, 34–20, in our fifth game of the 1994 season, after we turned the ball over five times. We went into the 1994 regular-season finale against Florida with a 9–1 record and were ranked number seven in the country. The Gators had a 9–1 record and were ranked number four. The Gators came out with five receivers and threw the ball all over us. We trailed, 31–3, going into the fourth quarter, and most of our fans at Doak Campbell Stadium left before the game ended. It looked like the score was going to get really ugly.

But Gators coach Steve Spurrier took his foot off the pedal, and our offense started making big plays. We scored four touchdowns in the fourth quarter, and Rock Preston's four-yard touchdown run cut Florida's lead to 31–30 with one minute, forty-five seconds to play. On the sideline, my players and coaches were pleading with me to go for a two-point conversion, which would have given us the lead. But I did not want to take a chance of losing the game after fighting so hard to come back. We kicked the extra point, and the game ended in a 31–31 tie. Our fourth-quarter comeback tied for the largest in college football history, and Florida State fans to this day still refer to that game as the "Choke at Doak."

Florida really replaced Miami as our biggest rival during the late 1990s. We played the Gators thirteen times from 1990 to 2000, and both teams were ranked in the top ten of the polls every time. After tying the

Gators in 1994, we played them again in the 1995 Sugar Bowl and beat them, 23–17. During the 1995 regular season, we lost for the first time to an Atlantic Coast Conference opponent, falling 33–28 at the University of Virginia after Warrick Dunn was stopped at the goal line on the final play. Florida beat us, 35–24, in the 1995 regular-season finale. We beat Notre Dame, 31–26, in the Sugar Bowl to finish the season with a 10–2 record.

Going into the 1996 season, I really thought we were going to have a team that might contend for a national championship. Thad Busby was taking over at quarterback, and I was excited about his future. Dunn was becoming one of the elite running backs in the country, and we had a dominant defense led by ends Peter Boulware and Reinard Wilson. In our team meeting on August 14, 1996, I told my boys there was only one goal for the upcoming season: to win a national championship. "All other goals are secondary," I told them. "You have to put the team first. It's not about 'I,' 'me,' or 'mine.' It's about the team. Lead, follow, or get out of the way!"

We won our first ten games in 1996, and only one of the scores was close. We beat Miami, 34–16, ending a twelve-year drought against them at the Orange Bowl stadium. Our defense forced three turnovers and sacked quarterback Ryan Clement eight times. Our defense allowed ten points or fewer in six of our twelve games in 1996. We avenged our 1995 loss to Virginia by beating the Cavaliers, 31–24, at homecoming in Doak Campbell Stadium. Before we defeated Wake Forest, 44–7, at the Citrus Bowl stadium in Orlando on November 9, 1996, I told my players about Reggie White, who was perhaps the greatest pass rusher in NFL history.

I coached White in the Japan Bowl after his senior season at the University of Tennessee, in 1983. White was an ordained evangelical minister and was known as the "minister of defense" during his fifteen-year career with the Philadelphia Eagles, Green Bay Packers, and Carolina Panthers. White's faith was tested when his church in Knoxville, Tennessee, was burned to the ground by arsonists. White spoke out against church burnings across the South, and he and his family received racist letters and death threats. "I am willing to die for the things I believe in," he said at the time.

In 1995, White helped lead the Packers to the NFL playoffs. But late in the season, White tore his left hamstring, and doctors told him he would need season-ending surgery. The Packers announced his season was over. But on Christmas Eve 1995, White was playing with his children and realized his hamstring felt better. He drove to Packers coach Mike Holmgren's house and told him he wanted to play. White underwent tests the next day, and doctors canceled his surgery. He played in three NFL playoffs games, leading the Packers to the NFC Championship game.

"Something miraculous happened," White said after returning from the injury. "I thank God for it. My legs were not hurting like they hurt before. The Lord healed me. God gave me an opportunity to do what He called me to do."

I wanted my boys to understand the sacrifices they would have to make to win a national championship. I also wanted them to know that even great NFL players such as Reggie White are not afraid to profess their faith.

* * *

We scored forty points or more in four consecutive games before playing the Gators at Doak Campbell Stadium on November 30, 1996. We were 10–0 and ranked number one in the country. It was probably Florida's best team. Danny Wuerffel won the 1996 Heisman Trophy and was as good as any quarterback I ever saw, and the Gators had great receivers, such as Reidel Anthony, Ike Hilliard, and Jacquez Green. Spurrier's "Fun-'n'-Gun" offense was really revolutionizing the way football was being played in the Southeastern Conference, where "three yards and a cloud of dust" seemed to reign forever. I was really concerned about my defense giving up big plays. Florida was averaging forty-nine points per game and could erupt at any time. "Our secondary has to play with confidence and stay disciplined," I told our team the night before the game. "We must stop the run first, but don't let their receivers get behind you. You will never catch them if they do."

Our defense was spectacular against Florida's passing game, and it probably helped that there were twenty-mile-per-hour gusts in the stadium that day. Safety Shevin Smith intercepted Wuerffel's pass to end the Gators' first drive, and that play really set the tone on defense. We sacked Wuerffel six times and intercepted three of his passes. Dunn had perhaps his best game at Florida State, running for 185 yards. We had a 17–0 lead at the end of the first quarter and held on for a 24–21 victory.

Needless to say, I was happy to get the Gators out of the way. They had become as much of a thorn in our sides as Miami was during the 1980s. Nebraska, the two-time defending national champions, was ranked number three in the country. We would play the Cornhuskers for the 1996 national title in the Sugar Bowl as long as they defeated unranked Texas in the Big 12 championship game in St. Louis. Arizona State, the Pac-10 conference champion, was contractually obligated to play Big Ten champion Ohio State in the Rose Bowl in Pasadena, California.

A week later, Florida defeated Alabama, 45–30, in the SEC championship game in Atlanta, and Texas upset Nebraska, 37–27, in the Big 12 title game. The Cornhuskers' stunning defeat knocked them out of the national championship race. Since Arizona State was going to play in the Rose Bowl, we were going to play the Gators again, in the Sugar Bowl. I did not like it. I thought beating a team you already defeated once was very difficult because the opponent had so much incentive to redeem themselves. And then Spurrier went on TV and complained about my boys hitting Wuerffel so much. He said we had several late hits during our first meeting and were trying to hurt his quarterback. Steve continued to complain about late hits even after both teams arrived in New Orleans a week before the game. At a pregame dinner on New Year's Eve, Steve pulled me aside and talked to me about the late hits. Steve told me he was only making a fuss to try to fire up his team.

The night before the 1996 Sugar Bowl, I talked to my players about the sacrifices they would have to make to beat Florida. I told them a story about Daniel Huffman, a high school student from Rossville, Illinois. I met Danny at ESPN's Espy Awards show in Orlando earlier that month. Danny was a promising high school football player and was probably big enough and talented enough to earn a college scholarship. Danny was raised by his grandmother, who was a diabetic and was suffering from kidney failure. Without his grandmother's knowledge, Danny talked to her doctors about giving her one of his kidneys. Danny's grandmother did not want him to do it, but surgeons transplanted one of his kidneys to his grandmother on July 8, 1996. Because Danny had only one kidney, he had to stop playing football. A few newspaper stories were written about Danny's ultimate sacrifice, and ESPN honored him with its first ESPN/Disney Spirit Award. During his acceptance speech in Orlando, Danny told the audience: "I'm for the Seminoles. I've always liked the Seminoles. I'm pulling for the Seminoles."

I told my players Danny could not make a greater sacrifice. I read my players John 15:13:

Greater love has no one than this, that he lay down his life for his friends.

I also read them a famous quote that legendary Green Bay Packers coach Vince Lombardi once said about his teams: "You've got to care for one another," Lombardi said. "You have to love one another. Each player has to be thinking about the next guy. The difference between mediocrity and greatness is the feeling these players have for one another. Most people call it team spirit. When the players are imbued with that special feeling, you know you have yourself a winning team."

I talked to Danny after the ESPN awards show and encouraged him to come to Florida State and become one of our student trainers. William "Bill" Proctor, who was a great football player at Florida State and later became a state legislator, helped arrange for Danny to receive a scholarship. Danny worked with us for a couple of seasons and worked in the school's sports information department. He left Florida State after a couple of years and returned to Illinois.

I wish I could say Daniel's story has a happy ending, but on December 6, 2004, Danny died from a self-inflicted gunshot wound. I never figured out why a young man who was willing to sacrifice so much for others would take his own life.

We did not have a chance against the Gators in the 1997 Sugar Bowl. Spurrier put Wuerffel in the shotgun to help keep our pass rushers away from him, and he passed for 306 yards and three touchdowns. Dunn was overcome by dehydration and ran nine times for only 28 yards. It was not the homecoming Warrick was hoping for. We lost the game by a 52–20 score, and the Gators were crowned college football's national champions in 1996. It was one of the most humbling defeats of my career.

The Gators cost us a national championship the next season, too. We were 10–0 and ranked number two in the country when we played Florida in Gainesville in our last regular-season game, on November 22, 1997. The Gators had already lost two games and were having all kinds of problems at quarterback. But Spurrier rotated Doug Johnson and Noah Brindise on nearly every play against us, and we lost the game, 32–29. Running back Fred Taylor really hurt us, rushing for 162 yards and the winning touchdown with one minute, fifty seconds to play. We beat Ohio State, 31–14, in the Sugar Bowl and finished the season with an 11–1 record.

We opened the 1998 season with a new quarterback, but Chris Weinke was hardly a rookie. Weinke was the country's most highly regarded quarterback during his senior season at Cretin-Derham High School in St. Paul, Minnesota, in 1989. We won a fierce recruiting battle for him, and he moved to Tallahassee in August 1990. But Weinke also was a highly regarded baseball prospect, and the Toronto Blue Jays drafted him in the second round of the 1990 amateur baseball draft.

Weinke left Florida State after being on campus for only four days. He spent six years in the Blue Jays' minor league system before finally deciding he wanted to give football a try. He called us late in the 1996 season. We were recruiting Drew Henson, who was a blue-chip prospect from Brighton, Michigan. Henson also was considering Michigan and a few other schools, and he told us if Weinke came to Florida State, he was signing with another school. We voted as a staff on which quarterback to take, but my vote was the only one that mattered. Weinke arrived at Florida State as a twenty-five-year-old freshman in the summer of 1997.

Weinke played in only two games in 1997, but took over the starting job the next season after Dan Kendra injured his knee. We opened the 1998 season against Texas A&M in the Kickoff Classic in East Rutherford, New Jersey. We struggled to pull out a 23–14 victory, but Weinke passed for 207 yards and one touchdown and played pretty well. The next week, Weinke threw a school-record six interceptions in a 24–7 loss at North Carolina State. It was only our second-ever defeat against an ACC opponent.

The next Tuesday, I called my players together for a team meeting and basically read them the riot act. We had lost many great players from the previous season, including defensive end Andre Wadsworth and offensive tackle Tra Thomas, who were NFL first-round draft choices. In fact, nine of our players from the 1997 team were drafted, and five more signed free-agent contracts with NFL franchises. I knew we had lost a ton of talent, but that was not an excuse.

"Boys, we're at a crossroads," I told them. "My last eleven teams were able to handle the pressure. Are you strong enough to handle it? Each team must build its own legacy. You cannot live on what happened in the past. You're trying to live on what the past eleven teams accomplished. They bled. They puked. They were exhausted from all of their hard work. One of you said football is not fun anymore. Since when is football fun? It takes hard work, dedication, and sacrifice. Winning games is fun!"

My boys responded to my motivational speech by winning their next seven games. We had an 8–1 record and were ranked number six in the country when we played Virginia at home on November 7, 1998. Late in the first half, Weinke did not see defensive end Patrick Kerney rushing him from his blind side. Kerney hit Weinke very hard, and Chris walked off the field at the half saying his neck hurt and complained that his right arm and hand were numb. Doctors initially diagnosed his injuries as a mild concussion and pinched nerve in his neck. But two days later, tests revealed that Weinke needed surgery to fuse two vertebrae and remove a bone chip from his neck. Weinke's season was over with two regular-season games left to play.

Sophomore Marcus Outzen was going to have to take over at quarterback, but he did not have much experience. My boys called him "Rooster" because of his red hair. He ran like a rooster, too, and had good mobility.

Outzen started against Wake Forest on the road the next week and played pretty well in a 24–7 victory. We closed the regular season against number four Florida at home, but I don't think many people expected us to win the game with an inexperienced quarterback. But Peter Warrick, our star wide receiver, caught a touchdown and threw for another score in a 23–12 victory. Our defense really dominated the Gators, not allowing them to convert a third-down play in the entire game.

After finishing the regular season with an 11–1 record, we had to sit and wait while other teams finished their games. Three teams were ranked ahead of us: number one Tennessee, number two UCLA, and number three Kansas State. At least two of them would have to lose their final games for us to play in the Fiesta Bowl for the national championship. It was probably pretty long odds that two of them would lose, but at least there was some hope.

A week later, Miami stunned UCLA, 49–45, and Texas A&M upset Kansas State, 36–33, in double overtime in the Big 12 championship game. We were going to play undefeated Tennessee for the national championship. The 1998 season was the first time they used the Bowl Championship Series to determine which two teams would play for the title at season's end. The complicated BCS formula included two human polls, three computer rankings, strength of schedule, and a team's number of losses to calculate rankings. Fans of Kansas State and Ohio State were upset that their teams were not playing Tennessee, and I thought they probably had as much of an argument to play the Volunteers as we did.

In the end, a few people might have believed we did not deserve to play in the Fiesta Bowl. Weinke was still recovering from his neck injury, so Outzen had to start against a very good Tennessee defense. Volunteers cornerback Dwayne Goodrich stepped in front of one of Outzen's passes and returned it fifty-four yards for a touchdown, putting us in a 14–0 hole. Outzen threw two interceptions, fumbled once, and was sacked four times. He did not get much help from anyone else, either. Tennessee's defense held Peter Warrick to only one catch. Tennessee quarterback Tee Martin was really sharp and threw a seventy-nine-yard touchdown to Peerless Price. Not many people believed the Volunteers were capable of winning a national championship in 1998. Quarterback Peyton Manning left Tennessee a year earlier, but the Volunteers definitely had the makeup of a championship team when we played them. And they beat us in the Fiesta Bowl, 23–16.

As I walked off the field on a cool, dry night in the Arizona desert on January 4, 1998, I wondered what it would take for Florida State to win its second national championship. Would Weinke be healthy in 1999 after recovering from neck surgery? Would Peter Warrick return to school, or enter the NFL draft as a junior? Most important, would my boys be willing to sacrifice everything to become a championship team?

CHAPTER 15

WIRE
TO WIRE

By the start of the 1999 season, I was getting pretty dadgum old, but my body felt great. I was entering my twenty-fourth season as Florida State's head coach and was nearing a couple of significant milestones. I entered the 1999 season with 292 career victories—only four other college football coaches won 300 games during their careers. I turned seventy years old on November 8, 1999, and Ann and I celebrated our fiftieth wedding anniversary and attended our fiftieth class reunion at Woodlawn High School in Birmingham. If that does not make you feel old, I guess nothing ever will.

But I was feeling so good and healthy I signed a five-year contract extension to remain Florida State's coach through the 2004 season. I honestly never thought I would coach for so long. In 1970 I was forty years old and was named head coach at West Virginia University. Six years later, Darrell Royal resigned as Texas's coach when he was fifty-one years old. A month later, Frank Broyles resigned as Arkansas's coach when he was fifty-one. Royal and Broyles were two coaches I really admired, so I figured I had about ten more years of coaching left in me. But when I turned fifty, I felt like I could coach five more years and retire. But then sixty came along, and then sixty-five came and went. As long as I felt good and my teams were winning games, I did not see any reason to retire.

Of course, if I ever wanted to see how much I had aged, I had only to look down our dinner table on Christmas Day. We had six children and twenty-one grandchildren. Three of my sons had become college football coaches. Terry, my third youngest boy, was head coach at Salem College in Salem, West Virginia; Samford University in Birmingham, Alabama; and Auburn University in Auburn, Alabama. My son Tommy was head coach at Tulane University in New Orleans and Clemson University in Clemson, South Carolina. My son Jeffrey coached for Terry and was later my wide receivers coach and offensive coordinator at Florida State.

Each of my sons played football for me in college. My oldest, Steve, played for two seasons at West Virginia University during the early 1970s but never played in a varsity game. If Steve had stuck with football, he would have played for the Mountaineers, because he was pretty talented. He just didn't like football that much.

Tommy walked on my team at West Virginia, earned a scholarship, and started at wide receiver for the Mountaineers in 1975 and 1976. During Tommy's junior season in 1975, West Virginia played California in Berkeley. The Bears were nationally ranked, but my team beat them,

28–10. Tommy caught a pass in the game and a defensive back just drilled him. He suffered a collapsed lung. Tommy came back and was able to play against North Carolina State in the 1975 Peach Bowl, but it was a very scary injury.

Terry walked on to my team in 1974 and was a special-teams player for us in 1975. The following year, Terry was hit so hard in practice that he had blood coming out of his mouth and ear. It scared me to death, because I thought he might have internal injuries. That's probably the biggest thing I learned from coaching my own boys; seeing them suffer made me realize that each of my players was somebody's son, and I think it made me take a more humane approach to coaching. I never asked one of my boys to play if he was hurt, and I think I was more cautious about injuries than other coaches who had never seen their own sons suffer.

I never wanted my sons to become football coaches. I didn't encourage it, partly because I didn't want to compete against them, but especially because I didn't want them competing against one another. Tommy decided very early—probably while he was still attending high school—that he wanted to be a football coach. He even wrote a term paper about it.

After Tommy graduated from West Virginia, he worked as a graduate assistant under Frank Cignetti in 1977. I made him a G.A. as my defensive backs coach in 1978, and two years later he left to work for Doug Barfield at Auburn. When Barfield resigned after the 1980 season, Tommy returned to Florida State as my tight ends coach.

I never really thought Terry would become a coach. I thought he was too intelligent to coach. Terry graduated magna cum laude with an accounting degree from West Virginia University. He then went on to do postgraduate work at the University of Oxford, in Oxford, England. Terry then enrolled at Florida State's law school and earned his law degree while working as a volunteer/graduate assistant coach for me from 1979 to 1982.

I tried to talk Terry out of going into what was fast becoming the "family business," but I guess coaching was just in his blood.

Terry was hired as head coach at Salem College, an NCAA Division II school in Salem, West Virginia, in 1983. At twenty-six years old, he was the youngest head coach in the country and Jimbo Fisher was his first recruited quarterback. Terry coached at Salem College for three seasons and hired Jeffrey as his offensive coordinator. In 1986, Terry left to work as an assistant at Akron University under Gerry Faust, who was a former head coach at Notre Dame. Terry was hired the next season as head coach at Samford University, my alma mater. He helped the Bulldogs make the transition from NCAA Division III status to Division I-AA and led his team to the I-AA national semifinals in 1991.

In 1993, Terry was hired as the head coach at Auburn University after Pat Dye was forced to retire because of an NCAA investigation. Tommy was Dye's offensive coordinator at the time. Tommy stayed on Terry's staff as offensive coordinator and they worked well together.

Terry went 11–0 in his first season and won his first twenty games at Auburn. After his first season, Terry won the Paul "Bear" Bryant Award as the national coach of the year. It was a trophy I always wanted to win because of my affection for Coach Bryant. But I never won it, and Terry makes sure he tells me about his trophy every time we get together.

Auburn finished 9–1–1 in Terry's second season in 1994 and then his teams won at least eight games in each of the next three seasons, playing in the SEC championship game in 1997. In 1998, Terry's team suffered a rash of injuries and he did not have a lot of depth because the NCAA took away some of Auburn's scholarships during probation. After a 1–5 start, Terry resigned as Auburn's coach in October 1998 and was replaced by defensive coordinator Bill Oliver.

I hated to see Terry's time at Auburn end that way because he can really coach and the boy can really motivate his players. Terry went into broadcasting and worked for ABC Sports as a studio analyst. He was very good at his job and was having fun, but his heart was always in coaching football. Before the 2009 season, Terry accepted a job at North Alabama, an NCAA Division II school in Florence, Alabama. He hired Jeffrey as his wide receivers coach and assistant head coach after Jeffrey had been out of the game for a couple of years. I always thought Terry could still do great things in coaching. His first year back, he led his team to an 11–2 season, finishing number six in the nation.

Jeffrey's tenure as my offensive coordinator at Florida State from 2001 to 2006 was the most difficult time of my career. When Mark Richt, who worked as my offensive coordinator from 1994 to 2000, told me he was leaving, I wanted to promote Jeffrey, who had served as my wide receivers coach since 1994. Dave Hart, our athletic director, told me Talbot D'Alemberte, the president of Florida State University, did not want me to do it.

In all my years of coaching at Florida State, the athletic director and president had very little input in my coaching staff. I met with President D'Alemberte and told him I was hiring Jeffrey. He let me do it but made sure I knew he didn't think Jeffrey was ready for the job.

We finished with an 8–4 record in 2001 and went 9–5 in 2002. We had some big wins, but college football fans are fickle. They always want to blame the offense when your team is not winning games. They don't understand that it takes nine coaches to be successful. It also takes an experienced quarterback to win games, and that was our biggest problem after Chris Weinke left following the 2000 season. When I first started coaching at Florida State we always had a junior or senior starting at quarterback. Guys like Jimmy Jordan, Wally Woodham, Rick Stockstill, and Danny McManus waited their turn. A big reason we won so many games during the 1990s was that we always had a quarterback ready to go when one left. We went from Chip Ferguson to McManus to Peter Tom Willis to Casey Weldon to Charlie Ward to Danny Kanell to Thad Busby to Weinke. I don't think any other team had a succession of quarterbacks that successful.

But after Weinke left, we missed on a few high school quarterbacks we recruited, and Florida State fans really started criticizing Jeffrey when we began losing games in 2005. The criticism of Jeffrey hurt me, but I have always known being judged—fairly or not—was part of the job. Jeffrey's philosophy was to devise a plan, stick with it, and not listen to people outside the program, but I knew the criticism had to be tearing him up inside. Ann was more outspoken about the criticism of Jeffrey, because he is her baby. If you want to make Ann Bowden mad, just say something bad about Jeffrey or me—it's that simple!

Wire to Wire

On November 11, 2006, Wake Forest beat us 30–0 at Doak Campbell Stadium. It was the first time one of my teams had ever been shut out at home. When I returned home that night, Jeffrey was standing in the kitchen. "Daddy, I'm going to resign," he told me. "We can't even score. I'm going to step out."

"Jeffrey, don't quit," I told him. "We still have some games left. We might be able to turn this thing around."

The next Monday, Jeffrey walked into my office and told me he had tendered his resignation. I told him that he needed to change his mind, that I didn't want him to quit and was willing to stand by him and go down with him. "Our family is more important than my job," I told him, but he wouldn't listen. We finished 7–6 in 2006, and Jeffrey did not return the next season.

After Jeffrey resigned, I sent him a note, which included a poem General Douglas MacArthur's mother sent to him while he was being questioned during a hazing incident at the United States Military Academy in 1900. My version of the poem went like this:

Do you know that your soul is of my soul such a part
That you seem to be fiber and core of my heart?

None other can pain me as you, son, can do;
None other can please me or praise me as you.

Remember the world will be quick with its blame
If shadow or shame ever darken your name.

Like father, like son, is saying so true
The world will judge largely of father by you.

Be this then your task, if task it shall be
To force this proud world to do homage to me.

Be sure it will say, when its verdict you've won
He reaps as he sowed: This man is his son!

The criticism that comes with coaching college football was another reason I never wanted my sons to get into the profession. There are so many variables involved with building a championship team, and you can never forget that you are always counting on eighteen- and nineteen-year-old boys to get the job done. Jeffrey stayed out of coaching for two seasons before joining Terry's staff at North Alabama. I knew he wouldn't stay out of coaching for very long—the boy just has too much Bowden blood in his veins.

Tommy probably paid his dues more than any of my boys. He worked as an assistant coach for twenty years at six different schools. He worked as running backs coach at Auburn, tight ends coach at Florida State, quarterbacks coach at Duke, and wide receivers coach at Alabama. He knew a lot about offense and became a very good offensive coordinator at Kentucky and Auburn in the early 1990s. In 1997, Tommy was named head coach at Tulane University. In his second season, Tommy guided the Green Wave to an 11–0 record, their first undefeated season since 1931. I must admit that I was really getting envious of my sons. Terry's team at Auburn went undefeated in 1993, and Tommy's team at Tulane accomplished the feat in 1998. I had been coaching for more than four decades and still did not have an undefeated season on my résumé.

After the 1998 season, Tommy was hired as Clemson University's coach. Of course, the Tigers were members of the Atlantic Coast Conference and played Florida State every season. As soon as Tommy was hired at Clemson, I started pondering October 23, 1999. It was the Saturday we were scheduled to play the Tigers at Death Valley in Clemson, South Carolina. It would be the first father-son coaching matchup in major college football history. The media dubbed the game the "Bowden Bowl." Everyone else was counting down the days to the game, but I wished I could just erase that Saturday from my calendar. I was not looking forward to glancing across the field and seeing my son coaching on the other sideline. I wanted to beat every opponent, but it was just an odd feeling knowing you had to beat your son's team to win a national championship.

But Clemson was one of twelve teams standing in Florida State's way in 1999, and I was determined my team would beat every one of them. And my boys weren't going to finish unbeaten without their old man doing it, too.

When I met with my Florida State players on August 12, 1999, Tommy's undefeated season at Tulane the previous season must have still been fresh in my mind. I told my players there was only one goal for the Seminoles in 1999: to finish unbeaten and win a national championship.

"I have never had a perfect season," I told my boys. "If you do everything we ask you to do, it will happen this year. Another coach told me the only way to stop Florida State this season is if it self-destructs. We cannot let that happen! Everyone has a role to play. We have to play together. We have to play as a team!"

Fortunately, our quarterback was returning. Chris Weinke, who seriously injured his neck the previous season, made a miraculous recovery. Only eight months after undergoing four hours of spinal surgery, Weinke was back at practice and was throwing the football very well. With Heisman Trophy candidate Peter Warrick and running back Travis Minor coming back on offense, we were going to be very explosive in 1999. Sebastian Janikowski was the best kicker in college football, and our defense led the country in nearly every statistic the previous season.

We were ranked number one in the polls heading into the 1999 season, and I thought we probably had the best team in the country. But I believed we also had the most talented team in the country in 1998, and we lost two games. I knew it only took a couple of injuries—or other unexpected events—to derail our national championship hopes.

We opened the season against Louisiana Tech at Doak Campbell Stadium on August 28, 1999. We were pretty banged up coming out of training camp, but it did not take Peter long to show why he was one of the best players in the country. Late in the first half, he took a handoff on a reverse and ran about one hundred yards to gain only twenty yards. After the game, I told reporters, "I went to get a drink of water and he was still running. I went to get a stick of gum and he was still running. I have never seen anything like it."

Peter ran for a twenty-one-yard touchdown to finish the drive and we blew open a close game against Louisiana Tech. Weinke threw for 242 yards with two touchdowns in his first game back and we won our opener by a 41–7 score.

Going into the 1999 season, Georgia Tech was supposed to be our biggest challenger in the ACC. After joining the ACC in 1992, we won seven consecutive ACC championships and won fifty-four of our first fifty-six games against league foes. But Coach George O'Leary was doing a really nice job at Georgia Tech, and Joe Hamilton was one of the most dangerous quarterbacks we ever faced. We had knocked Hamilton out of the game the previous two times we played him, but he lit up our defense in 1999. He completed twenty-two of twenty-five passes for 387 yards with three touchdowns.

We had a 41–28 lead early in the fourth quarter, but Hamilton threw a twenty-two-yard touchdown to Kelly Campbell to make the score 41–35 with one minute, thirty-five seconds left. We did not put the Yellow Jackets away for good until we recovered an onside kick in the final minutes. I was happy to get out of Atlanta with a victory, but I was surprised Georgia Tech moved the ball so well against our defense.

We played the ACC's Tobacco Road schools in our next three games and did not have much trouble. We beat North Carolina State by a 42–11 score, avenging our loss to the Wolfpack in 1998. We beat North Carolina, 42–11, after our defense forced six turnovers. We beat Duke, 51–23, in a game that was played in Jacksonville, Florida. The game was supposed to be played in Durham, North Carolina, but the city of Jacksonville paid Duke $500,000 to move the game to Florida. I certainly did not object to playing a game only two hours from Tallahassee.

After five games, my team looked a lot like my 1993 national championship team. We had scored forty points or more in every game, and our defense was creating turnovers and scoring points. Weinke was playing pretty well, but I believed he was just starting to hit his stride after knocking off the rust from his neck injury. We still had to play Miami and Florida—and the "Bowden Bowl" against Clemson was only three weeks away—but I was feeling pretty confident about our chances.

But my optimistic outlook changed dramatically on October 7, 1999. Peter Warrick and wide receiver Laveranues Coles were arrested on charges of grand theft after a young lady sold them $412 worth of clothing for only $21 at a Dillard's department store in Tallahassee. I was shocked because Peter had been a team leader and good citizen for four seasons. It made it that much more disappointing for me.

Peter was raised by his mother and aunt in Bradenton, Florida, and his father was not around. He made a big sacrifice by coming back to Florida State for his senior season in 1999. Peter probably would have been a first-round choice if he had entered the NFL draft after his junior season, but he returned to school because he wanted to win a national championship.

Peter was probably the leading candidate to win the Heisman Trophy at the time of his arrest, and I knew our offense would not be as explosive without him. I immediately suspended Coles from the team and dismissed him for good a couple of days later. He had previous off-field problems during his career and was already on team probation for legal and academic problems. Under the Florida State Athletic Association's conduct policy, Peter was suspended indefinitely until his legal case was resolved because he faced felony charges. He was allowed to practice with the team during his suspension but could not play in our games.

The night before we played the Miami Hurricanes at Doak Campbell Stadium on October 9, 1999, I talked to my boys about Peter's mistake. "I know you face a lot of temptations, but you have to be self-disciplined," I told them. "Ask God for guidance if you find yourself being tempted. He will show you the way."

I read my players James 1:12–15:

Blessed is the man who perseveres under trial, because when he has stood the test, he will receive the crown of life that God has promised to those who love him.

When tempted, no one should say, "God is tempting me." For God cannot be tempted by evil, nor does he tempt anyone; but each one is tempted when, by his own evil desire, he is dragged away and enticed. Then, after desire has conceived, it gives birth to sin; and sin, when it is full-grown, gives birth to death.

James teaches us that we are blessed even during our worst trials and tribulations. We must continue to turn to God while we are being tested. God does not tempt us, but He will forgive us for our sins. Even if we feel cursed, we must continue to turn to Him and seek His presence and His peace to guide us through whatever we are facing. We must count on God to lead us through it and we will be blessed if we have faith in Him and trust Him.

After reading the Bible verses to my team, I drew a boulder on the chalkboard and drew cracks through it. "If we allow these cracks to expand, the rock will crumble," I told our team. "We have to stick together! We can prove to everyone that we are rock-solid even when we are afflicted."

I read my players a quote from Miami tight end Bubba Franks, who said he hoped Coles and Warrick were playing in the game. "I hope they play so they won't have any excuses after we whip 'em," Franks said.

Peter apologized to his teammates in our locker room before the Miami game, and I believed his apology was genuine. Weinke made sure the Hurricanes did not whip us, as he completed twenty-three of thirty-four passes for 332 yards with two touchdowns in our 31–21 victory. He completed passes to eleven receivers and really distributed the football well even without Peter on the field. Our defense was sensational in the second half, forcing Miami's offense to punt five times in seven possessions.

Peter did not play in our 33–10 victory over Wake Forest the next week, which improved our record to 7–0. Peter's attorneys were trying to reach a plea agreement with the state district attorney, whom we hoped would reduce his charge to a misdemeanor. If he pleaded guilty to a felony, his career at Florida State would be over. Finally, five days before we played at Clemson, his attorneys reached a plea agreement. Peter would plead guilty to a misdemeanor and would spend thirty days in jail after the season.

Peter would return to the team immediately, as long as the plea agreement was approved by a judge and Florida State president

Talbot D'Alemberte. The judge approved the plea deal, but President D'Alemberte said he had to serve any jail time before he returned to action. Peter's attorneys had to go back to the district attorney and negotiate a new deal. The day before we played Clemson, Peter pleaded guilty to misdemeanor petty theft and was ordered to spend thirty days in a work program. He also had to pay restitution to Dillard's, pay court costs, and donate the clothes to charity.

By the time the "Bowden Bowl" arrived on October 23, 1999, even the circus atmosphere surrounding the game seemed like a welcome distraction. Tommy and I had fun talking about the game, but I knew neither one of us was looking forward to coaching against the other. Of all my sons, Tommy probably is the one most like me. In fact, when Tommy was coaching at Tulane, a researcher asked each of my sons and me to take a personality test. Not surprisingly, the tests revealed Tommy and I had very similar personalities. We were both very cautious, and both had strong faith. I badly wanted to beat Clemson because I knew we had to win the game to win a national championship. "We've got to go up there and play Ann's boy—not mine, but Ann's," I told the media before the game.

Tommy even joked to the media about my age. "Our management styles, our ways with the media, the way we do things is pretty similar," he said. "He's not like me on the sidelines now. I really get into it sometimes; he takes naps over there. Maybe he was more like me at forty-five than sixty-nine."

On the day of the game, Ann wore a sweater that was half Florida State's colors and half Clemson's colors. Each of my children was there, along with most of my grandchildren. I hoped most of my family was pulling for the Seminoles because we had more at stake. The Tigers had a 3–3 record in Tommy's first season. He was in the early stages of a rebuilding job. I had won 299 games in thirty-three years of coaching; he had won 21 games in three years. Tommy wasn't my only loved one coaching at Clemson. My son-in-law Jack Hines was coaching Tommy's defensive backs. Reggie Herring, one of my former linebackers, was Clemson's defensive coordinator. Rick Stockstill, one of my former quarterbacks, was coaching the Tigers' wide receivers. It was Jeff and me against everyone else.

Clemson ended up being our toughest opponent in 1999, and it did not surprise me a bit. We trailed by a 14–3 score at halftime, after Tommy called a fake punt to set up an early touchdown. Sebastian Janikowski kicked a field goal early in the second half to make the score 14–6, and then we tied the score on Travis Minor's one-yard touchdown run and Weinke's two-point pass to Dan Kendra III with ten seconds left in the third quarter. Janikowski's thirty-nine-yard field goal gave us a 17–14 lead with five minutes, twenty-six seconds to play, but Clemson lined up for a tying field goal in the final two minutes. Tay Cody tipped the forty-one-yard attempt and it sailed wide left to give us a 17–14 victory. I knew Ann was happy. She wanted me to win the game, but she wanted her son's team to keep it close. She prayed all week that it would not be a lopsided score. Of course, she was pulling for me because she knew who paid her credit cards.

Beating Clemson gave me three hundred career victories, which only four other major college coaches had accomplished. It was quite an honor to join the company of Paul "Bear" Bryant, Pop Warner, Amos Alonzo Stagg, and Joe Paterno. My players hoisted me on their shoulders and carried me to midfield, where I was greeted by Tommy. "Recruit hard, son," I told him. "That's the only answer."

And the dadgum boy went out and did it, too. We beat Clemson in each of the next three seasons, but Tommy came back and beat me in four of the last five games we coached against each other. After a while, the "Bowden Bowl" really lost its flavor. It just became too much for our family to bear once a year. You did not want to beat your son, but you did not want to lose to him, either. Tommy was starting to catch heat at Clemson, and Florida State was losing games, too. It seemed that every year, the game got bigger and bigger. It was too much for Ann. She did not even like going to the games in the end. She did not like seeing her husband and son competing against each other so often. Tommy resigned as Clemson's coach after six games in 2008. He had a 72–45 record in ten seasons with the Tigers.

After the 1999 "Bowden Bowl," we played the Virginia Cavaliers the next week. During practice before the game, Jim Gladden, our defensive ends coach, was hit on the sideline and broke his leg. Jim had been with me at Florida State longer than any of my other assistant coaches. He was a close and trusted friend. Jim did not make the trip to Charlottesville, Virginia, on October 30, 1999, and it was the first game he missed in twenty-five seasons. Before the game, I told the boys I wanted them to win the game for Coach Gladden. Weinke threw three interceptions in his first nine pass attempts, but stayed focused and threw three touchdowns to lead us to a comfortable 35–10 victory. Our big defensive tackle Corey Simon had a huge game against the Cavaliers, intercepting a pass and blocking a punt.

We had a 9–0 record heading into a much-needed bye week on November 6, 1999. During the bye week, Peter wrote a letter of apology to Florida State fans, which was published in the *Tallahassee Democrat* newspaper. "I don't want to send a message to young people that it is OK to break the law," he wrote. "Whether I choose to be or not, I have become a role model for other young athletes. In this situation, I regret that I did not set a good example."

I truly believed that Peter was contrite for his poor decision. When he rejoined the team, I told him to forget about winning the Heisman Trophy. There was so much negativity surrounding his arrest, he probably would not have won the award anyway. But I really wanted him to remain in the background and focus on more important team goals for the rest of the season. Peter never let the negative publicity affect him. He caught eleven passes for 121 yards against Clemson, and then caught a 50-yard touchdown against Virginia.

The night before we played Maryland on Senior Day at Doak Campbell Stadium on November 13, 1999, I told my players that God sometimes tested us to draw us closer to Him. I think my devotional was probably directed to Peter in many ways. I told my players I went through hell at West Virginia in 1974, but I came out of the situation a stronger man. I read my players four verses from the Bible. One of them was Proverbs 3:5–6:

Wire to Wire

Trust in the Lord with all your heart
and lean not on your own understanding;
in all your ways acknowledge him,
and he will make your paths straight.

The next day, Peter caught three of Weinke's six touchdown passes in our 49–10 victory over the Terrapins. He finished the game with nine catches for 134 yards, and our offense finally looked explosive again. Our defense forced five turnovers and blocked two punts. More than anything else, my boys played like they were having fun again.

After defeating Maryland, we had only one obstacle left between us and a trip to the Sugar Bowl to play for the national championship: we were going to play our last regular-season game against the Florida Gators at the Swamp in Gainesville. The Gators had wrecked our national championship hopes in 1997, when we were undefeated before losing, 32–29, at Florida. Every year, it seemed the winner of the Florida–Florida State game moved on to play for the national title. The Gators hardly ever lost at home under Spurrier, and we had won there only once in ten seasons, winning 33–21 during our national championship season in 1993.

Florida was ranked number three in the country after winning nine of its first ten games. The Gators' only blemish was a 40–39 loss to Alabama, in which Florida missed an extra point in overtime. In a 20–3 victory at South Carolina the previous week, Spurrier benched quarterback Doug Johnson and played Jesse Palmer against the Gamecocks. I suspected Spurrier would try to do what he did against us in 1997, alternating quarterbacks on every play.

There was so much at stake in the game. A week earlier, three unde-feated teams lost their games, including defending national champion Tennessee. Florida State and Virginia Tech were the only unbeaten teams left in the country, so there was a good chance the winner of our game would play the Hokies for the national championship. Officials from both schools knew tension would be high at the Swamp. Before our game against Florida at Doak Campbell Stadium in 1998, the Gators took exception to my players stomping on our midfield logo during pre-game warm-ups. A fight broke out, and two of our boys and one Florida player were ejected even before the opening kickoff. Throughout the week before our 1999 game, Spurrier and I did public service announcements on TV, asking fans of both teams to be polite before, during, and after the game, as difficult as that might have been for some of them to do.

To beat the Gators, I knew our defense would have to contain Gators running back Fred Taylor. He was an explosive runner and had a good offensive line in front of him. I was not sure how much Spurrier trusted his quarterbacks, and I wasn't even sure which one would play more. "You have to stop the run," I told our defense the night before the game. "You must stay in your gaps. You must pound the running back, receivers, and quarterback. They will make some plays. We will not stop them every down. Do not get discouraged. Get back up and go again!"

Our defense played exceptionally against Florida in the first half on November 20, 1999. Peter Warrick scored on a four-yard run to give us a 7–0 lead in the first quarter, and we had two more chances to score touchdowns in the first half. But our offense stalled inside Florida's five-yard line both times, and we had to settle for two field goals and a 13–6 lead. I never liked to leave points on the field, but I was happy to have a lead at the half.

Florida's Jeff Chandler kicked a twenty-two-yard field goal early in the second half to make the score 13–9, and then Weinke made a big mistake. We tried to rush a play in as Florida's defense was still getting lined up, and Weinke tried to throw a pass to Marvin Minnis. But Bennie Alexander intercepted the pass and returned it forty-three yards for a touchdown, giving the Gators a 16–13 lead with seven minutes, thirty-nine seconds to play in the third quarter. The Florida fans were going crazy, but my boys kept their composure.

Janikowski kicked a fifty-four-yard field goal to tie the game with four minutes, forty-five seconds left in the third, and then our defense made two big plays that really turned the game in our favor. Linebacker Tommy Polley blocked a punt to set up a short touchdown run, and then Chris Hope intercepted a pass at our two-yard line to preserve our 23–16 lead. Weinke drove us right down the field and threw a twenty-seven-yard touchdown pass to Marvin Minnis to make the score 30–16.

Johnson threw a three-yard touchdown pass with three minutes, thirty-three seconds to go to cut our lead to a touchdown, but then we recovered an onside kick. We punted the ball back to Florida and then knocked away their desperation pass on the final play to win the game, 30–23.

After a season filled with so many off-field distractions, it was hard to believe we finished with an 11–0 record. After Virginia Tech beat Temple and Boston College in its last two games, the Hokies finished number two in the final Bowl Championship Series standings. Virginia Tech had an exciting quarterback named Michael Vick and a stout defense led by Corey Moore. I really respected Hokies coach Frank Beamer, who produced one of the sport's great rebuilding jobs while turning around his alma mater. His teams were always known for having great special teams, too, so I knew we were going to face a great challenge in New Orleans. I also knew the Hokies would be a sentimental choice, since Florida State had been playing for championships for so long.

"Ya'll are tired of us," I told the media a few days before the 2000 Sugar Bowl. "We've been around here for a long time. They are the Cinderella team. They ought to be; they're the new kid on the block. People say 'Ya'll are up there every year. You've had all these chances, but you only won one. Ya'll must not be very good.' I'm not so spoiled that I can't live with being number three."

But in my heart, I really wanted to win a second national championship. I wanted to finish a season with an unbeaten record. I wanted Florida State to become the first team to go wire to wire as the number one team in the country. I wanted players such as Weinke and Warrick and Simon to become national champions. After going through so much during the regular season, I wanted to make sure my boys were focused in New Orleans. I banned them from going into the city's casinos and put security guards on every floor of our team hotel. I established a strict curfew, hoping to keep my players away from Bourbon Street and the other nightspots as much as possible.

On New Year's Eve 1999, five days before we played the Hokies for the national championship, three of my players missed curfew. Janikowski, the best kicker I ever had, was one of them. I didn't let two of the boys start in the Sugar Bowl, but I started Janikowski. I was ridiculed in the media for the decision, but I really did not care. "Sure, it's favoritism, but we have the international rule," I joked about my Polish-born kicker. "This isn't a democracy, and everyone doesn't have a vote. It's communism or whatever. I made the decision."

Peter ended up being the player who redeemed himself in the Sugar Bowl. He was a one-man highlight show against Virginia Tech, catching six passes for 163 yards with two touchdowns. He also returned a punt fifty-nine yards for a touchdown and caught a two-point conversion pass from Weinke. Peter scored twenty points in the game, helping us defeat the Hokies by a 46–29 score to win our second national championship.

Peter took over the game from the start. Weinke threw a sixty-four-yard touchdown to him late in the first quarter, and then Polley turned the tables on the Hokies by blocking a punt. Jeff Chaney recovered the ball for a touchdown, giving us a 14–0 lead with two minutes, fourteen seconds to go in the first quarter. Virginia Tech cut our lead to 14–7 on Vick's forty-nine-yard touchdown pass with thirty seconds to go in the first quarter. But Weinke threw a sixty-three-yard touchdown pass to Ron Dugans, and then Peter returned a punt for a touchdown to give us a 28–7 lead.

But Vick seemed determined that Virginia Tech would not lose. He probably had the best individual performance against us since quarterback J. C. Watts led Oklahoma to back-to-back Orange Bowl victories over us in 1979 and 1980. Behind Vick, the Hokies scored twenty-two consecutive points to take a 29–28 lead with two minutes, thirteen seconds left in the third quarter. But my boys proved they had the hearts of champions, scoring three times in the fourth quarter to win the game. Our last touchdown came on Weinke's forty-three-yard pass to Peter with seven minutes, forty-two seconds to play. Before Peter caught the pass with a defensive back draped all over him, he told me he was going to finish off the Hokies, and that was exactly what he did.

As much of a relief as it was to win our first national championship in 1993, the second national title, in 1999, felt like more of an accomplishment. No team had ever been ranked number one from start to finish. It felt great to go out every week and win every game. In more than forty years of coaching, I had never experienced what that felt like. It was a very trying season, but it also was a very satisfying season.

The morning after we beat the Hokies, I was asked by a reporter during a news conference if I thought Florida State would be back again to play for a national championship in 2000.

"Will we be back next year?" I said. "You bet your life we'll be striving to get back."

I didn't know if we would ever be good enough to win another national championship, but I was sure as heck going to keep trying.

CHAPTER 16

FERVENT PRAYERS

On the morning of September 10, 2004, about twelve hours before we kicked off the season against the University of Miami at the Orange Bowl stadium, I sat at a desk in my hotel room at the Miami Airport Hilton and wrote a letter to my six children. It was the most difficult letter I have ever written in my life.

Five days earlier, my fifteen-year-old grandson Bowden Madden, and his father, John Allen Madden, were killed in a terrible automobile accident on Interstate 10 near Quincy, Florida. Bowden was my younger daughter Ginger's child. She and John named their son Bowden because he was born during our 24–21 victory at Clemson on September 17, 1988, which was the famous "puntrooski" game.

Bowden and his father were returning to their home in Fort Walton Beach, Florida, after spending Labor Day weekend at our house in

Tallahassee. Much of the family was there to celebrate the nineteenth birthday of J. J. Madden, who is Ginger's oldest child. Our game against Miami had been postponed four days because of Hurricane Frances, a Category 4 storm, which made landfall for a second time at the Florida Panhandle shortly before Labor Day. The storm caused forty-nine deaths and more than $12 billion in damage.

Bowden and John were returning home because Bowden had football practice the next day. Bowden was a sophomore at Choctawhatchee High School in Fort Walton Beach. While they were driving on rain-slicked Interstate 10, John's car veered into a Dodge van in the adjoining lane. The accident sent both cars across the median and into oncoming traffic in the eastbound lanes. John's car was hit by a utility truck, which was traveling from Texas to Florida to restore power outages caused by the storm. Bowden and John were killed instantly.

I went to bed at about 6:30 P.M. on September 5, 2004. I was lying in bed watching TV when I heard a car pull into our driveway. I saw the car's lights through my bedroom window. I heard the doorbell ring and figured someone stopped by to visit. But then I heard Ginger running up the stairs and screaming, "Daddy! Daddy! It can't be true! It has to be someone else!"

Billy Smith, a former Florida highway patrol man, who was my escort at Florida State football games for more than three decades, came to our house with another state trooper to break the terrible news. I rushed downstairs, and Ann and everyone else in the house were crying. It was terrible to lose a grandson, but it had to be even worse to lose a son at such a young age. I was not sure how Ginger was going to handle it. It was the worst news I ever received in my life.

Bowden was a good Christian. He had been to a Fellowship of Christian Athletes summer camp, and I knew he had been saved. He sang in the church choir and was a pretty good athlete. In fact, if Bowden had not been killed, I think there was a good chance he would have played football for us at Florida State. His father was a starting center on our teams when he played at Florida State from 1978 to 1981. Bowden inherited some of John's size and athleticism. We had him in our football summer camps, and he was a tough little rascal. Bowden had a great sense of humor and was a very popular kid. Everyone really liked being around him.

We buried Bowden and John on September 9, 2004. I spoke at their funeral at the First Baptist Church in Fort Walton Beach. I told the people there that I knew Bowden had been saved and that he was in heaven. "I have talked to people who knew him, and I know he's in a better place than we are," I said. "He's in a place where there's no pain, no suffering, and where there is nothing but good."

I still remember when my daddy died. I went to his funeral and looked at him lying in his casket. I looked at him and said, "That is not my daddy." My daddy was always happy, but he no longer had that spark in his eye. He did not have a smile on his face lying in the casket, and he did not have that warm breath you could feel while you were sitting in his lap as a child. I just knew he was not there. I figured he had already gone to heaven. Sure, his body was sitting there in the casket, but that body is like everyone else's and is going to rot. I knew his body was going to rot in a grave, but *he* was already in heaven.

And I knew Bowden was with him.

"Even though Bowden is gone, everything is going to be okay," I told my family at Bowden's funeral. "The people who are going to suffer are us, because we're going to miss him so much. But he isn't suffering. He just beat us to heaven. We are all going to get there eventually and we'll see him again."

I tell my family that when I die, they are welcome to have a funeral for me, but I know only my body will be there. I will already be in heaven because I have surrendered my life to Christ. Like my friends and I used to imagine so long ago, lying on the grass in my parents' front yard, I tell my family "I'll be up yonder."

My son Jeff and I flew to Miami after the funeral to help our team prepare for the opener against Miami. When I awoke in my hotel room near the Miami airport, I felt I needed to write a letter to my children to help them understand why Bowden was gone. We were all struggling to understand why God would take him at such a young age.

My Dear Children,

When the tragedy occurred last week, I saw again the bond of love our family has for each other. I witnessed the inner strength of Ginger in a time of mortal crisis and love of her mother, brothers, sister, spouses, nephews, nieces, children, as well as in-laws and friends. Oh, how I love all of you!

This brought back the memory of when you were just children and your mother would stay up half the night each Saturday ironing and polishing your shoes. She would lay your clothes out systematically and we would go to church each Sunday morning. Now is a good time to reflect on where you came from. Ann and my number one goal was that we raise you in the same environment we were raised. I remember vividly the day you accepted the Lord and were baptized.

The good news of the tragedy is that John and Bowden were saved and today live again in the presence of God in their new Heavenly home. It has been said that when we die we can take nothing of ours with us, except . . . our children! Great job, Ginger!

Keep in mind, at this time, our family will be together forever, if we all trust in Jesus and surrender our lives to Him. I don't mean change jobs or schools, etc., but just make your life available to Christ as your grandparents did and Ann and I have tried to do.

When I die and go to heaven (I know I will) if all of you and your family are not there with me, when your time comes, I will consider myself to have failed in life. All the statues, trophies, championships, etc., will be in vain. Somewhere along the line I failed you, if you are not there.

Now is the time to recommit our lives to Christ just as you did as a child. Jesus said: "I am the way, the truth, and the life. No man comes to the Father except through me." I choose Jesus as my Savior and commit to Him.

Each night, this is my fervent prayer.

Love,

Dad

Coaching my boys against the Miami Hurricanes on that hot, muggy night in Miami in September 2004 was one of the most difficult days of my life. Bowden's death was still on my mind, but it was over, and there was nothing you could do about it. Everyone around me told me they could tell my mind was elsewhere. I am not exactly sure what they meant by saying that, but they said they could just tell I was somewhere else that night. After we lost to Miami by a 16–10 score in overtime at the Orange Bowl stadium, I told Rob Wilson, our sports information director, that it was the hardest thing I had ever been through in my life.

More than anything else, Bowden's death really put things in perspective for me. I had never lost someone close to me at such a young age. Losing my parents was difficult, but both of them had lived full lives. Bowden and John were both so young. I have helped many of my players cope with the deaths of their parents, siblings, and friends over the years, but until you suffer the pain of losing a loved one, you really do not know how awful the pain is.

After losing to Miami, we rebounded to win our next six games. We were ranked number five in the country when we lost to Maryland by a 20–17 score on October 30, 2004, and then we lost to Florida, 20–13, in our regular-season finale. We beat West Virginia, 30–18, in the Gator Bowl in Jacksonville, Florida, and finished the 2004 season with a 9–3 record.

The next year, we won our first five games and climbed to number four in the national rankings. But we lost our last three regular-season games, including a 34–7 loss at Florida. We upset number-five-ranked Virginia Tech, 27–22, in the 2005 ACC Championship game in Jacksonville, Florida, and then lost to Penn State, 26–23, in triple overtime in the Orange Bowl on January 3, 2006. It was really a bizarre game. Our kicker

Gary Cismesia missed an extra point in the first half and two field goals in overtime, which would have won the game. Penn State's kicker missed two field goals.

Of course, Penn State coach Joe Paterno and I were waging quite a battle at the time to finish number one in all-time victories among major college football coaches. After our loss to Penn State in the 2006 Orange Bowl, I had 359 career victories; Joe had 354. Joe passed me in all-time victories on September 20, 2008. Going into the 2009 season, Joe had a one-game lead on me. I do not think I ever would have caught him because I knew I would probably coach for only one more season, and it seemed like Joe was going to coach forever. I did not want to get out of the fight because I led him for so long. I thought it was a healthy competition between us and was good for college football. I really wanted to win four hundred games because Joe and I would have been the only guys to accomplish the feat.

I have never been big on trophies and titles, because I know those accomplishments last only until you lose your next game. You are not taking any of those trophies with you when you go to heaven, just like you're not taking your house, the money in your bank account, or the cars in your driveway. But I think finishing with more victories than anyone else would have been nice for my children and grandchildren. It would have been nice for them to be able to say, "My old man won more games than anyone else." You would like to have accomplished something for your grandchildren and their children to remember you by. But it did not happen, and I have not lost one second of sleep over it. The race with Joe was fun and just kind of happened. When both of us got into coaching,

I am sure neither of us set out to win more games than anyone else.

I can tell you there is not a more deserving coach than Joe Paterno. He has coached at Penn State for sixty years and has done a tremendous job there. He runs his program the right way, never breaks NCAA rules, and his players always graduate with degrees. Joe and I were inducted into the College Football Hall of Fame together on December 5, 2006. Under the old rules, coaches had to be retired or dead to be inducted into the Hall of Fame, but they changed the rules so Joe and I could go into it together. It was a very nice gesture and a great honor to go into the College Football Hall of Fame with Joe.

In many ways, the Florida State dynasty ended in 2001. From 1987 to 2000, Florida State won at least ten games in fourteen consecutive seasons and finished in the top five of the Associated Press Top 25 poll at the end of every season, which no other team has accomplished. It was a great honor for the boys who played on my teams and the men who coached with me. The Seminoles set an NCAA record by winning eleven straight bowl games from 1985 to 1995, and we played in twenty-eight consecutive bowl games from 1982 to 2009. You can set your goals before every season to play in a bowl game and finish in the top five of the polls and you will never come close. I am not sure how it happened; it just stacked up that way.

Near the end of the 2007 season, I was watching my boys practice from a tower above the practice fields. Florida State president T. K. Wetherell climbed up into the tower and said, "Boy, I have some bad news."

President Wetherell told me some of my boys had been caught cheating on a test for an online music course. He said the investigation involved sixty student-athletes, and twenty-five were football players. He told me the test was supposed to take about thirty minutes to finish, and some of my boys finished in five or ten minutes. Some of my boys did not even need help to pass the test, but every one of them had to appear before an academic committee and confess if they received improper assistance. About two dozen of my players were suspended from playing against Kentucky in the 2007 Music City Bowl in Nashville, which we lost by a 35–28 score. Many of those players also were suspended from playing in the first games of the 2008 season.

Florida State self-imposed two years of NCAA probation, but the NCAA came back in March 2009 and ordered FSU to vacate previous victories in ten sports, including five of my team's victories from the 2006 season and seven wins in 2007. So instead of trailing Paterno by one victory going into the 2009 season, I officially trailed him by thirteen wins. The race between Joe and me was over. I thought it was unfair for the NCAA to do it, and I hated to see them take away a national championship from our track and field team. Those kids had worked so hard to be the best in the country, and I really thought those kinds of cases should be handled by the university.

I coached for fifty-seven years and was never accused of cheating. But then the NCAA took away twelve of my victories for something I had absolutely no involvement in. I always wanted to retire and be known as someone who never believed in cheating. I always wanted to be remembered as someone who did things the right way and did not bend the rules. But the NCAA decided to tarnish my reputation for something I played no part in.

Near the end of the 2007 season, Florida State athletic director Bill Proctor came by my office. At the time, there was speculation that Jimbo Fisher, my offensive coordinator, might take the head coaching job at West Virginia. Rich Rodriguez had just left West Virginia for the University of Michigan, and Jimbo was born and raised in West Virginia, so he seemed like a logical candidate. I think Florida State administrators were getting kind of worried that they would lose him.

"Bobby, if you had to name a successor, who would it be?" Proctor asked me.

"Mickey Andrews," I told him.

Mickey had been my defensive coordinator since 1984 and was as much of a reason for Florida State's success as anyone else. I always promised Mickey I would support him for the Florida State job when I retired. Mickey passed up other opportunities to stay with us at Florida State and always had been very loyal.

"No, we need someone younger," Proctor told me.

"Well, I guess Jimbo would be the next-best candidate," I told him.

To be honest, I did not hear about the possibility of naming a successor again until a few weeks before we played Kentucky in the 2007 Music City Bowl. Proctor came back to me and told me they wanted to name a coach-in-waiting and they wanted it to be Jimbo. I agreed to do it more out of loyalty than whether I thought it was wise or unwise. I have always believed in being loyal, and if that was what President Wetherell wanted to do, I was going to support his decision.

On December 10, 2007, Florida State named Jimbo Fisher my eventual successor. They didn't tell me about the details of the arrangement before I read about them in the newspaper. Under Jimbo's contract, the school would have to pay him $2.5 million if he was not named my successor by January 2011. I thought the arrangement was fine because I planned to coach only a couple more years anyway. I thought I would coach through the 2010 season, and then Jimbo would take over after that.

I just never had a desire to retire because I have never known anything but coaching. I did not know what I would do with a free Saturday. Would I watch football games on TV? Would Ann and I go to the beach? Would we go out to dinner? I really did not know what I would do if I woke up on a Saturday morning and did not have a game to worry about. I really believe God called on me to coach, and that is the reason I stayed in it for so long. If God did not want me to do it, I would not have stayed on the sideline for as long as I did. But He wanted me to spread the things He taught me over seventy years to these young men.

During my last few seasons at Florida State, I would sometimes lie awake at night, praying to God to give me a sign that it was time for me to retire. I waited for Him to tell me that my work for Him was finished. Heading into the 2009 season, I was still waiting for that sign.

CHAPTER 17

THE FINAL SEASON

The 2009 season started exactly like my previous thirty-three seasons as Florida State's head coach. On July 28, 2009, I met with my coaching staff and support personnel for a three-day hideaway at the Varsity Club in the sky suites of Doak Campbell Stadium.

Near the beginning of the meetings, I gave my "State of the Union" address. We were coming off a 9–4 season in 2008, in which we beat the University of Wisconsin by a 42–13 score in the Champs Sports Bowl in Orlando, Florida. We finished the season ranked number twenty-one in the final Associated Press Top 25 poll, which was a step in the right direction. With the players we had coming back in 2009, I thought our team would be even better.

"Last season we improved to 9–4, but if not for two little things we could have been 11–2," I told my coaches. "Those issues were ball security against Georgia Tech and poor tackling against Boston College. These are two of our biggest objectives each fall and spring and yet we allowed them to beat us. Let's face it: our 2009 material is as good as anyone we play except Florida. If we can successfully play up to our potential, we could get back to the Dynasty Era of the 1990s. What is screwing us up? Poor tackling? Missed blocks? Fumbles? Bombs? Execution? Each of these areas is correctable. Do you have your priorities in order? Are you teaching the fundamentals first, or are you slighting them?"

With a veteran offensive line coming back in 2009, I thought our offense had the potential to be among the best in the country. We took our lumps by starting several freshmen on the offensive line the previous two seasons, and those players were going to be sophomores and juniors during the coming season. Our quarterback Christian Ponder (whose father, David played offensive line for me from 1980 to 1983) was the best passer and leader we had since Chris Weinke left Florida State in 2000. We had talented running backs and receivers around Ponder, but our offensive line had to play like gangbusters for us to return to national prominence.

"If our offensive line stays healthy all year, they could lead us to our resurgence," I told my coaches. "Alabama, the same team we beat in 2007, put their marbles on their offensive line in 2008 and was ranked number one in the country. They had slashing runners, a veteran offensive line, a veteran quarterback, and a great wide receiver. This year can be very exciting for us."

I tried to explain to my coaches what it would take from each of them for Florida State to return to its place among the country's best teams.

"Coaches must build confidence, enthusiasm, meanness, and toughness," I told them. "We must get better fundamentally. We must not turn the ball over, and our defense needs to score touchdowns like it did against Wisconsin in the 2008 Champs Sports Bowl. I can't wait! If this team can stay healthy and get great leadership, we will have a great year. Don't forget—it's the little things, and they are correctable!"

During our meetings, I also provided a staff organization plan for 2009. It consisted of more than two hundred points of concern, but the plan also was littered with famous quotes and parables that were important to me. The plan included a team slogan—"It's not about me! It's about us!" There also was a reminder to each of my coaches to encourage their players to participate in the FCA, which I believe was one of the most important things we did. The plan included philosophies from some of the coaches I tried to emulate through the years, including former Nebraska coach Tom Osborne, former Green Bay Packers coach Vince Lombardi, and Alabama coach Paul "Bear" Bryant.

I also laid out a plan for my coaches to have a successful life on and off the field:

1. Make time for yourself and your family.
2. Surround yourself with the best people possible.
3. Be open to new ideas and better ways to do things. Keep all lines of communication open with your staff.
4. Be prepared to take risks.
5. Like what you do and like what you sell.
6. Don't dwell on your mistakes or setbacks—learn and grow from

them, and then move on. Never let your mistakes defeat or discourage you. Never take criticism personally.

Going into the 2009 season, I was as excited as I had been in any of our previous thirty-three seasons at Florida State. I really believed Florida State was close to turning it around and returning to its place among the country's elite programs. During our first team meeting, on August 7, 2009, I told our players, "I was here in the 1990s when Florida State was winning national championships. I'm getting that same feeling now!"

We opened the 2009 season against the University of Miami at Doak Campbell Stadium on September 7, 2009. We kicked off the season against the Hurricanes four times after they joined the ACC before the 2004 season. The game was often a good barometer to how our season would play out and how we stacked up against the ACC's best teams. Unlike our great games against the Hurricanes in the 1980s and 1990s, most of our recent contests against them were defensive struggles. We lost by a 16–10 score in overtime at the Orange Bowl stadium in 2004. The next year, we beat Miami by a 10–7 score in Tallahassee and won 13–10 in Miami in 2006.

The 2009 opener ended up being anything but a defensive struggle. We trailed, 14–10, at halftime, but Ponder scored on a nine-yard run with twelve minutes, one second left to play in the third quarter. We missed the extra-point kick, which left us with a 16–14 lead. We took a 23–14 lead on Ponder's twenty-one-yard touchdown pass to Taiwan Easterling with about five minutes to go in the third quarter. But Miami's Matt

Bosher kicked an eighteen-yard field goal near the end of the third quarter, and then quarterback Jacory Harris scored on a one-yard run early in the fourth, giving the Hurricanes a 24–23 lead.

But then our defense provided what I hoped would be a game-changing play. Freshman cornerback Greg Reid blitzed on a passing play and hit Harris just as he was about to throw. The football popped into the air and was intercepted by defensive end Markus White. He returned the interception thirty-one yards for a touchdown, and Ponder's two-point pass to Richard Goodman gave us a 31–24 lead with eleven minutes, forty-five seconds to play.

But Miami's offense came right back, tying the score at 31–31 after Harris threw a twenty-four-yard touchdown pass to Graig Cooper. We kicked a forty-five-yard field goal to take a 34–31 lead with four minutes, eleven seconds remaining, but our defense just could not stop Miami's offense. Harris drove them right down the field, and Cooper scored on a three-yard run to put the Hurricanes ahead, 38–34, with one minute, fifty-three seconds to go.

I believed I was about to learn a lot about my football team during the next two minutes. There was still plenty of time for us to drive down the field and win the game. If we hadn't missed the extra-point kick early in the third quarter, we would have needed only a field goal to tie the score. But since we missed the kick, we would have to score a touchdown to win the game. Ponder seemed very calm on the sideline, and he went on the field and showed his grit. He led our offense to Miami's twelve-yard line with thirty-six seconds to play. We had five cracks at the end zone, but his last pass, to Jarmon Fortson, was a little low, but catchable.

The ball came out of Fortson's hands, and the game ended. We lost by a 38–34 score. The defeat was as painful as any of the "wide right" games against Miami during the 1990s because my boys had invested so much into winning the game.

But even though we lost the opener, I was still encouraged about our prospects for the 2009 season. The Hurricanes looked like a much-improved team—they would upset nationally ranked opponents Georgia Tech and Oklahoma en route to a 5–1 start—and my boys stood toe-to-toe with them for sixty minutes. Our offense looked explosive, and we had freshmen who were capable of helping us on both sides of the football.

In our pregame chapel the next week, Clint Purvis, our team chaplain, talked to the boys about the fine line between winning and losing and what it would take from each of them to rebound from the disheartening loss to Miami. He read the boys passages from Joshua 7:5, Joshua 7:8–9, and Joshua 8:1:

At this the hearts of the people melted and became like water.

O Lord, what can I say, now that Israel has been routed by its enemies? The Canaanites and the other people of the country will hear about this and they will surround us and wipe out our name from the earth. What then will you do for your own great name?

Then the Lord said to Joshua, "Do not be afraid; do not be discouraged."

"There is a huge difference between getting beat in a game and being a loser," Clint told the boys. "It was a really tough game on Monday night, but from the Old Testament God can teach us about coming back! We got beat, but you are not a loser! Listen to what Joshua has to teach us about the difference."

Clint reminded the boys of the characteristics of being a winner:

1. A winner still remembers that God never forsakes his own.
2. A winner must remember that it is always painful and costly to claim victory again.
3. A winner will always remember the source of all his blessings.

Because we opened the season against Miami on Labor Day night, we did not have much time to recover from our painful loss to Miami. Only five days later, we played Jacksonville State, an NCAA Football Championship Subdivision team from Jacksonville, Alabama. As an FCS program, Jacksonville State was permitted to award sixty-three scholarships each season. Florida State is an NCAA Football Bowl Subdivision program and awards eighty-five scholarships each season. Even though the Gamecocks were supposed to be outmatched against us, I knew from the early minutes of the game that my boys had not yet recovered from the disappointment of losing to Miami.

We moved the football up and down the field against Jacksonville State in the first half, but still trailed by a 9–7 score at the half. We could not muster much offense in the third quarter and trailed by the same score going into the fourth. With less than one minute to play, it seemed we would suffer an embarrassing loss. But Ponder threw a twenty-four-yard pass to Richard Goodman to set up Ty Jones's one-yard touchdown run with thirty-five seconds left. On Jacksonville State's next possession, Kevin McNeil scooped up a fumble and returned it thirty-three yards for a touchdown, which gave us a 19–9 victory. I knew we dodged a bullet and were fortunate to win, but that probably ended up being the game that made our fans and alumni so upset. They looked at Jacksonville State as a team from a lesser division, and Florida State was supposed to whip them. But people did not understand how much the opening loss to Miami hurt our team. In hindsight, it probably took my players a couple of weeks to really get over that loss.

We traveled to Brigham Young University in Provo, Utah, to play the Cougars on September 19, 2009. BYU had a really good team and was ranked number seven in the country. The Cougars have always been known for having a great passing game, and flying across the country to play is never easy. It ended up being our best game of the season. I believe we just had too much speed for BYU, and our offense scored every time we moved inside the Cougars' twenty-yard line. Our defense played great and forced five turnovers. We had a 30–14 lead at the half and blew the game open after Greg Reid intercepted a pass and returned it sixty-three yards for a touchdown early in the third quarter. We ended up winning the game by a 54–28 score, and I think my boys really wanted to redeem themselves after playing so poorly the week before.

But things really fell apart after we beat BYU. We lost our next three games, including a 17–7 loss to the University of South Florida at Doak Campbell Stadium on September 26, 2009. The next week, we lost at Boston College by a 28–21 score. Two days later, Jim Smith, who is chairman of the Florida State University trustees, told the *Tallahassee*

Democrat that he wanted me to retire at the end of the season. He said the arrangement with me serving as head coach and Jimbo serving as my eventual successor was not working. Jim told the newspaper, "We've got too many bosses out there. Jimbo is in a very, very tough situation where people assume he has a whole lot more authority than he really has. He's getting blamed for a lot of things [that are] just not his fault."

It really surprised me to hear Jim be so critical because we were always very close friends. At the time, I did not see any problems with the arrangement Jimbo and I had. In some cases, other coaches on your staff might not agree with having a coach-in-waiting. They might think, "Why him?" or "Why not me?" But I never sensed any problems with my coaches. Of course, you realized other coaches might want the job when you leave and they might be insecure because they are not getting it, but we all got along very well. We had good morale and worked well together. I did not know what each of my coaches was feeling inside, but as far as staff chemistry and our ability to work together, I did not see any problems.

My future as Florida State's coach became a national story going into our game against Georgia Tech on October 10, 2009. Early in the week, I met with Florida State president T. K. Wetherell, who assured me no changes would be made during the season. T.K. and I agreed we would talk about my future again once the season was completed. "Don't you give up, T.K.," I told him. "We still have a season to play."

I did a lengthy sit-down interview with ESPN the day before we played the Yellow Jackets, hoping to quiet some of our critics. We still had seven games to play, and the season was not over as far as I was concerned. "I'm not scared of the future," I told ESPN. "I'm not scared of what happened in the past. When our time comes, it will come. Now, I'd love to go out of here as a winner, but that might not happen. I'll survive somehow."

We played Georgia Tech in a nationally televised game at Doak Campbell Stadium on October 10, 2009. As we walked onto the field before the game, my players walked arm-in-arm with me in a show of unity. Before kickoff, I received a warm reception from the Florida State fans, which was a really nice gesture. The score was tied 7–7 early in the first quarter when officials had to stop the game for more than an hour because of lightning.

Once the game resumed, there were plenty of fireworks. Our defense could not stop Georgia Tech's triple-option spread offense, and the Yellow Jackets ran for 401 yards. We had a 38–35 lead late in the fourth quarter, but Georgia Tech scored two touchdowns to take a 49–38 lead with six minutes, twenty-nine seconds to go. Ponder threw a thirteen-yard touchdown pass to Rod Owens to make the score 49–44 with four minutes, fourteen seconds to play, but that was as close as we could get in a 49–44 loss. We had a 2–4 record, which was Florida State's worst start since my first season, in 1976.

But my boys refused to give up, and we came back and won four of our next five games. We beat North Carolina, 30–27, at Keenan Stadium in Chapel Hill, North Carolina, on October 22, 2009, after my boys rallied from a 24–6 deficit in the third quarter. Ponder was magnificent in the game, completing thirty-three of forty passes for 395 yards with three touchdowns. After a three-game losing streak, it was nice to get back on the winning side again. I think coming back from such a deficit—when everyone else was counting them out—really showed the character of my players.

We hosted North Carolina State at Doak Campbell Stadium the next week. Before we played the Wolfpack, Purvis held pregame chapel and talked to my boys about persevering through difficult times. He read them Matthew 5:13:

> *You are the salt of the earth. But if the salt loses its saltiness, how can it be made salty again? It is no longer good for anything, except to be thrown out and trampled by men.*

Clint explained to the players that salt is really a miracle of nature. Salt is actually composed of two poisons: chloride and sodium. If you ingest either by itself, you will die. But when they are combined, you make ordinary table salt. Clint explained the reasons salt is so important: it seasons, it creates thirst, and it preserves.

"Are you the hammer or the anvil?" Clint asked the boys. "Are you giving blows or taking them? Today, you decide. This is a great opportunity to put together back-to-back wins. In order to do it, you and our team will have to get salty!"

In what was another offensive shoot-out, we took a 38–28 lead over the Wolfpack early in the fourth quarter. But N.C. State quarterback Russell Wilson threw a pair of touchdown passes, giving his team a 42–38 lead with three minutes, fifty seconds left to play. Then Ponder led our offense down the field on another game-winning drive. On a

third-and-goal play from the Wolfpack three, Bert Reed, one of our receivers, scored a touchdown on an inside reverse. It was a pretty gutsy
play call by Jimbo, and it worked. N.C. State drove to midfield in the final
seconds, but Jamie Robinson intercepted Wilson's pass at our goal line.
We walked away with a 45–42 victory.

We lost at Clemson, 40–24, the next week, but we lost more than the
game after Ponder separated his right shoulder. He was already playing with bruised ribs and became frustrated after throwing his fourth
interception in the game's final moments. Ponder hit Tigers defensive
back DeAndre McDaniel during the interception return, and injured his
shoulder and was sidelined for the rest of the season. We were forced to
turn to redshirt freshman E. J. Manuel, who was one of the country's
most highly recruited quarterbacks when we signed him out of Bayside
High School in Virginia Beach, Virginia.

Manuel had not played much behind Ponder, who was leading the
ACC in passing and total offense at the time of his injury. Manuel
started his first game at Wake Forest, and we needed to beat the Demon
Deacons to stay in the hunt for a postseason bowl game. We could not
have asked for much more from Manuel when we played the Demon
Deacons at Groves Stadium in Winston-Salem, North Carolina, on
November 14, 2009. He passed for 220 yards and one touchdown and
ran for 45 yards and one score, leading us to a 41–21 victory. With a 5–5
record, we would have to win one of our last two games—home against
Maryland, or at rival Florida—to keep our streak of consecutive bowl
games intact.

We played Maryland at Doak Campbell Stadium on November 21,

2009, which was our final home game of the season. It was Senior Day, which was always a day of mixed emotions for me. Seniors such as Richard Goodman, Rod Owens, Caz Piurowski, Kevin McNeil, Dekoda Watson, Patrick Robinson, and Jamie Robinson had invested so much into our program over the past four years. Although our on-field results probably were not what they hoped for when they signed with Florida State, they did a great job representing our team and university on and off the field.

It also was the final home game for Mickey Andrews, our defensive coordinator, who announced his retirement earlier in the season. Mickey was the architect of so many great defenses that helped put Florida State on the map. He is one of my closest friends and was a loyal assistant coach for more than a quarter century. It was sad that our defense did not play better during his final season, because I know no one cared as much as Mickey did. He put his heart and soul into the Florida State program for many years and was always a man of integrity.

Before the Maryland game, Clint talked to the players about leading a life of integrity. He told them the Bible story of Job, whose integrity was challenged by Satan. Satan proposed to God that Job served Him only because God protected him. So God made Job vulnerable, and Satan took away his children, his health, and his wealth. Satan tempted Job to curse God, but Job never questioned God's will. As a reward for his steadfast faith, God returned Job's children and made him even wealthier, allowing him to live for another 140 years.

"Job was a man of integrity," Clint told my players. "His integrity is legend! A man with integrity stays focused and never gets distracted.

Integrity is defined as who you are when no one else is looking. Today's game is a game of and for integrity."

We trailed Maryland by a 26–22 score in the final two minutes, and it looked like the Terrapins would put our bowl chances in serious jeopardy. But then our speedy freshman Greg Reid caught a punt and returned it forty-eight yards to the Maryland forty-four. Manuel scrambled for a fifteen-yard gain on first down, and then gained twenty yards to the Terrapins' nine-yard line on the next play. Two plays later, running back Lonnie Pryor crashed into the end zone for a three-yard touchdown with thirty-two seconds left. The clock ran out on Maryland's final drive, and we escaped with a 29–26 victory. It was our sixth victory of the season, making us eligible for a twenty-eighth consecutive bowl game.

We closed the regular season against rival Florida at the Swamp in Gainesville on November 28, 2009. The Gators were college football's defending national champion, and they spent much of the 2009 season ranked number one in the country. Florida had beaten us badly in each of the previous two seasons, winning 45–12 in 2007 and 45–15 in 2008. Florida quarterback Tim Tebow was one of the greatest players we ever faced. I didn't think he was as physically gifted or as much of a polished passer as Charlie Ward, but I am not sure I ever saw a better leader on the football field than Tebow. He just seemed to will his team to victories and was willing to make whatever sacrifice was necessary to win.

Tebow beat us again in his final game at Florida's Ben Hill Griffin Stadium, throwing for three touchdowns and running for two scores in a 37–10 victory. Florida took a 30–0 lead early in the third quarter, then we were able to put up ten points to save us from a shutout. I was glad

I would never have to coach against Tebow again, since he was a senior. We finished the season with a 6–6 record, which certainly was not what I had in mind when the season started. After the game, I told reporters I wanted to return to coach Florida State in 2010, but would have to go home and do some soul-searching.

After returning home to Tallahassee, I went to bed that night believing that at least it would be my choice to make.

Of course, my coaching career ended after Florida State defeated West Virginia, 33–21, in the Gator Bowl in Jacksonville, Florida, on New Year's Day 2010. Winning the game was extra special because my boys came from behind to do it, and I really enjoyed ending my career on a winning note. I told reporters after the game that I had prepared myself for retirement.

"I ain't got to set no alarm no more, I'll get up when I'm darn good and ready, then like I say, go out and look for a job," I told them.

After my postgame news conference, Ann put her arms around me, smiled at me, and said, "Time to go home, baby."

It was time to go home, but my life's work is not finished. I continue to speak at churches and civic organizations around the country. I remain heavily involved in the Fellowship of Christian Athletes, trying to spread God's word to as many young people as possible. Even though I retired from coaching, I still believe that is my calling.

Because I'm eighty years old, I was more prepared for retirement. If I were fifty, it would have been terribly disappointing because I would have felt like most of my life was still in front of me. But now I can sit back and actually watch games on TV and enjoy them. I can spend more time with my family. Ann and I can go to the beach and take more trips together. We're planning our first trip to the Holy Land, which is something we've always wanted to do.

In a lot of ways, I'll always be a football coach. Shortly after I retired, Ann and I were visiting Rio de Janeiro, Brazil, where I spoke to a group of businessmen. While we were there, we visited the Christ the Redeemer statue, which overlooks the city at the top of Corcovado Mountain. While Ann and I were preparing to make the long walk up the mountain, I overheard a group of people talking and heard someone say "Bobby Bowden." "Are ya'll talking about me?" I asked them.

Sure enough, they were Florida State football fans.

"See you at the top," I told them.

I knew then that God still had a plan for me. It is up to me to follow His path and stay the course.

ACKNOWLEDGMENTS

BOBBY BOWDEN:

Do ya'll know how hard it is to put eighty years of life into one book? No matter how hard you try, there are only so many stories and so many people you can include. They didn't ask me to write a dadgum encyclopedia, you know it? Luckily for me I had my coauthor, Mark Schlabach, to help me sort through everything and pick out the events of my life that truly helped shape me into the man I have become. I've known for years that Mark is a great sports journalist, always covering the Seminoles and me objectively and fairly. But after reading our final product, Mark has shown me what a great writer he is. It surely isn't easy taking someone else's words and stories and turning them into a cohesive book that people can actually read. I am so grateful to Mark for his tireless work ethic, for getting this project together in record time, and for helping me to create a book that I am truly proud of.

I've been involved in several books over the years, but this one has given me the chance to discuss how important my faith is to me and how that faith has guided me through life's twists and turns. So for giving me this opportunity I want to thank my publisher, Simon & Schuster/ Howard Books. Their entire team embraced the idea for the book from the very beginning and have all worked tirelessly to see it come to fruition.

I know as well as anyone that putting together a great team is the key to winning at anything in life. I am so thankful to my attorney, Richard Davis, for overseeing all of the legal "mumbo jumbo" for me and for always looking out for my best interests. My new publicist, Kimberly Shiff,

ACKNOWLEDGMENTS

has been so helpful to me by coordinating my schedule, being my liaison with our publishing team, gathering the photos for the book, and for just keeping me very busy in my "retirement."

To my longtime friend Joe Paterno, thank you for taking the time out of your busy schedule to write one of the forewords for this book. I have always admired how Joe coached his teams with integrity and toughness, and I consider it an honor to be the second-winningest coach in major college history, behind only Joe. I wish you many more years of success on the field, my friend.

I am incredibly grateful to Tony Dungy, a bestselling author and the first African-American head coach to win the Super Bowl, for writing the other foreword for my book. His own books, like his coaching career, have inspired so many people, and to have Tony lend his support to my story is a great honor for me.

Of course, without my family, I probably wouldn't have anything to write about in the first place. I am eternally grateful to my wife, Ann, who is as pretty today as she was the first time I saw her. I am very thankful for her insightful input into many of these stories and for refreshing my memory about more than a few things. All of our children—Robyn, Steve, Tommy, Terry, Jeff, and Ginger—contributed with their support and offered suggestions on the manuscript. I may not have listened to all of them, but I certainly did appreciate all of it.

I am so grateful to still have such strong friendships with many of the men I've written about in this book. There are too many to name, but without all the boys that I went to school and played football with from Woodlawn High School and then Howard College, I don't think I would have developed the depth of love for the game that I did. My father taught me to love the game of football, and it was the friendships with those boys from Alabama that taught me what it meant to be a good teammate.

The men that I had the privilege of coaching at South Georgia College, many of whom I still see every year, taught me that treating players with respect would pretty much ensure getting respect in return. Looking back, I think the fact that many of those guys were actually older than I was ended up making me a better head coach. Getting war veterans to trust me and follow my plan for our football team is probably one of my proudest accomplishments.

I had the honor to work with so many incredible coaches throughout my coaching career, including three of my own sons, and I know that without the contributions of each and every one of those coaches I could not have had the successes that I did. To every volunteer, graduate assistant, assistant coach, and coordinator that I've ever coached with, I want each and every one of you to know how grateful I am for your contributions and dedication to all of our teams over the years at South Georgia College, Howard College, West Virginia University, and Florida State University. My sincere thanks also extend to all of my support staff—trainers, doctors, administrative staff (especially my longtime administrative assistant and dear friend, Sue Hall), equipment personnel, video crew, and every other person that did their part to help our programs be successful.

And last, there is no way I can ever express the amount of pride, satisfaction, and love that I received from coaching every young man who ever suited up for me on the football field. For being given the chance to coach young men in the 1950s, 1960s, 1970s, 1980s, 1990s, 2000s, and for one day in the 2010s, I am incredibly blessed. I hope that I taught them as much as they taught me. To all of my players, thank you for choosing me to be your football coach.

MARK SCHLABACH:

I asked the question during the end of one my interview sessions with former Florida State football coach Bobby Bowden.

"Coach, you wouldn't happen to have copies of any of your pregame speeches, would you?"

Bowden walked to a desk in the front room of his house in Tallahassee, Florida, and returned with a file folder that appeared to be about twenty inches thick.

"Here you go," he told me. "You might be able to get a couple of things out of there."

Inside the folder, I discovered a treasure chest of information. The folder contained an outline for nearly every pregame speech Bowden delivered to his teams during his thirty-four-year career as Florida State's coach. There were also copies of many preseason speeches and his legendary "state of the program" speeches he delivered to his coaches and support staff before each season.

The speech outlines and actual speeches were written on pages from steno and legal pads, on the back of parking passes, and even on napkins. The speeches provided never-before-revealed insight into one of college football's legendary coaches, as well as the blueprint for how Bowden built Florida State into one of the sport's greatest dynasties.

During his thirty-four seasons on the sideline, Bowden led the Seminoles to two national championships, twelve Atlantic Coast Conference titles, and fourteen consecutive seasons in which FSU won at least ten games and finished in the top five of the final Associated Press poll.

Like most football pregame speeches, Bowden's outlines included keys on offense, defense, and special teams for every game. But the outlines also revealed so much more about Bowden as a man, mentor, and Christian.

ACKNOWLEDGMENTS

When Bowden was a young coach at South Georgia College in Douglas, Georgia, in 1955, he started a ritual he followed until his retirement as Florida State's coach at the end of the 2009 season. Each night before a game, Bowden had a team meeting at the team's hotel or in the locker room. Each meeting would begin with a devotional. Bowden would often deliver the devotional, but his coaches and players sometimes told the team about things that were important to them.

Many of the devotionals that Bowden delivered to his teams over the years became the blueprint for this book. In the preceding pages, you have read stories such as "Unseen Eyes," "Transfusion," and other parables that Bowden used to teach his players about the importance of faith and morals. As much as Bowden wanted to win games and championships, he was equally interested in his players becoming good men, fathers, husbands, and professionals.

I would like to thank Bowden for giving me the opportunity and having the confidence in me to cowrite his memoir. It is a tremendous honor and privilege to have my name on his book. Bowden was one of the reasons I became a sports journalist. I remember watching his Florida State teams play during the 1990s. The Seminoles were one of the reasons I became so interested in college football.

After graduating from the University of Georgia in 1996, I went to work as a staff writer at the *Atlanta Journal-Constitution*. I still remember the first time I met Bowden while working for the *AJC*, and he was very cooperative and gracious in welcoming a young journalist into his office. I was fortunate to spend even more time with Bowden as a staff writer for the *Washington Post* and ESPN.com. During his final season at Florida State, I conducted several TV interviews with Bowden and worked as a sideline reporter during his games. He was always very cooperative and professional, even when asked difficult questions.

More than anything else, I learned Bowden is a man of integrity and moral fabric. He genuinely cared about the welfare of his coaches, play-

ACKNOWLEDGMENTS

ers, and fans. I am not sure college football will ever have a coach quite like him and he will be sorely missed during the coming seasons.

I would like to thank several people who were instrumental in making this book happen. Kim Shiff, who works as Bowden's publicist, helped persuade him to tell his story. She was very valuable in acquiring photos, letters, and other correspondence from Bowden's life. Kim also became a great listener during the writing process and is a good friend.

Frank Scatoni, my agent at Venture Literary, did a great job of putting together the deal quickly. Becky Nesbitt and Jessica Wong are fabulous editors and never let a detail fall through the cracks. Terry Bowden, the head coach at the University of North Alabama and one of Bowden's sons, provided me with many details about his father's life. Chris Carson, my pastor at Madison Presbyterian Church in Madison, Georgia, gave me great insight and spiritual guidance.

I would like to thank my editors at ESPN.com—David Albright, David Duffey, Brian Kelly, and Conor Nevins—for allowing me to take on this project and giving me the time to complete it. I'd like to thank my colleagues at ESPN.com—Pat Forde, Ivan Maisel, and Chris Low—for providing encouragement when it seemed like the project would never end. Joe Drape of the *New York Times* and Tony Barnhart of CBS Sports also have served as tremendous mentors to me over the years and are good friends.

More than anyone else, I would like to thank my parents, brother, and sisters for their love and support. My wife, Heather, and my children, Caroline, Jane, and Jack, whom I love dearly, made a lot of sacrifices while this book was being completed. I am forever grateful for the sacrifices they make every football season.

I can only hope my children one day find a mentor like Bobby Bowden.